# OCEANS BETWEEN US

# OCEANS BETWEEN US

Pacific Peoples & Racism in Aotearoa

Edited by Sereana Naepi

AUCKLAND
UNIVERSITY
PRESS

First published 2025
Auckland University Press
Waipapa Taumata Rau
University of Auckland
Private Bag 92019
Auckland 1142
New Zealand
www.aucklanduniversitypress.co.nz

© Sereana Naepi and the contributors, 2025

ISBN 978 1 77671 125 3

A catalogue record for this book is available from the National Library of New Zealand

This book is copyright. Apart from fair dealing for the purpose of private study, research, criticism or review, as permitted under the Copyright Act, no part may be reproduced by any process without prior permission of the publisher. The moral rights of the authors have been asserted.

Design by Carolyn Lewis
Cover artwork by Vasemaca Tavola, 2025
This book was printed on FSC® certified paper
Printed in Singapore by Markono Print Media Pte Ltd

*For those who tirelessly work to transform the future of our Pacific communities – your dedication and hope inspire us all and pave the way for generations to come.*

# CONTENTS

**Foreword** ix
*Ashlea Gillon Aramoana*

**Artist's Note** xiii
*Vasemaca Tavola*

**RACISM**
Why We Need to Talk About It  1
*Sereana Naepi*

**HISTORY**
'They Call Me a Bunga'
Colonialism, History and Stereotypes in Aotearoa New Zealand  9
*Marcia Leenen-Young*

**ECONOMY**
Is the Migrant Dream a Capitalist Dream?
Pacific Peoples and the Economy  37
*Sereana Naepi, Lisa Meto Fox, Dylan Asafo and Evalesi Tuʻinukuafe*

**EDUCATION**
Structural Racism and Education in Aotearoa  53
*Jean M. Uasike Allen, Toleafoa Yvonne Ualesi, David Taufui Mikato Faʻavae and Fetaui Iosefo*

**MIGRATION**
Time and Race
Pacific Migration Journeys to Aotearoa  81
*Evalesi Tuʻinukuafe*

**CLIMATE JUSTICE**
There Can Be No (Climate) Justice on Stolen Land
Pacific Peoples, Climate Change and the Law in New Zealand   97
*Dylan Asafo*

**HEALTH**
'We Need to Get Real'
Structural Racism and the Wellbeing of Pacific Peoples in Aotearoa   117
*Caleb Marsters*

**HIGHER EDUCATION**
The Pacific Pipeline
Structural Racism and Pacific Peoples in Higher Education   153
*Sereana Naepi*

**JUSTICE SYSTEMS**
Recognising Stories of Suffering in Section 27 of the Sentencing Act 2002   175
*Barbara-Luhia Graham*

**THE NEXT GENERATION**
To Weave Dreams of Liberation   195
*Chelsea Naepi*

**Notes**   206
**Contributors**   239
**Index**   243

# FOREWORD

*Ashlea Gillon Aramoana*

Haere mai, haere mai, haere mai rā.
Haere mai e ngā whanaunga o Te Moana-nui-a-Kiwa nei e.
Whakatau mai ki runga i ngā kaupapa o te
    whakawhanaungatanga, o te mana motuhake,
    o te rangatiratanga e.
Nau mai, haere mai, kōrero mai, noho mai, whakatau mai,
    karanga mai rā.
Tēnā rā koutou katoa.
Manawa mai te mauri moana, manawa mai te mauri whenua,
    manawa mai ngā mauri katoa.
Tihei mauri ora.
Ko te Mana Moana te kaupapa o tēnei pukapuka. He kohinga kōreo tēnei kia akiaki i ngā tangata moana kia whakapapare tonu i ngā pūnaha whakakōmau. Ko tēnei whiti he karanga, he pōwhiri mō tēnei kaupapa, mō ēnei whanaunga hoki, nā reira, nau mai, piki mai, kake mai.

*Welcome, come forth, welcome to the relations of Te Moana-nui-a-Kiwa for connecting, building relationships, for self-determination and sovereignty. Welcome, share your truth, sit with us, settle, and call forth. Greetings to you all. Bring forward the essence and power of the ocean, bring forward the essence and power of the land, bring forward the essence and power of all things. It is done. The purpose of this book is the agency, sovereignty and power of the Pacific Ocean peoples against the systems of oppression that restrict us. This section is a call, a welcome for these conversations, for these relations. And so, come forth, climb ahead, ascend forward.*

KIA ORA. Here, I present a karanga, a call, a welcome, a declaration, a ceremony in its own right. I welcome our whanaunga, our relations of the moana, Te Moana-nui-a-Kiwa, I welcome them to speak, to discuss, to share, to rest, to settle, and to call here. I do not speak for all Māori by any means, nor do I pretend to have the power to declare anything definite or permanent, or immovable. Much like Te Moana-nui-a-Kiwa, I move and flow with our ocean that connects us. What I offer here is a toka tū moana, a rock in the ocean to rest upon; I offer a type of pōwhiri, a type of spiritual and cultural safety, connection, and welcome to have these kōrero in this space; I offer this with my ngākau and my puku, to ensure that our whanaunga o Te Moana-nui-a-Kiwa are safe and welcome.

A pōwhiri is a process of connection, of relationship, of nurturing and (re)moving tapu, of nurturing and (re)establishing noa, so that conversation, relationship, coming together, and sharing and conceiving new and old ideas may take place. These things often happen within marae, within our wharenui, a space often understood as a body that may conceive and receive newness and abundance, a space within which to have easy, moderate, difficult, excruciating, blunt, purposeful or hilarious conversations. A place within which children and young people are meant to be disruptive, inquisitive, to disturb the dust, to learn, to argue, to deliberate; a place within which questions are meant to be asked, to challenge, and to seek answers. A pōwhiri is tikanga within which one may talk absolute poetry and truth, and in the next moment, when in good relation, utter shit talk, mockery and joking. It is a tikanga within which safety, mutuality and respect can be (re)created. Within pōwhiri, there are often mana whenua, the people who have agency, the responsibility of guardianship and hospitality, and who whakapapa to the place within which the pōwhiri is being held; and manuhiri, visitors, guests or extended relations who may not have the same responsibilities of manaaki for a space, but may find a home there, and may seek to be in relation. I am re-writing or perhaps, (re)creating pōwhiri here for these purposes, for relationship, for connection, for enabling and (re)creating cultural and spiritual safety to engage in kōrero that may be taumaha. I am (re)creating pōwhiri to offer a safe, welcome, relational space for the authors within this book to kōrero tūturu, to speak, wholly, their truths, their experiences, their feelings, their histories, their commonalities, their differences. I offer a welcome to our Pacific whanaunga, our kaihana, to kōrero their tika, their pono.

It is a privilege to write the foreword for this book. I have known many of the authors for a long time; we have had many kōrero and wānanga about the racism of New Zealand towards Māori and Pacific Peoples. We kōrero as whanaunga; we discuss in depth the ways in which institutional and structural racism deny, restrict and undermine us and our agency. We kōrero about the ways in which stereotypes and colonialism form racial slurs that seek to disempower us. We kōrero about the ways in which the failures in climate justice inequitably impact Pacific Peoples. We kōrero about this government's utter failures, and about white supremacy, racism and violence towards us. Honestly, brutally, truthfully, transparently. We kōrero utter shit talk, mockery and joking about the sheer idiocy that is racism as a means of carrying the weight of it. We kōrero. And it is a privilege to be a part of that kōrero, along with this foreword, to offer safety and connection to my tuākana in this space so they may kōrero.

This book is a truth-telling of Pacific Peoples' navigations of racism in New Zealand. It brings together Pacific Peoples across disciplines, rohe and histories. This book reiterates the rights that enable Pacific Peoples to tell their truths, to tell of their experiences, to share the genealogy of racism that has controlled and restricted their realities, much like ours as Māori. The chapters of this book flow together, like our oceans, to (re)centre Pacific Peoples in ways that our Westernised, colonial world could not dream of.

Just as a pōwhiri offers critical space to have direct conversations, this book provides the perfect time and space to have these critical, direct conversations about the many promises that New Zealand has broken for Pacific Peoples because of its racism. The stories shared within this book may be difficult for racists to read, which is all the more reason to read this book, to honour our Pacific whanaunga and their truths, to challenge the structural racism that is embedded within our world, and, quite frankly, to be like our tamariki and learn through disruption and disturbing the dust. In this instance, I see the dust that needs to be disturbed as the dusty, crusty racists who will be mad about this book.

The editor and authors have come together as a rōpū, as whanaunga, to create a book that is critical, transformational, generative, and a beautiful koha to all of us in Aotearoa New Zealand. With koha, comes a commitment to being in good relation. In receiving this important, critical koha, we as readers are making a commitment to Pacific Peoples, and to having ongoing whanaungatanga. As readers, much like when we engage and commit to pōwhiri, we have a responsibility to honour, build and move in good relation, in solidarity, with Pacific Peoples in Aotearoa New Zealand, with all those who experience the violence of oppression, and to work towards unlearning and undoing racism. This is the whanaungatanga and the koha we commit to and can reciprocate for our whanaunga o Te Moana-nui-a-Kiwa.

Ki a koutou, e ngā whanaunga
nau mai
kōrero mai
werohia mai.
Tēnā koutou
tēnā tātou katoa.

*And so, to you, the relations*
*welcome here*
*speak here*
*bring forth your challenges here.*

# ARTIST'S NOTE

Vasemaca Tavola, *Na Wasawasa e Vamatana, na Wasawasa e Weisemati – Oceans Have Eyes, Oceans Connect Us All*

Textile assemblage: cotton, polycotton, synthetic felt, ric-rac trim, 1185 × 1260 mm.

THE TITLE OF THIS WORK REFERENCES the *i seru* motif at the centre of the assemblage. It is an abstraction of a traditional Fijian hair comb. In the Fijian language, the gaps in between the teeth of the comb are known as the comb's eyes. Here, the *i seru* and its many eyes offer a kind of visual scaffolding, a means to connect, reinforce and offer structure for the space between oceans, lands, bodies, hearts and minds.

I was introduced to Sereana Naepi via a textile banner I made in 2023 that simply said the words 'racism is tiring'. It was a work that spoke to the frustrations and fatigue of racism in all its forms. While firsthand experiences of racism can be confronting, embodied and infuriating, anti-racism work involves decoding, describing and translating these experiences in attempts to raise awareness and call it out. This is a form of largely unpaid and undervalued cultural/colonial labour that people do in their workplaces, in homes, schools, lecture halls, boardrooms, galleries, museums, hospitals, libraries, cafés and restaurants. This labour is necessary for attitudes, behaviours and systems to change, but before systems change, the obstacle course of shame, blame, erasure and white fragility can be a bruising affair.

Books like *Oceans Between Us* help with this burden of cultural labour. Making the artwork for this book cover was a way to honour those who have created this important resource. A book like this can help us navigate emotional, historical and systemic thresholds by articulating evidence-based arguments in the context of Aotearoa New Zealand.

I was inspired by the notion that the space and scale of that which needs to be crossed to find a place of understanding is a measurement of water: an ocean. I thought a lot about those places where waters meet, like what can be observed from Te Rerenga Wairua where the Tasman Sea meets the Pacific Ocean, and the scene in Disney's *Moana* (2016) when Moana parts the ocean to confront the fiery goddess Te Kā. As the late Teresia Teaiwa reminds us, 'We sweat and cry salt water, so we know that the ocean is really in our blood.'[1] I liken the scale and weight of an ocean to the work needed to confront racism in all its forms; unravelling the deep systemic rootedness of racial inequality has to start with the work individuals must do within themselves.

A textile assemblage is a laborious act; every stitch is a commitment to the vision and the kaupapa. I use this medium as a symbolic honouring of the undervalued and unseen work of women. I use the aesthetics of banners – as a medium of revolution and activism – to speak directly to issues that confront and disrupt our everyday lives. In this work, I honour the geometry, design and labour of floor mats made by Fijian women who commonly use fabric scraps from garment factories. They represent a level of creative integrity, entrepreneurship and technical skill that is literally walked all over. These thrice-folded fabric squares make a border of 253 triangles and speak to the falsehood of 'unskilled' labour – the backbone of Pacific migrations to Aotearoa to fulfil colonial and capital needs. In this assemblage of symbolic references, I hope this multicoloured, hand-made object can remind us of the human aspect of confronting racism and the life-giving potential of overcoming the oceans between us.

— *Vasemaca Tavola, Tāmaki Makaurau, January 2025*

# RACISM

## Why We Need to Talk About It
*Sereana Naepi*

RACISM. THERE, WE SAID IT. You can let your shoulders drop now that you know we will say the word and not sidestep it to protect people's comfort. Or, you can raise your shoulders in preparation for tension as you realise that this book will not talk about unconscious bias or other terms that enable us to excuse ourselves from our own complicity in, inaction on, or upholding of racist structures. Racism is the discrimination of peoples based on their socially constructed race. Racism can come in many forms and is a highly adaptive social practice that can be elusive to address. This book is here to raise awareness of racism, despite the stance of our previous prime minister, Chris Hipkins, that the word is a barrier to productive engagement.[1] I disagree with him; racism is an extremely helpful word. The word racism enables us to pinpoint not just moments of exclusion, such as racial slurs, but also long-term, proactive and complicit exclusion that is embedded into our systems. My call to our allies, accomplices, friends and collaborators is that if you are going to use the word racism, you need to be precise – open-heart surgery precise. The word racism enables us to open old wounds and begin to work through blockages that are preventing Pacific peoples from living their full lives. The analysis of structural racism offered in this book enables us to move away from focusing on individuals doing bad things towards an honest conversation about how foundational racism is to New Zealand;[2] how racism is part of the very structure of this country. Importantly, this book also explores how structural racism impacts Pacific peoples' prospects in this supposed land of milk and honey that promised hope for Pacific migrants to change our communities' futures: 'Niu Sila, the land of milk and honey. Niu Sila, the land of opportunity. Niu Sila, the land of education. Niu Sila, the land of good jobs'.[3]

The final draft of this manuscript came together in December 2023, just as the National, ACT and New Zealand First coalition agreement had been finalised. The National Party had no Pacific Members of Parliament and designated Dr Shane Reti (Ngāti Maniapoto, Ngāti Wai) as their Minister for Pacific Peoples.[4] During the campaign period, a number of public comments by party leaders raised concerns for Pacific peoples, including incidences of 'dog whistling' (where a politician uses coded language to get support from groups such as racists without actually using racist words).[5] ACT leader David Seymour joked in national media that he would like to 'send a guy called Guy Fawkes in there and it'd be all over' when discussing the dismantling of the Ministry for Pacific Peoples[6] in an ongoing campaign by his party against 'demographic ministries'[7] and 'ending division by race'.[8] The racial division that ACT is so against comprises equity measures designed to undo the systemic racism that results in Pacific peoples having disproportionately low life expectancies, low educational achievement, low home ownership rates, low levels of wealth, and high incarceration rates.[9] New Zealand First also campaigned on ending race-based policies.[10] As soon as the results for this election became clear, political commentators raised concerns about what this would mean for Pacific communities.[11] The final coalition agreement aims to end 'race based policies',[12] many of which have been put in place to end race-based inequity.

As we finalise the text of this book, the 2024 Budget has just been released, revealing that Pacific funding has been cut by

$26 million a year, and that some of the programmes impacted were designed to ensure Pacific peoples' access to housing, skills, training and business development.[13] More general policies, such as tax cuts and pro-rated sick leave, will negatively impact Pacific communities disproportionately.[14] Perhaps the most insulting aspect of some of these announcements was the fact that they were staged in Pacific community spaces, with community members smiling behind announcements that will create poor outcomes for their peers.[15] These stagings are perfect examples of just how structural racism works – while we look included, as we are in the announcements, what is being said and operationalised will harm our communities.

Our political landscape is showing us that the fight for equity and against racism is far from done. Sir Collin Tukuitonga has resigned from government-appointed board positions citing no confidence in the current government and wanting to be in a position to critique their policies.[16] Other Pacific leaders have supported Sir Collin's stance,[17] and launched their own critiques.[18] In the months prior to the general election, the late Fa'anānā Efeso Collins lost the Auckland City mayoral race, having noted that 'some of our research groups came back and told us quite clearly that one of the biggest issues I would face is the colour of my skin'.[19] This bubbling up of sentiments that have, for so long, been considered socially unacceptable to say out loud shows us that racism never went away – people just became better at hiding it. This shift back towards public racism means that it is more urgent than ever that we begin to question why and how we do certain things in our places of work, play and influence, or we will continue to be complicit in the further entrenchment of racism in our social structures.

The arrival of this book feels timely, as Pacific communities weigh up aligning ourselves with tangata whenua (people of the land) or attempting to participate in the model minority[20] story and the settler state.[21] Pacific peoples were initially allowed into New Zealand because there were labour shortages here.[22] As authors, some of us are the children of those who made the migration, whose parents and grandparents had aspirations for us in this new place. We have fulfilled those aspirations and then some – yet New Zealand has not rewarded our communities with the land of milk and honey. Pacific peoples as a whole do not have the opportunities, education and good jobs that inspired the initial migration. This situation is not an accident; it is evidence of how structural racism persists in New Zealand. The system is working by design and New Zealand will continue to break its promise of milk and honey to our ancestors and future generations unless structural racism is addressed.

## Structural Racism

Racism as an idea has a long history, particularly in how scholars debate, utilise and come to know the term. One issue that we often run into in conversations about racism is that it has become a term with multiple definitions and uses, and so recent efforts have called for the development of a language to discuss race and racism in New Zealand.[23] While we will not be able to explore every definition in this book, I do want to lay some foundations for where and how we speak about racism in this book. By doing so, I hope to make clear what this book will address, while also noting that there are many other experiences and ideas around racism that will not be accounted for in this book.

So, why structural racism when there are countless examples of personal racism? To answer that, I ask us to turn to Sara Ahmed's depiction of the world that we inherit and exist in as shaped and determined by its histories.[24] These histories shape our world and who gets to be at home within it. As Marcia Leenen-Young shows in her chapter, 'History', the histories of the New Zealand settler state, within the Pacific and here in Aotearoa New Zealand, have created narratives where Pacific peoples are weak, lazy, poor, criminal and violent. These colonial stereotypes carry over into contemporary perceptions of Pacific peoples and shape how structural racism operates and is responded to. Structural racism is shaped by and exists because of our histories. These histories shape our laws, education, migration, economy and health systems. As Charles Mills explains, this world is only possible because of the idea of White supremacy.[25] For Mills, our current world is built on racism as a 'political system, a particular power structure of formal or informal rule, socioeconomic privilege, and norms for the differential distribution of material wealth and opportunities, benefits and burdens, rights and duties'.[26] This structure means that Pacific peoples' poor statistics in this country are not a result of either their poor individual choices or mis-held stereotypes, but are actually evidence of racism within the system – if White supremacy is the worldview that made this world, then every interaction that we have with an institution is one that is rooted in this ideal, even if it is not outwardly practised anymore. The chapter 'Education' by Jean Uasike Allen, Toleafoa Yvonne Ualesi, David Taufui Mikato Fa'avae and Fetaui Iosefo provides insight into how structural racism has shaped their everyday experiences as educators and how they speak back to structural racism in their roles. We see further evidence of this process in the chapter 'Economy', co-authored by myself, Lisa Meto Fox, Dylan Asafo and Evalesi Tu'inukuafe, which calls into question the wider economic drivers in New Zealand and how they lead to overwhelming structural disadvantage for Pacific peoples. Our chapter interrogates the devaluing of Pacific peoples and their labour, and asks us whether we truly wish to be fully integrated into this system.

Structural racism can be understood through macro-processes, or what Eduardo Bonilla-Silva terms racialised social systems, where 'societies in which economic, political, social, and ideological levels are partially structured by the placement of actors in racial categories or races'.[27] In short, the colour of your skin or your nationality shapes what you can access within society. We see one such example in Evalesi Tu'inukuafe's chapter, 'Migration', which explores New Zealand's migration policies and how they operate to devalue Pacific labour while simultaneously laying claim to be acting in the Pacific's best interests. Dylan Asafo's chapter, 'Climate Justice', showcases this on a global scale through the idea of 'legal violence', where capitalism and racism operate hand in hand to create an unjust system for Pacific peoples.

Structural racism can be tracked and measured using both quantitative and qualitative data. When we track structural racism, we enable a pattern of evidence to be built that can help to convince others of the need to change and also guide where we can invest our limited resourcing.[28] Caleb Marsters' chapter, 'Health', showcases how health has tracked structural racism over time and developed frameworks for change. It is particularly common in education to track how racism impacts access and success.[29] In my chapter, 'Higher Education', we see how data can enable us to visualise patterns in our overall structures. By considering the higher education space, we can track the impact of structural racism on Pacific peoples and come to understand the power of data in addition to our own experiences. Barbara-Luhia Graham's chapter, 'Justice Systems', provides insight into the power of qualitative stories for understanding how structural racism shapes not only a single experience in the courtroom but somebody's entire life. When we track and measure structural racism, we provide much-needed evidence for change.

Overall, these chapters come together to story the many different ways that Pacific peoples experience and have their lives shaped by structural racism. The final chapter by Chelsea Naepi, 'The Next Generation', weaves together all of the preceding chapters to ask what they mean for Pacific peoples and what our next movements can be if we all agree that it showcases a reality for Pacific peoples that is simply not acceptable.

We came together as a collective of authors as we all knew in our different spaces that structural racism was impacting our communities. We all knew that our communities' aspirations were not being supported by today's systems. We wanted to provide a space where we could document our collective evidence and make a strong call for change, particularly during a time when hard-fought-for gains are being systematically disestablished under urgency. We came together knowing that this book would enable us to say the unsayable:

*racism*

# HISTORY

# 'They Call Me a Bunga'
Colonialism, History and Stereotypes in Aotearoa New Zealand

*Marcia Leenen-Young*

We live in a racist society. If you are of Pacific descent and you live in Aotearoa New Zealand, this is inescapable. But this reality is also heavily denied by the majority of the country. There was an uproar in 2018 when Māori director Taika Waititi, in an interview with *Dazed*, suggested that New Zealand is racist. He stated, 'if you're Poly then you're getting profiled'.[1] And there is a distinction here; Waititi was not just calling out racism as an ingrained part of our society but illuminating that there is a framework of prejudice in New Zealand that is based on being Polynesian, infused with negative stereotypical ideas of what it means to be from the Pacific.[2]

That these stereotypes are pervasive in Aotearoa New Zealand society is without doubt. They have been seen in previous years by journalist Heather du Plessis-Allan's reference to the Pacific Islands as leeches in 2019[3] and the widespread class- and race-based vitriol targeted at a Pacific family in 2020 in South Auckland due to a COVID-19 outbreak.[4] Social media in particular allows people to openly show their racial prejudices. In 2023, it was found that the New Zealand Government's 2021 apology to Pacific peoples for the historic Dawn Raids of the 1970s was hollow because there was no real change to the methods of Immigration New Zealand (as a government agency), which was, at that time, still conducting raids at dawn.[5] While this in itself shows an alarming disregard for the trauma of the Dawn Raids era, responses on social media to this report included statements like 'Stop? They need to return' and 'Apologising to the dawn raids illegal overstayers is like apologizing to someone who got arrested for stealing your car'.[6] Even political leaders in this country display racist attitudes towards Pacific peoples, as shown by ACT leader David Seymour's comment on sending Guy Fawkes into the Ministry for Pacific Peoples in the lead-up to the 2023 election – an election that made him co-deputy prime minister.[7]

Comments such as this show that racial prejudice is alive and kicking in Aotearoa New Zealand, but what is less realised is that this racism has deeply ingrained historical origins. It is rooted within our institutions and social fabric, borne from the past shared by the Pacific and New Zealand. This is the crux of the issue – how can Pacific peoples prosper in a society that still, clearly, has deeply ingrained racial prejudices and believes in these stereotypes? So much of our history – the history of Pacific peoples and New Zealand – is simply invisible to the majority of the population living in New Zealand. But history can tell us many things about this deep-seated racial prejudice that defines the way many New Zealanders see Pacific peoples. The lack of understanding of our shared history is a concern, because without an understanding of the historical connections between us, there can only be limited understanding of the place that Pacific peoples have in New Zealand society today and the deeply held responsibility that New Zealand has to the Pacific and to Pacific peoples. History is crucial to the way we see ourselves and how we connect to people and place, but history is also a curated picture of the past that forms and establishes key cultural narratives that become part of a collective consciousness – and this is where stereotypes take root.

This chapter is an exploration of these racial prejudices and their historical foundations, many of which were created in the colonial period and have been perpetuated in New Zealand society to the point where they are now part of the social fabric and structures within which we live – both perpetuating and reinforcing the negative stereotypes commonly thrown at Pacific peoples. But how are these racial prejudices and stereotypes connected to this book and the structural racism Pacific peoples face daily in Aotearoa New Zealand? The connection between racial stereotypes and systemic racism is circular. Racial stereotypes historically justified how the systems within which we live were built; these systems contribute to the continuation of these racial stereotypes by confining access to opportunity to those it was built to serve – Pālagi (Pākehā).[8] Our realities are inherited from what has come before, so history and, significantly, colonialism have shaped the world we live in – including the narratives that remain from this period through stereotypes. In this world, race is a social construction that determines what we have access to, and according to Sara Ahmed, 'whiteness is an orientation that puts certain things within reach'.[9] Structural racism determines this access, or lack of access, both historically and in our contemporary society.

The system of government in Aotearoa New Zealand was built on the convictions that Indigenous peoples were unable to govern themselves and that Pākehā had the qualities needed to build a nation and lead it. This is linked to the colonial conviction that Europeans were superior because they were 'civilised' – which was, of course, racially determined. Historically, then, racial convictions of superiority drove the development of a system that privileged the powerful in these early societies, contributing to the development of government systems, policies and law – structures within which we still live in New Zealand. Racism is historically 'baked in' to the structures of our society. Additionally, this created historical precedents, defining particular memories, attitudes and beliefs as the fabric of this system and contributing to the development of a cultural narrative that defines the roles and hierarchies of people within society. This system determined how society was organised, which means that the fabric of our social and political systems in Aotearoa New Zealand, like many Western countries globally, is founded on ideas of racial difference and superiority. Stereotypes supported the building of these systems, but they also work to uphold the status quo in societies to ensure continued oppression based on racial prejudice.[10] History functions within this space to support the cultural narratives established through colonisation, empire-building and the development of nationhood, which has harmed Indigenous peoples for hundreds of years through narratives made to reinforce the 'truth' of racial stereotypes.[11]

Pacific peoples have faced these stereotypes for decades, although the reaction to racial slurs such as bunga, freshy, FOB and coconut has varied. This response has changed, generally, by generation, with many of our parents and grandparents brushing these stereotypes aside as just part of living in the 'land of milk and honey'.[12] But as successive generations have been born and raised in New Zealand, the tolerance of racial slurs thrown at Pacific communities has worn thin. Like many Indigenous peoples, Pacific peoples have inverted racist stereotypes for both humour and empowerment.[13] This process can be seen, for instance, in the early 2000s with the success of *bro'Town* as satire that loudly displayed the tensions between different Pacific stereotypes, or the flipping of derogatory terms by labels such as PopoHardWear.[14] Such acts of assertion are part of a period of time that Melani Anae refers to as the 'browning' of New Zealand, where Pacific peoples and cultures became entwined with New Zealand's national consciousness and identity.[15] But we are now 20 years past this 'browning', and while Pacific peoples and cultures are part of the New Zealand infrastructure and its national identity, racist stereotypes of Pacific peoples are still pervasive. This must change.

While successive generations have reacted differently to Pacific stereotypes, SWIDT's *Bunga* represents the Pacific youth of Aotearoa today, clearly and unapologetically shouting that enough is enough. Released in 2019, *Bunga* is a short film developed by a group of young Polynesian men collectively known as SWIDT.[16] *Bunga* is more than a song; it is visually and audibly a push against racism towards Pacific communities. Its style is assertive and confronting, with the main actor, Chris Alosio, staring at the camera while he undergoes transformation from a young Tongan man eating dinner with his family to an activist in the guise of the Polynesian Panthers of the 1970s, greeting police at the door as they demand to see his ID (in reference to the Dawn Raids and police harassment based on racial profiling in the 1970s). While Pacific music often reflects the realities of our communities, rarely has it done so in such a confronting and polemic way. The lyrics of *Bunga* highlight a number of stereotypes aimed at Pacific peoples – lazy, weak, poor, criminal and violent. It calls out New Zealand society as one that embraces Pacific peoples when we have something to offer (as in sporting achievements or labour) but otherwise devalues us as a community and relegates us to 'the have nots and the have less'.[17] *Bunga* is the collective cry of Pacific youth in Aotearoa New Zealand against unfair and *untrue* stereotyping of our communities. As Allyssa Verner-Pula, a young Samoan woman, states in a piece she wrote for *Craccum*, the University of Auckland's student magazine:

> In my mind, SWIDT's *Bunga* is an act of reclamation, speaking to the Pacific experience in New Zealand, while retorting back against such ideas, subliminally highlighting the inaccuracies and falsities of these fabrications about Pacific peoples. Conclusively, *Bunga* helped jumpstart my journey of dismantling how I reckon with being labelled a 'bunga'.[18]

*Bunga* is a confronting picture of Pacific realities. For many non-Pacific in New Zealand, this is both uncomfortable and shocking. This was seen when broadcaster John Campbell, a fan of SWIDT, asked if, in the largest Pacific city in the world, Pacific peoples really had such experiences. In response, a member of the

SWIDT collective, SPYCC, stated that *Bunga* was a 'generalisation of collective lived experiences of Pasifika in New Zealand'.[19] SmokeyGotBeatz, another MC, spoke of *Bunga* as being from their grandparents' perspective with the visual focus on the Dawn Raids, stating that these experiences 'linger down on us'.[20] And they do. Pacific peoples in Aotearoa have inherited the trauma of our ancestors' experiences in trying to survive in the so-called 'land of milk and honey'.[21]

That is why *Bunga* is an ideal vehicle for exploring stereotypes Pacific peoples face today, with lyrics that point to Pacific peoples as lazy, weak, poor, criminal and violent. All these stereotypes that New Zealand society applies to us as Pacific peoples are referenced in *Bunga*. In this chapter, I am going to explore these four stereotypes, inspired by the words of SWIDT, and trace the historical foundations of these stereotypes, which have now become part of the way Pacific peoples are viewed nationally.[22] I will then look briefly at the contemporary implications of these stereotypes and how they still, to this day, impact the experiences of Pacific peoples. Inescapably, Pacific peoples appear in all negative statistics in this country – but, in the words of Teresia Teaiwa and Sean Mallon, this is 'historically-produced disadvantage'[23] and not a reflection of the 'truth' of these stereotypes. For anything to change for Pacific peoples in this country, it must be understood that we currently live in a context created by the historical relationship between New Zealand and the Pacific, lest these racist stereotypes of Pacific peoples continue to represent our communities for wider, Whiter New Zealand.

## Historical Blind Spots

Despite living in a settler colony, New Zealanders see colonisation as a distant phenomenon unconnected to us as a country and as a people. The largest historical blind spot that New Zealand has is its own position as a colonial power in the Pacific.[24] Somehow, since New Zealand did not colonise on the scale of Britain or the

US, it is seen to have been 'less' than other colonisers – less violent, less traumatic, less horrific overall. And in some ways, this may be worse – New Zealand has styled itself as a benevolent coloniser that, really, did no harm and instead improved the lives and prospects of the people it colonised.[25] But it would be an error to think that this colonial past did not (still) impact Pacific peoples both in the Pacific and here in Aotearoa New Zealand.

Samoan historian Damon Salesa highlights this historical blind spot and advocates for a clear identification of New Zealand as an empire-state.[26] This ascription would seem ludicrous to some – New Zealand as an empire?! But this label connects not only to New Zealand's colonial past, but also to the clear and extended imperial ambitions held by those who led New Zealand from the mid-1800s towards what they believed was New Zealand's Pacific destiny.[27] From the 1840s, New Zealand aggressively pursued opportunities that increased its power and territory in the Pacific. In 1845, Charles Buller made a speech to the British House of Commons that made this ambition clear: 'a British Colony in New Zealand would be the natural master of this ocean . . . and from that new seat of your dominion you might give laws and manners to a new world, upholding subject races, and imposing your will on the strong'.[28] In 1848, Governor George Grey proposed that New Zealand annex Fiji and Tonga, a request that was denied by the British Colonial Office – but this set the tone for the following fifty years as New Zealand politicians attempted time and again to gain a foothold in the Pacific.[29] As Salesa states, the British are the ones who actually curbed New Zealand's ambitions to create a 'Little Britain' in the South Pacific, without which New Zealand's empire would have been far larger.[30] In the end, New Zealand's empire included the Cook Islands, Niue, Sāmoa, Nauru and Tokelau; all through different circumstances, but all in order to increase the prosperity and power of New Zealand.

This historical blind spot has supported the development and perpetuation of key aspects of New Zealand's international and national identity: first, the idea that New Zealand is a leader in positive race relations, and second, that its presence in the Pacific, and support of Pacific peoples in New Zealand, is altruistic and benevolent. New Zealand's historic reputation for being a leader in race relations stems from a settler-colonial belief that their dealings with Māori were successful. From the perspective of Māori, this is of course not true, but it is a fallacy that New Zealand has carried for a long time. It followed New Zealand into the Pacific, where they believed that this 'success' made them ideal colonisers of a people who shared ancestry with Māori. This belief was also wrapped up with the eugenics movement and racial classification ideas of the late 1800s and early 1900s, according to which Polynesian peoples were 'nearly Caucasian' and so able to be more easily 'civilised' and become part of a Western society, although obviously without the privileges afforded to Whiteness.[31]

American psychologist David Ausubel wrote a book, *The Fern and the Tiki: An American View of New Zealand National Character, Social Attitudes, and Race Relations*, based on his time as a Fulbright scholar in New Zealand in 1957–58.[32] While the research that this book is founded on reflects the questionable research ethics of the time, its conclusions had lasting impacts in an era of increased awareness of Indigenous rights in the 1960s and 1970s, and called into question New Zealand's claim to be a leader in 'positive race relations'.[33] Ausubel states:

> The most striking impression an American receives of race relations in New Zealand is that although they are generally much better than in the United States, they are not nearly as people think or claim they are. New Zealanders abroad, as well as those who shepherd tourists around within the country, describe the situation, both orally and through official Government publications, as: 'The most successful mixing of two races yet achieved. This is one thing we New Zealanders are really proud of – the way we handle our race relations.'[34]

Peter Meihana traces the idea of Māori privilege and the idea that many still hold in New Zealand that, comparatively, the experiences of Māori are not as bad as those of other Indigenous peoples.[35] This belief of superior race relations feeds into the image of New Zealand as benevolent and altruistic. Colonisation is frequently framed within the parameters of benevolence, with the 'civilising' of the Indigenous peoples primarily being done out of concern for their 'best interests'; which always happened to be the best interests of the colonisers. This argument is often accompanied by the image of the coloniser as the 'father' and the Indigenous people as the 'children' needing to be brought into the 'light' of civilisation. The paternalism that underlies New Zealand's actions in the Pacific is minimalised within the frame of 'good intentions', masking the significance of this image in gaining and maintaining influence. But there is no other way to spin it. New Zealand's paternalistic attitude towards the Pacific was born from an initial belief of racial superiority and an ingrained conviction that New Zealand deserved to lead the Pacific into the modern, civilised world. This paternalism is *still evident* in our society, embedded in the framings of Pacific peoples – as *Bunga* portrays – as poor, criminal, lazy, unskilled, weak and violent.

## Pacific Peoples in New Zealand and the Birth of Stereotypes

Damon Salesa points out that 'the circumstances of New Zealand are so very different from those of the islands that Pacific people who have migrated have had to remake their lives and adapt their cultures and lifeways in all kinds of ways'.[36] Pacific peoples in contemporary Aotearoa New Zealand have done this remaking, and now occupy a pivotal place that sits outside the rhetoric of 'diversity' or 'equity' often used to justify measures that support the non-White population of Aotearoa New Zealand. While Māori and Pacific are often lumped together, our place and rights are different, with Māori as tangata whenua. While Pacific peoples are not from this land, we are not simply another ethnic group; we are now part of the fabric of New Zealand's national identity. Initiatives and programmes that support Pacific peoples in this country are not equity measures to help those who are 'underachieving', but instead recognise New Zealand's responsibility to Pacific peoples and the systemic issues that have been endemic since New Zealand began colonising the Pacific and its peoples. The existence of Pacific peoples outside the structures that focus on 'equity groups' in Aotearoa New Zealand is evidenced by the existence of the Ministry for Pacific Peoples, first established in 1990 as the Ministry of Pacific Island Affairs, in recognition of the growing Pacific population. It is also evidenced by the formation over the last 20 years of multiple Pacific/Pasifika Education Plans by the Ministry of Education. Yes, we do feature in all the statistics of underachievement, but the reasons for this lie in our deep colonial past with New Zealand and the fact that we are part of a structure that was made for Pālagi to prosper – not us. Additionally, we must remember that there are parts of the Pacific intimately entwined with the territory of New Zealand. Tokelau is the northernmost point of New Zealand, as a dependent territory. Niue and the Cook Islands are both self-governing in free association with New Zealand, and, significantly, have automatic New Zealand citizenship. These unique connections demonstrate that New Zealand's connection to the Pacific and Pacific peoples goes beyond the framework of 'equity' and instead towards a deep-seated responsibility for the wellbeing and prosperity of Pacific peoples – a responsibility that New Zealand actively sought in the campaign to become the 'Britain of the South Pacific'.

Stereotypes of Pacific peoples can be traced through historical periods in the Pacific, from the earliest arrival of Europeans to the formation of colonial governments, to more recent experiences of Pacific peoples in Aotearoa New Zealand. Stewart Firth claims that one of the most significant achievements of the coloniser in the Pacific was the creation of the image of the 'Native'.[37] This was the development of an image of Pacific peoples in opposition to

Pālagi, with characteristics that were diametrically opposed. Albert Wendt, in his 'Towards a New Oceania', explains the character types that Pacific peoples were cast as by early Europeans: 'the colonisers prescribed for us the roles of domestic animal, amoral phallus, the lackey, the comic, lazy and happy-go-lucky fuzzy-haired boy, and the well-behaved colonised'.[38] By comparison, the Pālagi was civilised, intelligent, controlled, masculine, strong – everything that the Islander was not. This initial dichotomy drawn by colonisers in the Pacific has directly contributed to the stereotypes of Pacific peoples that still exist today in Aotearoa. That these depictions of Pacific peoples have endured shows us that in the last 200 years, despite all that has happened in the world, Pacific peoples are still cast as inferior. And that is what the continued belief in these stereotypes means – calling someone a bunga, coconut or freshy is not harmless; the historical connotations of these words **have weight** in today's society.

So, what does bunga mean? According to Te Papa Tongarewa, bunga is a racist term for a person of colour, especially a Pacific person.[39] Alice Lolohea of *Tangata Pasifika* refers to bunga as 'a word used with the intent to emotionally harm and demean Pacific people'.[40] The origin of the term bunga is not as easy to find as coconut or freshy, which are kind of obvious, but it seems to be a slur particular to New Zealand. Bunga as a term beyond the Pacific links to sex parties held by Italian former prime minister Silvio Berlusconi, to a racist joke about being captured by an African tribe, and to a blackface 'practical joke' from 1910 called the Dreadnought Hoax where a group of British aristocrats pretended to be the Emperor of Abyssinia (Ethiopia) and his entourage.[41] It is uncertain whether these contexts link to the use of the word in the Pacific and Aotearoa, but one thing that can be agreed upon is that it is a derogatory term used to refer to Pacific peoples in New Zealand. This usage is what features in SWIDT's *Bunga*, a slur against Pacific peoples, associated with all of the negative stereotypes thrown at us in Aotearoa New Zealand. Unless, of course, you are a Pacific person who achieves national fame and are then claimed as a New Zealander, as SWIDT state:[42]

> ... *they only love us if its sports achievements*
> *Siana, see a bungas what they call that, unless you scoring*
> *tries for the All Blacks then you kiwi* (lines 5–6)

But the question remains, what are the historical foundations for these stereotypes? And how have these stereotypes contributed to the systemic and personal racism that Pacific peoples face today in Aotearoa? Part of the difficulty in writing history is that there are always multiple layers, and it can be difficult to feel like you are covering things adequately – this is the way I feel about the following sections; there is so much to discuss and it is complicated. And, as a historian, my instinct is always to search for more information, but the space here is limited. These stereotypes overlap and feed into each other, but for the purposes of analysing each stereotype, the divisions (although somewhat arbitrary) are necessary. The depth of history dealt with in the following sections is only the trunk of the coconut tree – vital and useful, but bare without the palms, fruit and flowers. This is the start of a story that, still, is yet to be fully told.

### Stereotype 1: Pacific People Are Weak ...

> *We have to die before they pay homage*
> *Just a inter-generational cycle where we don't make progress*
> ... (lines 15–16)

> *Tyrants with a smug affliction*
> *Embedded too deep into drug addiction and gambling ...*
> (lines 18–19)

> *See there's little to no hope g, emotions isn't manly*
> *You don't understand me, bunga* ... (lines 21–22)

Weakness as a stereotype is at the heart of the historical image of 'the Native' in the Pacific: weak-minded, weak morally, weak in all ways that the opposing European was strong. The idea of Pacific peoples as 'weak' may seem ridiculous considering the physical strength that is often associated with people of the Pacific, as exemplified by celebrities like Dwayne 'The Rock' Johnson. Early colonisers also saw Pacific peoples as physically strong and large, with French explorer Louis-Antoine de Bougainville commenting on his arrival in Tahiti: 'furthermore the race is superb, with men 5 feet 10 inches tall, many reaching six foot, a few exceeding this'.[43] But the weakness of this stereotype was not physical; it applied to the mind and character of Pacific peoples.

According to colonisers, the 'Native mind' was weak. This applied to the perceived 'intelligence' of Pacific peoples and also their ability to comprehend development – a 'fault' linked to a perceived lack of industry. There are many historical aspects to this image, which began with the characterisation of Pacific peoples by early explorers as pure, uncorrupted by modern society, and childlike.[44] This characterisation of Pacific peoples as childlike implied a lack of civilisation, intellectual ability, or ability to develop in Western terms, and also designated the coloniser as a 'father-like' figure who knew better and had to guide Pacific peoples out of their uncivilised ways, as a father would do. Paternalism limits the rights of the colonised *for their own good* because they are not able to look after their own interests.[45] We see this in the Pacific with the arrival of the first permanent missionaries from the 1700s, who tried to 'save' heathens by converting them, and we also see this through the taking of formal control by colonial governments such as New Zealand. New Zealand's colonisation in the Pacific was framed within this altruistic notion of paternity, where it supposedly acted for the good of Pacific peoples as a benevolent master rather than in self-interest. So, the actions of New Zealand and other colonisers in colonising Pacific peoples were directly linked to this idea of Pacific peoples as weak-minded and unable to determine their own political futures.

This perceived weakness connects to the notion that non-Europeans were inferior and has its roots in the Enlightenment in Europe in the late 1700s and early 1800s, which cemented ideas about race.[46] This was the era of European exploration of the Pacific, so these ideas coloured early interactions between European voyagers and Pacific peoples, many of which were led by men who were part of this 'intellectual revolution' (such as Captain James Cook). In essence, the Enlightenment in its search for knowledge introduced the idea of quasi-'scientific' racial categorisations that laid the foundation in the Pacific for further divisions imposed on Pacific peoples by Europeans. In 1832, Jules Durmont D'Urville published his division of the Pacific Ocean based on his observations – Polynesia: many islands; Micronesia: small islands; Melanesia: black islands.[47] In the late 1800s and early 1900s, these 'scientific' classifications built towards the eugenics movement, which seemed, again, to 'prove' the superiority of Pālagi.[48] The search for knowledge at these points in history has only served to reinforce racism, despite intentions – first through theories of humanity, and then, while colonisation was sweeping the globe, through claims of biological superiority based on science. 'The Brain of the Native', published in 1938 anonymously in the *Pacific Islands Monthly*, stated that the Melanesian brain is markedly different from the brain of the European, and that the 'animal instincts of uncivilised people, which we know to be a dominating influence in the general racial character, [are] in reality due to an anatomical excess from which there can be no escape'.[49] The Native, then, was biologically inferior, primitive in thought, and weak-minded, much like a child. This justified the colonial structures that early nations were built on, and within these structures the subjugation of Indigenous Pacific knowledges and people.

This 'weakness' included an inability to be responsible or control base instincts. In 1919, the Australian governor of New Guinea wrote that 'the Native is a primitive being, with no well developed sense of duty or responsibility. A full belly and comfortable bed are his chief desiderata'.[50] In 1923, the Methodist mission chairman in Fiji pointed out that Native ministers did not want to manage their own stipends for fear of their Indigenous chiefs, seeing the European as the ideal person to manage finances, stating 'you must take the NATIVE MIND into consideration when attempting to put responsibility on him'.[51] This sentiment illustrates a perceived weakness in terms of responsibility, in this case for managing finances and keeping them out of the hands of Fijian communities. The childlike image of Pacific peoples was linked to a lack of ability to control impulses and desires; the weakness of the Native mind meaning that the primitive Pacific person could not be trusted to regulate their own behaviour.

This ingrained belief that there was a weakness in the mind and character of Pacific peoples limited opportunities and access, as Pālagi confined us to what they decided was appropriate. This was central to the way governments and social systems were built, and informed an education system that did not encourage Pacific peoples to aim beyond their 'limited' abilities. In 1905, Walter Gudgeon, the New Zealand Resident Commissioner in the Cook Islands, spoke on the education system:

> In such communities education can only create a desire for things unattainable. At the best only one in twenty of the boys will obtain employment as clerks or storemen, and the rest will be spoiled for the work for which they are best fitted – viz., the cultivation of the soil.
>
> I would point out that the principles of education and evolution have not yet begun to work among the Polynesians; their only idea on the subject of education is that they may thereby acquire wealth and avoid work.[52]

A couple of decades later, New Zealand was luring Pacific peoples from their homelands specifically to fill the unskilled labour market that they had educated us for, informed by this idea of our 'weak minds' being inferior to those of Pālagi. The implications of this in Aotearoa in the current context are clear. There are systemic barriers to education for Pacific students predicated on this initial failure to see beyond manual labour and built on racial prejudice. Such attitudes were prevalent in the Pacific until after World War II, with limited opportunity beyond primary school in New Zealand's colonies. This is an intergenerational issue based on limited access to education but also on the prevalence of the idea of differing intellectual ability in our society. Many still believe that Pacific peoples are best suited for work in the fields and factories. Pacific peoples have been told, generation after generation, that they only have the ability to reach a certain level of education. This stereotype has not only infected society generally in Aotearoa New Zealand but has also seeped into the consciousness of our own Pacific peoples with disastrous results.

### Stereotype 2: Pacific People Are Lazy . . .

> *Unemployed not because these employees aren't hiring*
> *or cos we not tryin*
> *But because we dole bludgers, down low dirty soul*
> *suckers . . .* (lines 10–11)

> *Life's devalued in my section, you see we reproduce and have*
> *kids, only to neglect em*
> *We using our kids as a weapon*
> *We the minority, whom should be government funding*
> *priority*
> *But they perplexed about a flag, only to raise it sky high*
> *on stolen land . . .* (lines 23–26)

The belief that Pacific peoples are 'lazy' is deeply anchored in multiple historical eras, from the invasion of the Pacific by Europeans to the colonial era and the introduction of moneyed economies based on the commodification of agriculture. It is common to hear about 'island time' in Aotearoa, which implies a lack of concern for structures of time that dictate the rhythms of life in a Western society – connected to the idea that Pacific peoples value leisure above productivity. This has always seemed like a particularly unfair stereotype to me, having been raised watching the incredible labour that our families perform for each other, our churches, and our communities.

Historically, this stereotype is linked to the Western lens through which early European explorers viewed our societies – as places concerned only with pleasure and relaxation. In comparison to the societies they had come from, the difference would have been stark, especially after the months they had spent at sea confined to a ship. But this judgement has very little to do with us as lazy and a lot to do with cultural disconnection, Christian moral structures, and rampant romanticisation of early Pacific cultures by Europeans. French explorer Louis de Bougainville characterised Tahiti in 1767 as New Cythera, after the birthplace of the Greek goddess of love, Aphrodite. It does not take much imagination to figure out why, but this image is one that has been enduring.

The image of Pacific peoples as lazy was bolstered further in the colonial era with the formal development of a moneyed economy that demanded the development of a labour force. By the 1860s, industry had entered the Pacific and labour was a commodity, especially on whaling ships. With this shift came the development of large-scale plantation agriculture in the Pacific driven by Europeans, which demanded a large labour force. The problem was that there was limited appeal for Pacific peoples to work on these plantations – they had their own land to work and community to support, which gave them all they needed to thrive. Of course, some Pacific peoples did decide to forgo subsistence farming and work on these plantations, but this did not fill the demand for labour. With these large plantations came seizure of land from Indigenous peoples and the development of more centralised power platforms for Pālagi, which, in many places, eventually led to formal annexation and colonial governments. But cheap labour was necessary for the success of these plantations, increasingly in the form of indentured labour where people agreed to work off (extremely low-pay and high-living-cost) contracts over a set number of years in exchange for passage to the Pacific. These agreements attracted people who were looking for a better life and led to widespread migration from Asia and India into the Pacific, particularly Fiji, Sāmoa, Hawai'i, Guam, New Caledonia and New Guinea. A by-product of this process was the bolstering of the image of Pacific peoples as lazy, since they did not immediately jump to provide the labour force necessary for Pālagi industry – and so entered the image of Pacific people lying under coconut trees while other people laboured in the sun to meet the demands of this new, increasingly Westernised society.

When New Zealand began to colonise the Pacific, this image of lazy Pacific peoples was already part of the international landscape. New Zealand administrators in the Pacific could not understand the lack of industry that they observed from Pacific peoples, specifically in what they considered was not 'correct' use of land. In the Pacific at this point in the early twentieth century, land was a shared commodity to provide for the community, not an asset to make profit from. This context led to efforts by the New Zealand Administration to regulate land 'ownership' to create prosperous plantation-based economies based on their priorities as a colonial power to establish Western types of industry. This was seen through the efforts of the early New Zealand Resident Commissioners in the Pacific, who turned their attention to regulating land 'ownership' before almost anything else.[53] This process links to the image of Pacific peoples 'bludging' off the system, a Western system that historically has seen us as less able to participate in a capitalist society and so *consciously* relegated us to low-skilled positions.

This historically determined image of us as lazy has also been an easy target for blame towards Pacific peoples, and has been for over 100 years. In the influenza outbreak of 1918 in Sāmoa, the New

Zealand administrator, Colonel Robert Logan, blamed the Samoan people for the high death toll, claiming they had not helped themselves.[54] The idea that we are inherently lazy and unable (or unwilling) to help ourselves has taken root in the institutions and structures of society in New Zealand. The healthcare, education and justice systems all perpetuate these ideas, as does wider society. How many times have we heard that if we just helped ourselves, we would be healthier and more successful? But this is a simplistic argument that denies the racist systems we live within, which were never made for us and decided very early on that the *lazy Islander* would never prosper in a Western society.

### Stereotype 3: Pacific People Are Poor . . .

> *They call me a bunga, they poke fun at the accent, yet only speak one language*
>
> *See I'm a bunga, the have nots and the have less, a park bench for an address*
> *A bunga, we always blessed with some bad press, our living situation average*
> *Just a bunga, I share a room with 6 relatives, we draw heat from a stove top element* . . . (lines 1–4)
>
> *We spend our rent on the pokies, we give a fuck about our families* . . . (line 20)

This stereotype of Pacific peoples as poor has many different links to history. First is the link to our perceived lack of industry mentioned above, which for the Pālagi meant we would never be successful. From the 1790s, industry entered the Pacific, with Europeans searching for resources such as bêche-de-mer and sandalwood, or hunting whales, the biggest industry in the Pacific in this period. While Pacific peoples did take part in whaling, it was not on the same scale as Pālagi, and often Pacific people on whaling ships had the most risky and dangerous jobs.[55] Many early colonisers in the Pacific were in search of resources to exploit (the sealife, the moana, the land, the people), and this objective meant that, very early on, they built monopolies around those resources. Key examples of this are the Colonial Sugar Refining Company, which opened in Fiji in 1882, and the Dole Pineapple Plantation in Hawai'i, which grew from a farm purchased in 1899 in the wake of the American seizure of Hawai'i.[56] The rise of large plantations in the Pacific led to large-scale exporting ventures dominated by Pālagi, which in many cases led to political intervention by Europeans and European nations in order to protect the financial prosperity of these plantations. The drive to exploit resources pushed colonialism all over the world, and the Pacific was no different. Pacific peoples were also actively blocked from participating in this industry to any large extent, with small Indigenous plantation owners often paid at rates below their larger Pālagi counterparts. A good example of this is the creation of the Tonga Ma'a Tonga Kautaha in 1909 to stop the monopoly of European traders who were getting rich off exports while paying a pittance to Tongan growers. Hand in hand with the rise of these European monopolies came the relegation of Pacific peoples to the role of labourer and Europeans to the role of owner, which set the tone for who was financially prosperous in the Pacific in the nineteenth and early twentieth centuries.[57]

The education system was established to aid this placement of Pacific peoples into the 'labourer' category – supported, as mentioned above, by colonial ideas of ability and intelligence, which were racially informed, with Whiteness associated with the pinnacle of these traits. This means that perceived ability was determined by skin colour, with access to opportunity and education limited to Pālagi or those Pacific people who were deemed to be 'exceptional'.[58] Although there were exceptions, colonisers in the Pacific largely trained us specifically to fill low-skill and low-wage positions, because they believed education was something that was not necessary for Indigenous Pacific peoples

– first, because they believed we had limited capacity, and second, because they did not need us to be highly educated to fill the roles they saw for us in these new societies they were creating.

In New Zealand's Pacific colonies, there is a clear connection between the conviction that Pacific peoples were best suited for unskilled roles, the level of education we were allowed, and the needs of the coloniser. In the 1950s, New Zealand was in the midst of the post-war economic boom and sought cheap, low-skilled labour on a large scale. Workers for these jobs were needed immediately, but they were jobs that the majority of the New Zealand population did not want – they were low-skilled, low-paid jobs, mainly in factories, and hard on the body. People migrated from all over the Pacific, but largely from countries that New Zealand controlled as a colonial power. This flood of Pacific peoples, lured with the promise of a 'land of milk and honey', led to the growth of a Pacific population in New Zealand who were, from the point when we first entered the country, relegated to low-paying roles in society. With no intergenerational wealth to build upon, with limited education, and with an expectation in New Zealand society that we were particularly suited to low-skilled jobs, Pacific peoples had limited ability to prosper and so were seen by society more widely as poorer – we arrived here on the back foot and have been kept there by limited opportunity and education, and by the narrow expectations society has of us. The idea of Pacific peoples as 'poor' was built on the idea that we loved leisure and were not capable of being more than unskilled labourers. It is a stereotype decided by the form of migration Pacific peoples had to New Zealand – one based on our provision of cheap labour and exacerbated by the huge influx of Pacific peoples to the factories of New Zealand.

Theoretically, ability leads to opportunity that leads to education (or training) that leads to success in financial terms, which in turn leads to the ability to participate in a Western society. But what happens when 'ability' or 'intelligence' is judged by a racist system that has actively told you, for generations, that you only fit into one small part of this society – as the labourers, the factory workers, the agricultural workers? It has been difficult to break out of this role society assigned to us decades ago, leading to a cycle of poverty. Damon Salesa, in *Island Time*, talks about locked-out segregation in Auckland and how school zoning and property prices mean that Pacific communities only occupy certain areas of the city, which has implications for the quality of education our children have and access to employment.[59] It is easy to point to education as a way to break out of these cycles, and it can be, but our communities often have competing priorities and are torn between getting an education to get a better-paying job and the immediate needs of supporting our families. This can be seen starkly post-COVID-19, as many of our young people now see education as a luxury beyond their reach because they must work fulltime in the same places and industries as their parents to provide for their families in a cost-of-living crisis. Pacific peoples are also often in precarious jobs and are the first to lose employment. This phenomenon is global, recognised as 'migrant sickness' – a cold after-effect of the COVID-19 pandemic.

All of this means that in our society this stereotype is not only an image of Pacific peoples perpetuated over decades, but is one that is directly tied to the structures of society in which Pacific peoples are trying to survive in New Zealand.

## Stereotype 4: Pacific People Are Criminal and Violent . . .

> *Bunga, our only meetings are court proceedings, they only love us if its sports achievements . . .* (line 5)

> *Women clutch purses, cross roads when they see me*
> *And if they see me then it's usually on the TV*
> *Police 10/7, see police been stressin and profilin . . .*
> (lines 7–9)

> *Dark complexion so they don't trust us, dark complexion so*
> *they don't love us*
> *English broken, fingers groping, unpaid product*
> *Hood pharmaceuticals the only way we make profit . . .*
> (lines 12–14)
>
> *Don't forget we silent, when it comes to abuse and domestic*
> *violence . . .* (line 17)

The stereotype of Pacific peoples as criminal and violent is arguably the most prevalent in New Zealand society. This stereotype is not one that is difficult to trace historically, since violence has been an accusation levelled at us since European explorers first landed without invitation on our shores. Savage, primitive, uncivilised – each word carries with it the impression of uncontrolled violence linked to the stereotype of weakness. An inability to control base emotions is a common characteristic used to paint Indigenous peoples globally as animalistic, dark and in need of saving.

There are many accounts of violence in early encounters between Europeans and Pacific peoples. For example, the first encounter between Māori and the Dutchman Abel Tasman in 1642 led to him naming the location Murderers Bay after some of his crew were killed, while Captain Cook named Niue Savage Island after its inhabitants failed to welcome him with open arms in 1774.[60] Not only were we violent, but there were also many examples in the Pacific of people 'taking' from early explorers. Such an instance led to the death of Captain Cook in Hawai'i in 1779, when he tried to force the return of a cutter (a smaller boat) from the *Resolution* by kidnapping Kalani'ōpu'u, an important ali'i, (chief) and was instead killed in a skirmish with the Kānaka Maoli (Indigenous Hawaiians) in defence of their chief.[61]

Early European visitors to the Pacific believed that they brought peace to a people who were violent by nature and unable to achieve that peace without foreign intervention. One example of this was in 1899, when the British, Germans and Americans in Sāmoa decided that Samoans could not be relied on to rule themselves and overcome their base nature. These three imperial powers made a tripartite agreement to separate the territory and instil permanent European styles of government, leading to the annexation of Sāmoa by the Germans and the claiming of American Sāmoa by the US. This decision was made by Pālagi based on their interests, because they were worried the 'warlike' nature of the Samoan people and their perceived inability to be at peace would harm Pālagi economic interests in the profitable and growing plantation economy in Sāmoa. But this image of Pacific peoples as warlike was wrapped up in the image of us as barbarians, cannibals, lacking control and ruled by instinct – we were uncivilised people before Europeans brought peace through civilisation and Christianity. The paternalism of this period of history in the Pacific is clear, as Europeans became parental figures who brought Pacific peoples, as unruly children, into the modern world to save us from ourselves.

This early image of Pacific peoples as violent and uncontrollable contributed to the later development of the image of Pacific peoples as criminals in Aotearoa. A specific period of New Zealand history inflamed this image to the point where it is now a prevailing stereotype. There are many contributing factors here, such as poverty and opportunity, but the image of criminality, drunkenness and violence can be linked directly to the era of the Dawn Raids in the 1970s when the New Zealand Government consciously cast Pacific peoples in a negative light. The economic recession of the 1970s changed the position of Pacific peoples in New Zealand drastically. Suddenly, Pacific peoples were being rendered as villains as unemployment rates rose and Pākehā New Zealand now needed the low-skilled jobs Pacific peoples had been asked to do only a few decades before. The lax immigration policies of the 1950s and 1960s were now being blamed for the lack of jobs, and Pacific peoples – all Pacific peoples across the country, regardless of status – were labelled as overstayers and targeted by the police and the government as criminals from 1974 onwards. The targeting of Pacific peoples in this way cast us, all of us, as criminals, with Dawn Raids used as a measure to catch us and deport us back to our Pacific homelands. It soon became a crime to be Brown and walking the streets of Auckland – police powers were extended in 1976 to allow them to stop any Pacific person they chose on the street and ask about their immigration status.[62] The image of Pacific peoples as criminals was reinforced by this targeted police harassment, but the New Zealand Government also has much to answer for in terms of developing this stereotype.

In the 1975 election campaign, the National Party encouraged this fearmongering among the New Zealand population through blaming immigrants for changing the country into a place where New Zealanders no longer wanted to live. In an election advertisement produced by the American cartoon company Hanna-Barbera, Pacific people were depicted as stealing jobs, causing overcrowding in cities, and contributing to poor schooling, impacting the way of life of the 'ordinary' New Zealander. Violence was directly connected to these issues; an immigrant – Brown, wearing a factory uniform, with a big afro – was shown drinking and becoming violent. This election was a landslide win for National, as the New Zealand population supported a government that pledged to stop immigration and bring back the traditional way of life by vilifying Pacific peoples. The stereotype of the violent, criminal Pacific person is one that has harmed Pacific peoples in Aotearoa New Zealand significantly. It changed the way Pacific peoples were viewed by New Zealand society, casting us in a role that we are still seen in. This is obvious in the way people talk about places like South Auckland, where there are high numbers of Pacific peoples. It impacts the way Pacific peoples are treated in society, especially in a justice system that has been used within living memory to cause harm based on race and perceived criminality. This stereotype is one that is entrenched in our systems, reinforced in our media, and ingrained in the way Pālagi New Zealand sees people from the Pacific – still, to this day – as criminals.

## Conclusion

In writing this conclusion, I have been thinking about what is important for me, as a Pacific historian born and raised in Aotearoa, to reiterate in a book on Pacific peoples and racism in New Zealand. Racism is frequently expressed through belief in stereotypes that characterise a people as distinct from others, but these stereotypes are always borne from history. In the case of Pacific peoples in Aotearoa, these prejudicial beliefs are deeply rooted in a colonial past that has informed the structures in which Pacific peoples live in this country, relegating us to a position that is 'less' from the time we first arrived on these shores. Colonisation and racist ideologies have had lasting impacts on New Zealand society, even if there is a thin veneer of shine that commonly hides the ugly racism that underpins our institutional systems and social structures. Even liberal New Zealand will believe in at least one of the stereotypes listed in this chapter; they have been so heavily socialised as 'the truth'. Think about what you truly believe, reader. Do you clutch your bag if you see a young Pacific man walking towards you on the street? Are you surprised when you see a Pacific person get a scholarship or a high-paying job?

SWIDT's *Bunga*, in a heartbreaking way, makes clear that Pacific youth in this country are aware of how we are seen by a large sector of society: lazy, weak, poor, criminal and violent. These stereotypes have traversed time and place to be just as pervasive today as they have been in the past. These perceptions of Pacific peoples are now part of the fabric of New Zealand society, part of the structures that determine how we live our lives. But no longer. Pacific people are, more and more, refusing to accept the roles assigned to us by these stereotypes. In the words of SPYCC from SWIDT:

> People need to check themselves, and we need to check them too . . . I feel often in New Zealand we let a lot of light hearted racism or . . . sly remarks, you know, slide, but I feel like it's our job now to check people and not even let . . . them have that voice.[63]

Young Pacific peoples are leading towards unapologetically claiming our place and rights in New Zealand society, pushing against these racist stereotypes that have harmed our people over and over again. Part of this is understanding the historical foundations of these stereotypes and how far in the past they originate, building over the centuries to positions of power in our society. It is recognising that these were stereotypes that the people who formed our governments truly believed in – that informed the way our societies were created. History has power unrecognised by the majority of society, but I have shown in this chapter how the reach of history is still felt by many of us today. Even with the power of *Bunga* as a battle cry, the final line of the song speaks to a type of helplessness, a type of internalised racism that – even for the staunchest Pacific person – is still a whisper in the back of their mind.

> *I'm speechless, they really be calling us leeches*
> *The audacity, but I guess it is warranted, until they need us,*
> *bungas* (lines 27–28)

Is it warranted? By looking back at history, we can see where these stereotypes have come from and how they have been informed by colonial racism and the priorities of the Europeans – those who landed on our shores and set up their structures of government in our Pacific homelands, and those who lured us away with promises of a better life to fill their own needs and priorities. No, it is not warranted. But it is important for us as Pacific peoples to understand this history so that we know these are not true reflections of our peoples. Only then will we be able to prosper and flourish as Pacific peoples in Aotearoa.

*The audacity.*

# ECONOMY

## Is the Migrant Dream a Capitalist Dream?
Pacific Peoples and the Economy

*Sereana Naepi, Lisa Meto Fox,
Dylan Asafo and Evalesi Tu'inukuafe*

EVERY AUTHOR ON THIS PAGE EXPERIENCES A PAY GAP. Every author on this page has a degree or multiple degrees from a reputable university. Every author on this page is Pacific. And despite being highly qualified Pacific people, our labour is deemed less valuable than that of others. The economic system that we exist in rewards labour by Pacific peoples in inequitable ways, a process that is visible in Pacific peoples' disproportionately low home ownership, employment and wealth rates. Pacific peoples in Aotearoa New Zealand collectively contribute $8 billion to the national GDP each year and provide 27,000 hours per week of unpaid labour and volunteer work.[1] However, Pacific peoples have a median annual income over $7,000 less than the average of the total Aotearoa New Zealand population, are the least likely ethnic group in Aotearoa New Zealand to own their own homes, and have an unemployment rate 3 per cent higher than the total population of Aotearoa New Zealand.[2] These examples showcase that Pacific peoples contribute to Aotearoa New Zealand in a variety of ways, yet are still not rewarded evenly within our current economic system.

We wanted to include a talanoa on the economy in this book as this inequality has become an unquestionable reality of modern society. This chapter brings together a talanoa between three Pacific people (Dylan Asafo, Lisa Meto Fox and Sereana Naepi, with the support of Evalesi Tuʻinukuafe to create the chapter) who have all worked in and around efforts to record and disrupt the unequal ways the economic system rewards Pacific peoples. In the tradition of other chapters in this book and previous Pacific collaborations,[3] this chapter has engaged the authors in talanoa and then converted the talanoa to the chapter you are now reading. Throughout this chapter, there are quotes from the talanoa that are intentionally not attributed to individual authors, partly because some of us enjoy academic freedom but not all of us have this privilege, and questioning the logic of the current economic system and the inequity that is perpetuated by the system is still a dangerous stance to take. Italicised quotes like the one below are comments from the talanoa that contributed to the thinking around the chapter and how it is we came to consider how racism operates in the New Zealand capitalist economy.

*Somebody's going to be exploited for capitalism to survive.*

The economic system is an all-encompassing structure that impacts our engagement with law, education, health and migration:

> *All those things that people were talking about in the other chapters are impacted by our access to wealth and if the economic system's set up in a way that means we can't access that wealth, then we can't address those other issues.*

Capitalism is unquestionable today; to raise concerns about how capital flows in inequitable ways causes concerns in many circles in Aotearoa. However, it is the myth of meritocracy, which tells us that if we do the right thing and make the right choices we will be rewarded with increased wealth,[4] that this chapter aims to illuminate. We also believe that 'racism is foundational to capitalism',[5] and this chapter is going to focus on the structural racism that is built into the economic model that we currently engage in.

> *Sometimes it is difficult to say I want more pay, especially when I earn about five times the median income of the average Pacific woman. Society frames my professional success as me earning A LOT for a Pacific woman and this frustrates me because it shows that the inequity in the economic system means that I'm incredibly privileged compared to the rest of my family, but I am not as privileged when compared to the Pākehā I work for and with.*

This chapter will first explore how capitalism as a system is predicated on the exploitation of labour and resources. In particular, these resources across the globe are racialised and Indigenous bodies and land are exploited in order to benefit a settler state, its settlers, and their descendants. To understand how this global phenomenon is intertwined with Pacific peoples and New Zealand, we will consider Banaba, Pacific peoples' labour in New Zealand, and the pay gap. We then consider how the pursuit of being middle class is often a pursuit of Whiteness; before, finally, offering solutions.

## Capitalism, Racism and the Pacific

Capitalist systems perpetuate racial hierarchies. Capitalism as we experience it today is dependent on the exploitation of labour and resources in order to enrich oneself.[6] New Zealand's own agricultural economy was, and is, dependent on the exploitation of Pacific peoples' lands and bodies. The wealth we experience today as a nation was dependent on land theft (for example in Aotearoa) and on continuing labour exploitation (such as the Recognised Seasonal Employer or RSE scheme).

> Europe needed to essentially colonise Indigenous societies and Indigenous lands. That was the only way they were going to survive.

Additionally, Pacific peoples experience this exploitation in remarkably different ways. While some of us are used for cheap labour, others lost their land or sovereignty in the colonial process.

> I also think it's actually important to understand that experiences of colonial capitalism vary across the different Pacific Island countries. For example, in Niue, while the land may have not been the main site of exploitation, it was labour, it was racialised bodies.[7] When we look at other countries like Banaba, Marshall Islands, Papua, all of those projects were essential to the survival of the British capitalist empire and still are to this day.

### New Zealand and the Exploitation of Pacific Lands

New Zealand's economic wealth is firmly tied to exploitation of Pacific lands. Beyond the existence of the settler state of New Zealand on Māori whenua, there is also the decimation of entire islands in order to build our agricultural economy. The history of Banaba is one that is not readily spoken about in New Zealand, despite the impact of this island on everything we eat today. In 1900, the world's highest-grade sources of phosphate rock were identified in Banaba in the Republic of Kiribati (and also in Nauru) by New Zealand prospector Albert Ellis.[8] Phosphate is an incredibly important ingredient in fertiliser for modern farming techniques. Shortly after this discovery, Ellis acquired the exclusive right to mine Banaba for £50 per year (about NZ$10,000 today) for 999 years. Additionally, Ellis assured Banabans that their crops would be left alone, their land would not be destroyed, and that they would be paid royalties.[9] The exploitation of Banaba was seen as inevitable;

it was considered humanity's right to access the resources. As the *Sydney Morning Herald* wrote in 1912:

> Naturally some think the native owners are right, yet it is inconceivable that less than 500 Ocean Island-born natives can be allowed to prevent mining and the export of a product of such immense value to all the rest of mankind.[10]

These assurances were never realised. Instead, 90 per cent of Banaba's surface was mined, leaving the island uninhabitable and leading to the forced relocation of Banaba's people to Rabi (an island in Fiji).[11] To understand the level of exploitation, we can simply consider the levels of profit collected by those (including the British Phosphate Commission, an equal three-way partnership between the UK, Australian and New Zealand governments) who owned the mining rights. Between 1900 and 1913 the company made profits in excess of £1.75 million (NZ$440 million today), and, in the same period, paid Banabans less than £10,000 (NZD$2.5 million today) for land, trees and phosphate. The phosphate that drove these profits was spread all over New Zealand, feeding the land and enabling the level of farming that the New Zealand economy became dependent on to grow its wealth.[12]

Often, when faced with stories such as Banaba, people will retort that this happened in the past and therefore any impact has long since passed. However, unkept promises to restore the island and inadequate compensation for the mining has meant that the people of Banaba continue to experience intergenerational loss, in terms of both their land and the lack of any economic gain.[13] Additionally, the island of Rabi occupies a legal loophole of sorts, where international law prevents the people of Rabi claiming compensation for their loss from the UK, Australia and New Zealand.[14]

## New Zealand and the Exploitation of Pacific Peoples

> . . . *they couldn't exploit our land, so they exploited our people, they exploited our labour because they didn't see value in our land.*

Pacific peoples occupy the lowest-paid professions in the country and disproportionately struggle to meet their basic needs in many ways. Yet, we know that key to Pacific peoples' overall wellness is our access to the economy.[15] As Litia Tuiburelevu and Hugo Wagner-Hiliau write, Pacific peoples' labour exploitation is a key aspect of the New Zealand economy: 'New Zealand has benefited from colonial conquest and exploitation of the Pacific, not just through material extraction of land, resources and unequal trade agreements but also by strategically pigeonholing Pacific peoples into low-paid, manual work for sub-par wages.'[16]

Importantly, many people do not know that Pacific peoples' relegation to manual and servant labour was intentional. When New Zealand was setting up education in the South Pacific, the curriculum was designed to ensure that Pacific peoples were only trained in manual labour and servitude, thereby guaranteeing a labour force wilfully limited in scope to fill gaps in the New Zealand economy.[17] This ongoing exploitation of Pacific peoples beyond the initial colonial period has impacted our ability to receive an equitable share of the economy. Pacific peoples' access to the New Zealand settler state has always been predicated on the exploitation of our labour, from the large migration in the 1960s for factory and warehouse labour that led to the Dawn Raids to the RSE scheme.

> *And you know these systems are built upon the exploitation of racialised bodies, but that I think it's really hard for some to accept that fact.*

> *One of the things I was also thinking about in terms of the future is in the current inflation rate; all the economists*

are like, 'we need some unemployed people'. And you know they're talking about Pacific people, you know that the jobs that they're imagining need to go are our jobs. They're not talking about getting rid of the mass amounts of wealth that the bank has attributed to the economy, they want to get rid of low-paid, low-skilled labour for six months to cool down the economy. But those aren't the people who are blowing the economy out.

### The Pacific Pay Gap

The Pacific Pay Gap Inquiry highlighted that racism plays a significant part in economic inequity. Pacific men earn $0.81 and Pacific women earn $0.75 per dollar that Pākehā men earn.[18] Importantly, the inquiry also was able to show that occupation, industry and education only accounted for 27 per cent of the gap for Pacific men and 39 per cent of the gap for Pacific women.[19] This result leaves a significant amount of the pay gap unexplained – or, as the authors argue, racism has a significant role to play in ensuring that Pacific peoples are paid less for the same labour as Pākehā men. We want to be clear, here, that Pacific peoples experience these inequities differently. The pay gap we experience as Pacific professionals impacts our lives differently from how a Pacific labourer may experience the pay gap. For example, Pacific peoples in manufacturing in 2023 were receiving a median hourly income of $26, compared to their European counterparts receiving $33.95, whereas Pacific peoples in professional and administration services were receiving a median hourly income of $30 compared to their European counterparts receiving $38.60.[20] While there is a difference in median income within both industries, there is also a difference in median income between industries, meaning that Pacific peoples in professional and administration services still have more income entering their households than those in manufacturing, resulting in a different experience of the pay gap.

> These systems are premised and defined by the exploitation
> of racialised bodies.

Before and after Pacific peoples migrate to New Zealand, we are promised upward economic mobility based on access to and engagement with the New Zealand economy. This idea of economic prosperity and the notion that you will be rewarded if you work hard is reflected in these promises. Yet, the Pacific pay gap shows us that our reward is inequitable, and that you can be employed as an RSE worker, a manual labourer, a professional, or an academic,[21] and still get paid less than your Pākehā counterparts.

> Further to this point of upward mobility, it is arguably relative to gender and ethnicity. For some who did all the right things, getting a good education and getting a good job, the financial struggles do not end here. And there is definitely a divide between Pākehā professional success and Pacific professional success. Simply put, Pacific peoples in the same professions as Pākehā peoples are paid less despite being part of the middle class. This is seen as a position of privilege to other Pacific peoples who aspire their work to be valued more and their wages increased.

Taken together, the exploitation of Pacific land and Pacific labour and the Pacific pay gap show us how structural racism in the economy works. The economy is dependent on exploiting Pacific peoples. Our farmers relied on the exploitation and destruction of entire Pacific Islands to grow their crops and they now rely on imported Pacific labour and legislation that enables them to pay Pacific peoples significantly less.

> I like your point on the migrant dream, right? Because the dream is that we get to engage in the economy that is why we come here. We get an education. We get a good job. We can send money home, and we can support our wider community.

> *Pacific migrants are taught that the way to liberation is to seek upward mobility, to aspire to Whiteness rather than questioning the hierarchy as a whole and the systems as a whole.*

However, for first-generation Pacific people and their children, there has definitely been a perspectival shift towards confronting systemic racism while still engaging in economic mobilisation. For the children and grandchildren of Pacific migrants, there is a critical understanding that in pursuing economic wealth or financial prosperity you are also pursuing Whiteness. And what is the danger in this for future Pacific generations?

> *Our older generations were sold on the migrant dream, which is this idea of economic wealth as the fruits of one's labour . . . I still think that there's a real danger with our generation, even younger generations in aspiring to Whiteness and to wealth because these capitalist systems are extremely seductive, and although the younger generations are more radical, they are still somewhat invested in that migrant dream as a survivalist tactic to escape financial insecurity. Any misstep and you fall down the middle-class ladder.*

## Recommendations for Change

Initially in this talanoa, we began to explore structural mechanisms for addressing racism in the economy, such as the Fair Pay Agreements, and Pacific inclusion.

### Fair Pay Agreements

> *I think Fair Pay Agreements are really important; they could prioritise industries where Pacific peoples are concentrated.*

> She talked about her mother as a cleaner on an award
> having a decent paid job, being able to support family
> well, being able to have security, and then, as soon as
> the Employment Contracts Act came in and replaced the
> awards, all of a sudden she had insecure work, could be
> paid the minimum wage, and that was the reality for a
> lot of Pacific and Māori families who were in these kind of
> vulnerable jobs. And so the Fair Pay Agreements are trying
> to bring back something similar to the awards.

Fair Pay Agreements provide a mechanism for addressing pay inequities by industry. The legislation was designed to provide a mechanism for collective bargaining that would impact entire industries.[22] There was hope that if industries with high numbers of Pacific people could enter negotiations, then this would help to address the national pay gap. Within our talanoa, we had disagreements about Fair Pay Agreements' ability to address structural racism, for while Fair Pay Agreements could have been negotiated in sectors with high numbers of Pacific people, the pay inequity within those sectors would have remained. It is also important to note that, since we had this talanoa, the newly elected government has repealed the Fair Pay Agreements Act 'with effect from 20 December 2023', and it is unclear that they have any plan to ensure equitable economic reward as they grow the economy.[23]

> I don't see how the Fair Pay Act will address racism in
> remuneration.

### Pacific Inclusion

> The Brown and bougie class is a thing, right? There's a
> class of Pacific people who have the opportunity to speak to
> Ministers, to push for change, to do all of these things on
> behalf of our communities.

We hope that having Pacific people in influential positions means that we can drive change from within the system. Often, Pacific people's inclusion is seen as one way of addressing inequity within inequitable systems. For instance, if we have more Pacific academics, more Pacific public servants, more Pacific engineers, doctors, lawyers, accountants, consultants, then we will start to see the wider structural change needed to address racism in the economy, as not only will Pacific people be earning more in professional occupations, but they will also be positioned to advocate for Pacific communities. This inclusion, in some ways, is an easier solution: train more Pacific people to enter the middle classes and address inequity over time.

However, in our talanoa we raised concerns regarding whether inclusion will really change anything for Pacific peoples more broadly, or if inclusion operates to benefit a select few Pacific people.

> *They don't have race loyalty, they have class loyalty. And so can we expect radical economic change that benefits Pacific people when everyone who has the ability to push radical economic change benefits from the current system?*

> *It is clear that the system is designed to reinforce class loyalty over so-called race loyalty. It really makes you question whether you are willing to put your job on the line when speaking out against systemic racism, like in our universities. Or do you quit your job to earn less money so that you have the somewhat freedom to say whatever you like about them? It is a difficult position to contend with.*

> *I was so disheartened at the Pacific Pay Gap launch where our Minister said 'thank you for this, this is really important', but essentially, he needs social licence to do something right? I thought 'are you kidding me?' You've got literally pages of evidence that you can give to your colleagues. But you're still not going to put it on the table*

> because it's not impacting [the] majority of Labour voters
> and because there are Labour voters who benefit from our
> exploitation, there are people who employ Pacific people who
> don't want to close the pay gap, because that means that
> they'll lose more of their profits. It becomes an interesting
> report with no impact.

## Beyond?

> *Colonial capitalism limits our collective imaginations.*

It became increasingly clear that these solutions were simply tinkering around the edges of a significant problem. Solutions that can be overturned in a single election rely on people acting in ways that are not beneficial for their own progression, and rely on surface-level inclusion over structural change. While we can put in place many different strategies and programmes to compensate for disproportionate access to the economy, the reality is that without significant reform not only to the economy but also to the settler state, we are unlikely to realise economic equity.

> *It is clear that as Pacific people we'll never be free in the*
> *system. For example, the Pacific pay gap is and will always*
> *be in settler-colonial politics and its economy.*

At some point, we also have to question if seeking economic redistribution via policy adjustments will truly deliver on the aspirations of Pacific communities. Do we truly aspire to economic equity if it means that we participate in the exploitation of other people on a global scale, including other Pacific peoples? Perhaps we must have an honest conversation about how our consumption of goods and services contributes to climate change, which is an existential threat to the Pacific. Should we want economic equity that is built on the theft of land from our whanaunga?

> The Pacific pay gap, all of these unjust conditions, will always persist, no matter what reform, whatever legislation and Fair Pay Agreements come along. Settler-colonial politics and economies, the way that they work is that [these measures] will always be reversed. And you know these systems are premised and defined on exploitation of racialised bodies.

Pacific peoples are indeed beginning to question the migrant dream narrative. Is it truly empowering to migrate to another country to simply be valued less based on skin colour and ancestry? Or does Pacific peoples' liberation lie in destroying the economic system that not only actively exploits us but rewards others for their exploitation of us?

> If we are our parents' dreams, did they truly dream that you would be in a university learning colonial theory to get a job at the bank?

> We need to radicalise and encourage a collective imagining beyond this current system.

## Conclusion

If we cannot begin to honestly address these questions, then we will simply be making superficial changes, asking to be included in a system that relies on the exploitation of other people and their lands. We have spoken up to say that we have had enough of being exploited, but we need to ensure that this does not lead us to exploit others for our own gain. In order for there to be a tomorrow for those yet to come, we need to think outside of the confines of what capitalism offers us and instead engage in what our ancestors have gifted us – the knowledge of how to ensure that everybody has enough, that everybody is cared for, and that everybody has a future.

*Just one final thing I wanted to say is that there's more than enough. There's more than enough for everyone to have a decent home that they can live in, to have decent food, to access the doctors. There is more than enough to go around. But it's because some people, the one per cent, want to hoard all of that wealth, that we don't have that. And I think that that's the thing that always gets to me, we're the most developed as a human race that we ever have been, and it's by design that some people have nothing.*

# EDUCATION

# Structural Racism and Education in Aotearoa

*Jean M. Uasike Allen, Toleafoa Yvonne Ualesi, David Taufui Mikato Fa'avae and Fetaui Iosefo*

ALL GOOD CHAPTERS START WITH A DISCLAIMER, RIGHT? Well, here is ours: we are Pacific academics with diverse positionalities, working within colonial institutions that privilege dominant Western knowledge systems. In this chapter we are unpacking some of our ideas around the challenges presented to us through systemic racism in higher education settings and through our experiences as educators – how they impact us, and how we, at times, work to create pockets of disruption. Some of the authors in this chapter talk about the 'colonial gaze' or what Frantz Fanon calls 'the white gaze'.[1] This idea is about how educational institutions have made us feel like we are monitored, while also being put on display, as if we are a spectacle, or to use Stuart Hall's words, 'the spectacle of the Other'.[2] The spectacle of the Other is predicated on the use of binaries; that we, as Pacific academics, are often compared to our Western (read: White) counterparts. However, Hall, reflecting on Jacques Derrida,[3] suggests that it is not only this comparison that marks difference and positions us as Other, but also the power that is present between binary oppositions, positions of either/or. He argues that we should really write these binary oppositions as follows: '**white**/black, **men**/women, **masculine**/feminine, **upper class**/lower class, **British**/alien to capture this power dimension in discourse.'[4] Like Hall and Derrida's examples above, we as Pacific people, people with brown skin, have felt the way we are gazed upon, positioned as Other, and compared across a range of European markers within educational spaces.

Our brown skin, our grounded and localised knowledge systems and ways of being, are sought after for the ticks of diversity they provide our institutions, while we and Pacific peoples more generally occupy temporary roles of employment where we are often underpaid and excluded – or when we are included, are often expected to speak on behalf of 'our people' as if we could possibly occupy such a position. However, we also acknowledge the role we play as members of our educational institutions and as educators. We are not without our own agency. We choose to work in these spaces, and, as such, we often occupy ambivalent spaces where we are attracted to learning, knowledge and teachings while often being repulsed by the injustice, racism and discrimination we and others face.[5] This chapter draws largely on experiences that have repulsed us and how these experiences, these aggressions which continue to mark us as different, have led us to push back and challenge racism within our educational institutions and the roles we occupy in initial teacher educational spaces.

Stuart Hall articulates that:

> Difference has been marked. How it is then interpreted is a constant and recurring preoccupation in the representation of people who are racially and ethnically different from the majority population. Difference signifies. It 'speaks'.[6]

The marking of difference in our society and within educational institutions is an ongoing phenomenon. This phenomenon, which is underpinned by racist assumptions and stereotypes, impacts various minorities around the world on a daily basis. Within

Aotearoa New Zealand, the context in which the authors of this chapter are writing, minorities such as Indigenous Māori, Asian and Pacific are constantly confronted and must grapple with this marking of difference. This marking, which may be overt but also subtle, can be enacted on the individual level or on a collective level and works to inflict daily aggressions on minority groups in the form of racism. Racism can be experienced by various minority groups in a range of ways, such as through name-calling, physical aggression, being ignored, or being denied access to goods and services.[7] This chapter focuses on the way racism is perpetuated through practices in compulsory and tertiary education. Compulsory education has long been a vehicle of assimilation to Western ways of knowing and doing.

For minority students, educational spaces have been spaces that exclude and marginalise their ways of being, knowing, seeing, doing and feeling in the world. Challenging racism is a justice issue, and, as such, the concerns of the authors lie in identifying how power operates through a plethora of interactions and spaces. Employing a grounded and Indigeno-centric, Pacific-inspired approach centred on the ethical relational practice of talatalanoa, the authors reflect on our experiences of education in Aotearoa New Zealand as students of Pacific heritage. Talatalanoa, a largely Poly-centric method, can be found in both Sāmoa and Tonga. In Gagana Sāmoa (Samoan language) the term 'tau talanoa' is used as a directive. To 'tautala sa'o' is to talk frankly and directly. Hence, 'tautalanoa' is to speak straight, to address a topic with the necessary layers of knowledge. Through our sense-making, we expose the power working across these sites, drawing on Fanon's theory of colonial domination and racism alongside a range of Pacific scholars to explore how our experiences have shaped our pedagogical practice within the very institutions that marginalised us as students.

## Racism, the Marking of Difference and Compulsory Education

Throughout the world, and especially in the Global South, diverse peoples are confronted daily with racism that positions their ethnic groups on the margins of society and within various institutional spaces. Racism has far-reaching consequences and is a 'complex phenomenon whose markers – stereotypes, prejudices, and discrimination – are distinct but interwoven'.[8] These markers are often underpinned by the process of comparison and categorisations to define minority groups as possessing specific characteristics; a way of signifying individuals who are not like the White majority.[9] In Aotearoa, racism is often understood as a result of colonialism, which has legitimised and continues to legitimise the view that the Pākehā race is superior.[10] By viewing the Pākehā race and culture as superior, Pākehā ways of life become naturalised, developing power through privilege. As Wetherell argues, 'power develops through "normalization", through defining what is usual and habitual and to be expected, as opposed to the deviant and exceptional'.[11] The viewing of ourselves and others is fundamental in examining power, for it is a marker of who is included and who is excluded socially.[12]

### Categorisation and Comparison – Processes of Othering

For the purposes of this chapter, we draw on Fanon's notions of colonial domination and racism through the process of categorisation and comparison to unpack our experiences of racism as underpinned by comparison to White Western norms and cultural practices. This comparison works to position minorities in particular ways and within specific, narrow, stereotypical representations.[13] Furthermore, categorisation and comparison, or what Hall articulates as the 'marking of difference',[14] also marks Otherness – power works to categorise and compartmentalise people according to race and gender, thus making judgements on whether they have power and knowledge.[15] Fanon theorises that this process results not only in the marking of difference by those in power, but also the internalisation of this difference to the point where minorities make moves to assimilate into dominant cultures. Writing of his own context, he states that:

> For him there is only one way out, and it leads into the white world. Whence his constant preoccupation with attracting the attention of the white man, his concern with being powerful like the white man, his determined effort to acquire protective qualities – this is, the proportion of being or having that enters into the composition of an ego ... He requires a white approval.[16]

This internalisation is underpinned by a desire to be human within the boundaries of colonial power, leading many minorities to negate their cultural practices as part of the process of acquiring status, success and achievement, as defined by Whiteness.[17] Within Aotearoa New Zealand, this process can be seen between the colonised and the colonisers, where the 'consciousness of Māori as a people was forged through the crucible of colonisation and continues to be realised in relation to Pākehā and New Zealand identity'.[18]

Although comparison of the empowered and the marginalised is a key focus of both Fanon and Hall, this chapter also recognises the importance of self-definition or self-determination. For example, individual definitions of success differ but, by Western standards, socioeconomic capital is a signifier of success.[19] In contrast, Fanon's definition of success – one which we identify with – is tied to dignity:

> Dignity is not located in seeking equality with the white man and his civilization: it is not about assuming the attitudes of the Master who has allowed his slaves to eat at his table. It is about being oneself with all the multiplicities, systems and contradictions of one's own

ways of being, doing and knowing. It is about being true to one's self.[20]

## Privileging of Pākehā Culture and Maintaining Segregation

Colonisation is a process that is ongoing and continues to impact Indigenous groups. However, colonisation also impacts minority groups, like those from the Pacific, in colonial contexts such as New Zealand. The privileging of Pākehā knowledge above other minority group knowledge, such as Māori knowledge, is a continual tension in wider society but also within educational institutions. This tension is also discussed by Darin Hodgetts and others, who argue that '[u]nexamined Pākehā assumptions concerning what is "real" and what counts as legitimate knowledge come to frame public debate and establish a common sense against which Māori views of the world struggle to gain legitimacy'.[21] We have seen this struggle for legitimacy in our institutions through ongoing debates regarding what some scholars call 'disciplinary knowledge' vs 'social knowledge'. More recently, educational institutions have come to be somewhat more inclusive of Indigenous perspectives, exemplified by the inclusion of teaching focused on te Tiriti o Waitangi and informed by Te Whare Tapa Whā (a Māori wellbeing model that is part of our health and physical education curriculum), or the newly legislated public holiday marking Matariki. These inclusions are a result of a long history of struggle in Aotearoa, where Māori activists and scholars such as the late Moana Jackson, Linda Tuhiwai Smith, Dame Whina Cooper, and a plethora of others have worked to challenge the Crown and hold it accountable for promises made via te Tiriti o Waitangi. However, even with this movement and the inclusion of te reo Māori (Māori language) and Indigenous Māori perspectives in our educational systems and curriculum, there are still debates and outright racism towards Māori people, Māori knowledges, and Māori language. As this chapter is being written, there is currently uproar throughout Aotearoa New Zealand as many White New Zealanders are upset that a national chocolate brand has used te reo Māori to market their brand. Additionally, the use of te reo by national news anchors has resulted in a range of complaints where some, underpinned by racism, positioned te reo as belonging outside of national news. These are just two examples of the racism that is ongoing in Aotearoa New Zealand towards its Indigenous population. While the authors are not Indigenous Māori, we acknowledge the ongoing struggle for land, self-determination, participation in decision-making, respect for and protection of culture, and equality and non-discrimination that the people of the land which we live on are going through.[22] While we, as Pacific people, also experience racism, discrimination and prejudice, we acknowledge that our experiences are different to those of Indigenous Māori. Still, like Māori, we continue to be compared to White colonial norms.

Fanon states that the use of comparison and prioritising of White norms is a means of oppression, as it focuses predominantly on what minority groups are not and how they should be more like the majority group.[23] He argues that 'it is not that we deny that blacks have any good qualities, but you know it is so much better to be white'.[24] This privileging of Western/White norms can be seen throughout Aotearoa New Zealand's society and history in the ways that minority groups, such as Pacific peoples, have been represented and positioned as Other and thus treated in discriminatory ways. For example, we can see the privileging of Western norms historically through the examination of attitudes towards Pacific people in the 1970s during the time of the Dawn Raids. During this time, Pacific people who had migrated to New Zealand for work and had overstayed their work permits were used by the government as scapegoats for the decline of the economy.[25] The representations provided by the media during the Dawn Raids presented all individuals with brown skin as overstayers, and Finau 'Ofa Kolo argues that because of the frequency and commonness of this representation, overstayer is a label still attached to the Pacific population today.[26] The continual representation of particular dominant racialised group ideologies encourages stereotypical racial perceptions. As 'Ofa Kolo illustrates, the use of media power meant that society's perceptions regarding the Pacific community in Auckland led to the creation of negative stereotypes including criminals, rapists and overstayers.[27] A decade later, Damon Fepulea'i echoed 'Ofa Kolo's findings by identifying that many media articles involving Pacific people linked them to crime and violence.[28] Both studies demonstrate the power of dominant representations to privilege ideologies that not only influence perceptions of a nation, but also maintain racial segregation between Pākehā and Pacific people. As Pacific people, we have often been confronted by such negative stereotypes.

A consequence of the privileging of Pākehā norms is that minority groups are compared to and thus categorised and represented as inferior to the dominant group.[29] One of our concerns with the development of stereotypical representations is that in becoming the norm, they become more naturalised and believable.[30] This can result in these stereotypes being internalised, resulting in beliefs of inferiority within minority groups when compared to dominant White groups. Fanon describes this internalisation and assimilation when he states:

> I begin to suffer from not being a white man to the
> degree that the white man imposes discrimination on
> me, makes me a colonized native, robs me of all worth,
> all individuality, tells me that I am a parasite on the
> world, that I must bring myself as quickly as possible
> into step with the white world, 'that I am a brute beast,
> that my people and I are like a walking dung-heap that
> disgustingly fertilizes sweet sugar cane and silk cotton,
> that I have no use in the world'.[31]

Thus, comparison, categorisation, stereotyping, and the internalisation of these stereotypes are all processes of colonisation that contribute to the assimilation of minority groups into majority worldviews. One of the largest vehicles of assimilation is the education system.

## Compulsory Education in Aotearoa

In Aotearoa New Zealand, schooling is compulsory for students between the ages of six and sixteen, but most students start school at the age of five.[32] Prior to the first Education Act in 1877, New Zealand was in a state of desperate need to build cohesion. At the time, land wars and divisions between Indigenous and settlers, rural and urban, and Catholics and Protestants were rife.[33] Furthermore, New Zealand's infrastructure, geography and economy were weak, with poverty and social disorder exacerbated by the activity of larrikins (youth criminals). This unrest led to calls for a united and democratic nation enabled by education. Hence the Education Act 1877 was used as a medium to create citizens who would contribute to building the nation and society, while also integrating different groups into the social contract. In addition, the use of education to improve the lives of individuals would ultimately develop and improve the economy.[34] During our talatalanoa session, Fetaui discussed these educational beginnings in Aotearoa New Zealand, highlighting her belief that education was and continues to be idealistic, and questioned whether anything has really changed. She shared:

> *So up to the age of 16 that you have to go and then 16, you're a free agent . . . I think compulsory education dates back to 1877 . . . The Education Act, where it was free, compulsory and secular and universal dates back to that. So, the New Zealand school system is compulsory for children aged 6 to 16. But, you know, what is it? Nothing's changed, really. If we think of what happened way back then, they said all these beautiful, idealistic things, but pragmatically it wasn't . . . And now, years later, it's still*

*the same. But this time we've got migrants, like now we've got the Pasifika people, you know, and our children. So, years later, it's still idealistic but still not pragmatic for our people. Still a dud system.* (FI)

Education has been positioned as the great equaliser, the way that low socioeconomic people get themselves out of poverty. As Pacific scholars have highlighted, narratives of movement from the Pacific Islands to nations like Aotearoa New Zealand and Australia are often underpinned by notions of educational opportunity.[35] However, the systemic practices within compulsory educational institutions work to 'fix' or collapse particular identities into Western framings and understandings. For example, Jean draws attention to her experiences of compulsory education where the process of selecting ethnic identity when enrolling students in school reflects compartmentalised, hierarchical framings:

*I'm just thinking off the top of my head, like, but you know that whole thing when you enrol your kid [in school] and whatever ethnicity you put down first is what they come under? You can't even put a whole range. Pacific/Pasifika is collapsed.* (JA)

In Aotearoa New Zealand, the more commonly practised categorisation for ethnicity allows for multiple ethnic identifications into broader ethnic groupings. Classification of multiple ethnic identities is complex and divided into two broad categories, as described by Esther Yao and others: 'mutually exclusive methods, where multi-ethnic participants are allocated to a single ethnic group; and non-mutually exclusive methods, where multi-ethnic participants are allocated to two or more overlapping ethnic groups'.[36] The concern here is that by using mutually exclusive prioritisation you are collapsing a range of diverse ethnic groups into one single group, and this could impact on people's ability to express their ethnic ties in ways that are meaningful to them.

The Ministry of Education use Stats NZ's standards of definition and classification of ethnicity. Enrolment forms for schools only allow students to identify with up to three groups, and they are then assigned to a 'prioritised ethnicity' group based on rankings by Stats NZ.[37] At the first level, ethnic groups are ranked with Māori as first, Pacific peoples as second, and Asian as third. A further, second-level ethnic group ranking for prioritised reporting ranks New Zealand Māori as first, followed by a breakdown of Pacific ethnicities.[38] While the Ministry of Education asserts that this approach has been phased out in favour of a total response ethnicity method allowing students to select all ethnicities they identify with, this new model may have implications for funding.[39] Some are against this ethnicity-based funding – as Teresia Teaiwa and Sean Mallon argue, '[o]pponents of "race"-based assistance seem to miss the point of historically-produced disadvantage'.[40] Migrants to Aotearoa New Zealand from non-Western countries, especially those from the Pacific Islands, are disadvantaged by New Zealand's colonial systems that place importance on socioeconomic status. Arvind Zodgekar shows an understanding of the difficulties that occur for immigrants to New Zealand when he explains, 'these ethnic groups [Asian and Pacific], with very different cultural and religious backgrounds and practices, may initially experience certain difficulties while trying to settle in New Zealand'.[41] While we are not necessarily critiquing the use of targeted funding to particular groups, we are concerned about how this approach plays out and the impacts it has on children and their families. The erasure of particular ethnic identities due to the hierarchy that is employed in schools is upsetting and harmful, particularly to ethnic groups where culture comprises a large part of our being.

Jean further believes that this kind of practice, while underpinned by racist undertones that privilege funding and monetary gain, also results in a form of erasure or ignoring of who the children are and where their ancestors came from:

> *So does that kind of link with your initial, like, erasure? . . .*
> *You know, like, the erasure of specific identities is a racist*
> *practice in our compulsory education and our schools,*
> *and . . . it starts from as soon as kids are enrolled before*
> *they even set foot in the [classroom].* (JA)

While these practices can be – and often are – dismissed as merely processes that have been around for a long time, they work in a manner that, as Hall argues, marks difference.[42]

The development of decile ratings within our school system is another way that difference is marked. Until January 2023, decile ratings were measures of localised socioeconomic status used by the government to determine its distribution of funding. These decile ratings contributed to and reinforced the definition of various areas, and by extension the various groups of people who live in these communities, according to the dichotomy of deprived/privileged. Popular discourse associates decile rating with the educational prestige of a school. In 2014, for instance, broadcaster Mike Hosking noted that 'white flight is alive and well. White flight is driven by a belief that a number matters. Decile 1 is poison, decile 10 is aspirational.'[43] These connotations are important to note – the more these discourses are perpetuated and reinforced, the more widely they are believed, and so the more that people who occupy low-decile areas are positioned as Other. Although the government is now phasing out the decile system, the residue of this institutional and hierarchical racism still lingers, and likely will for many years to come.

## Talatalanoa

Talatalanoa is the Indigenous Pacific approach we have taken to capture our deep critical reflections regarding structural racism across educational contexts and collective critical pedagogies as educators in the tertiary sector of initial teacher education.

We situate our talatalanoa as an Indigenous Pacific approach to make visible the ways in which tertiary institutions and related systems reinforce and perpetuate neutral recruitment policies that continue the underrepresentation of ethnic minority lecturing staff. The repetition of 'tala' (to talk, to story) in tala-talanoa emphasises the significance and continuity of talking and storying in order to understand 'noa' (something or nothing or an unknown phenomena).[44] The practice of talatalanoa, from a Tongan perspective, has a collective intention: a gathering of people in the community who come together to discuss a particular concern. Talatalanoa is ongoing and can be carried out in a range of ways: in person and face to face as well as online, using digital tools and platforms, where people contribute their ideas and interact with others' perspectives in an iterative way.[45]

There are subtle differences between tautalanoa and talatalanoa due to context which takes into careful consideration the role and responsibility of the collective within ongoing sense-making, discussion, and problem-solving in Samoan and Tongan societies.[46] The practice of talanoa in a research context is structured in a manner that often sees the researcher doing the research with others or talking with others. But, for tautalanoa, speaking together as a collective as opposed to one person holding power in the meeting or gathering is of shared significance, making space for the visibility and expression of our similar yet distinct voices and experiences as female and male educators, researchers, and parents who hold ethnic affinity to Tonga, Sāmoa, Niue, Fiji, Tokelau and Europe.

In Lea faka-Tonga (Tongan language), 'tau talatalanoa' is connected with a group's shared conversations. In this chapter, we are deliberate about unpacking the layers of ongoing talatalanoa and 'tau' is critical to our goal. The context of this talatalanoa is linked to our experiences of racism – both the subtle and overt in compulsory and higher education – as a collective concern, something we continue to experience together as Pacific scholars seeking to confront practices and situations that undermine our knowledges and practices. Bringing together our thoughts and connections through tau and tala, we are going to unpack the various faces of racism across the contexts in which we work. Talatalanoa in Tongan communities, for instance, is largely informal, not often governed by a fixed agenda, though its purpose is to collectivise and provide a space for shared and ongoing conversations in search of possible solution/s. The talatalanoa space allows people to unpack their thoughts and talk with each other about what they think the issue is and any associated concerns.[47] Again, talatalanoa and tautalanoa feels fitting for us as a group of Tongan/Samoan/Niuean/Fijian/Tokelauan/Pālagi scholars.

In Samoan and Tongan, the term tau also means to battle, or battle together. Tau talatalanoa involves drawing from our stories, words and lived experiences of battling and speaking back to the impacts of racism and the racialised attitudes, behaviours and practices in higher education. Here, we engage in tautalanoa and talatalanoa as part of our process within this intellectual space and collective writing as we come together to share our lived stories and do battle against racism.

## Tau Talatalanoa – (On)going into Battle
## Tau as Speaking Back to Racism: Pacific in Tertiary Institutions

> *They want us here, but they are not really willing to put in the work to keep us here.* (FI)

The battle, or tau, was experienced by the authors within their tertiary institutions at various points in time across their academic journeys as students and as staff. This (on)going talatalanoa section unpacks our concerns, sharing moments of 'going into battle' and ways we speak back to racism. The feeling of institutional racism was captured during our talatalanoa through a range of stories. We share examples below of how some of the authors have experienced institutional racism during their employment at their institutions and have not necessarily been supported in the growth of their own careers and vision for the Pacific collective.

> *When I started there, I felt hopeful that they were going to create the space for our Pacific postgraduate students and undergraduate students, and really for Indigenous Pacific knowledge to flourish in our division. And they were talking about having the space that all our students can go into and growing our scholars over time. When I converse with leadership about the things that matter to Pacific . . . they don't always get it. They don't always get the whole vision around what it means to enable Pacific to thrive.* (DF)

> *Unfortunately, the way we have been treated reflects institutional racism, it's not like people don't know that there's a gap between Pasifika woman academics and inequality. Everybody knows, Sereana's research is published and she has been on TV and talked about it, but even though it's been highlighted in the media, what has been done about it?* (FI)

The development of our careers as Pacific academics is not focused solely on us as individuals. Rather, when we discuss our career development, we are constantly thinking and aware of those we are in service to, our āiga/kāinga (nuclear, extended and collective family), and our communities. This concept reveals itself as misunderstood through our storying of our experiences of institutional racism. Neoliberal educational institutions continue to privilege the individual above the collective, which is problematic for Pacific peoples, as our collectives are at the heart of what we do. Similarly, Joanna Kidman and Cherie Chu describe the problematic way that Pacific scholars are embedded in the cultural politics of New Zealand's universities through an academic prestige economy, where Pacific scholars see themselves as 'not the hottest ethnicity'.[48] The unequal relationships that Kidman and Chu highlight are reflected in Westernised positioning, as in David's and Yvonne's stories below:

> *In my previous workplace, they used to say things like, 'what can we do for you so that you can stay here?' Even though I've shared that it's not about me, it's the role that I'm in and creating more tenured academic roles for Pacific. And making sure that, the role I was in is going to grow and help others [Pacific academics] come [into the tenured academic position in university]. But every time I have a conversation with [them, they] keep focusing on . . . 'what can we do to make sure that you stay?' [They've] totally missed the whole vision because it's not about one person.* (DF)

> *You know, in my previous workplace there was an expectation that I go over and above all the time and I think what they did was capitalise and take advantage of our cultural service, right? They knew that I was going to be the humble Brown person who likely wouldn't say anything, and we just continue in an under-resourced environment often doing the cultural labour.* (YU)

Both David and Yvonne discuss how their tertiary spaces continue to perpetuate power dynamics in a manner that disregards the importance of the collective and the community, instead choosing to reinforce the systemic status quo. One of the authors saw this power dynamic reflected via the guise of norms, where the use of 'names' is called into question:

> *Even something as simple as your name can be an issue. I got an email asking if how I'd written my name [to be published in a university document] was purposeful because the norm is just to have your first and your last name. Whereas I wanted to have 'Uasike' in there. And so,*

> *I got asked if that was actually purposeful, if I'd done that correctly, or if it was an error.* (JA)

Being confronted about our names is problematic – from the authors' perspectives, as well as Indigenous and Pacific worldviews, there is power in names. Names are bestowed upon us, are alive with knowledge of our ancestors and those who are part of us.[49] Therefore, to be challenged over the use of our names is a traumatic experience. As Fetaui so simply but eloquently articulates:

> *That is because for Pasifika, a name holds everything, it is tapu [sacred] and holds the mana and genealogical connection of our families.* (FI)

Acknowledging the collective and actively working with others while in awe of those who have gone before us, our ancestors, is part of who we are and what we do. However, Fetaui felt a level of discomfort with the common saying 'we stand on the shoulders of giants':

> *I hate that. I really hate the notion of standing. We stand on the shoulders of our giants, our ancestors. Fuck off. That is so rude. We do not stand on their shoulders, you know, like. Like. Okay, metaphorically. It might be bliss, but actually there's no way. We don't even stand on their graves. You sit at their feet. Yeah. Yeah. And I was thinking, actually this is going to sound stupid, but like, I heard Josh's [her son's] speech the other day and it was, actually, we carry them on our shoulders. We don't stand on them. We are them. They are with us. We embody them.* (FI)

While we stand with our ancestors and learn from them, we also acknowledge, as educators, that education has become a vehicle for assimilation into Western knowledge and ideologies. More recently, education, and specifically tertiary education, has shifted from a focus on knowledge and learning to a model of business and money-making. Administered by the Tertiary Education Commission Te Amorangi Mātauranga Matua (TEC), the purpose of the Performance-Based Research Fund (PBRF) is to fund tertiary education organisations (TEOs) on the basis of their performance – that is, performance aligned with quality or 'excellent research' in the tertiary education sector as set out by the governing body of the TEC.[50] Recently, the criteria for the PBRF have changed, and research funding Māori and Pacific outputs is now worth more than previously. This change means that staff within these groups have now become sought after as they have an increased monetary value to the university. As David articulates, having increased financial value has further reflected the racism present in the university, as, again, it feels that the value of Pacific staff has been reduced to a monetary amount:

> *I feel like certain leaders in institutions don't value what it means for Pacific to thrive. Maybe it's too much work? It's all about meeting goals because for them, seeing a Pacific person do well is a tick in the right box. And because the next PBRF round is coming, that's what universities are focused on more, you know, it feels like subtle racism to me because all they're worried about is getting more money into faculties, and they're not worried about the people that need to come to strengthen Pacific ways of knowing, seeing, being, and doing. That kind of practice is from a genuine tauhi vā lens, a Tongan respectful and generative way . . . to look at opening more doors for the next generation.* (DF)

> *Pacific are often given teaching fellow roles that do not allow them to supervise Pacific postgraduate students. There is a need for master's and doctoral supervisors with knowledge of Indigenous Pacific research ideas, methodologies, and methods. I know of institutions where a couple of our Pacific*

*teaching fellows left universities because teaching fellow roles were 'teaching heavy' and had very little or no research time. The pay was less than what they earned as high school teachers. A few of them left and had to give up their doctoral studies. It seems like they're [universities are] not open to supporting them further. It's important for Pacific students and teachers to see their own Pacific people not only occupy tenured academic positions but... [also] succeed and thrive in them. That requires a genuine investment by schools, faculties, and universities. But instead, I'm hearing more of the, 'they're not good writers. They're not deep enough intellectually. They can't do this and that.' I hear stuff like that. COVID-19 and lockdowns highlighted such deficit views of Pacific students as well. What about the things Pacific students can do and bring to the learning? There's a lot! Institutional racism is ongoing in universities. It's ongoing and embedded in university course design and delivery.* (DF)

Here, we see a lack of understanding of the core issue in this case – the educational system being structured in a manner that resists ways to genuinely support equity, despite the so-called 'equity approaches' or strategies often described on tertiary institution websites and in strategic plans and ministerial reports. These patterns beg the question: is our educational system or structure inherently racist? And, if so, what can we, as authors, scholars and academics, collectively do to dismantle the status quo?

Our stories culminate in a collective feeling and understanding of our presence within tertiary institutions as tokenistic. We are often appreciated for the 'diversity' we bring, but mentoring and support for ourselves and the collective to further develop careers and pathways that allow us all to thrive are lacking for several of our authors. As Fetaui articulated at the beginning of this section, we are often the Brown faces at the interface of our institutions, but also, we are often underpaid and stuck with fixed-term contracts. In 2020, Tara McAllister and others found that Māori and Pacific women academics were paid significantly less than non-Māori and non-Pacific male academics: $7,713 less in 2018, coupled with 65 per cent lower odds of being promoted to the professoriate between 2003 and 2018.[51] Concerningly, their findings suggest that inequities for Māori and Pacific academics, like the authors, will continue to persist unless there are structural shifts in New Zealand's universities. Further, Māori and Pacific make up over 30 per cent of 'other' academic staff, reflecting an excess of precarious workers on short-term contracts, likely including a significant proportion of tutorial staff who are PBRF ineligible.[52] It is with this in mind that we collectively share how structural racism in tertiary institutions continues to socially disadvantage minoritised ethnicities.

The authors understand the power that circulates in our institutional spaces as a form of cyclic reproduction where dominant representations or processes are employed to recycle power, privilege and positions of Otherness. In line with Graham Hingangaroa and Linda Tuhiwai Smith, we argue for a decolonised academy and further assert the need to Indigenise our institutions through our Pacific lecturers in an authentic approach.[53] As Yvonne and David noted:

> You know, broken promises. In my last workplace, we knew we needed more Pasifika staff on a degree that had 'Pasifika' in 'name' underpinned by Pasifika values and knowledge systems, but they failed to recruit Pasifika staff. Okay, so it might have not been a 'language' degree which was what they argued, but I said you cannot separate language, culture, and identity. I believe you need the appropriate staff who can speak to their Pasifika epistemological [knowledge] and ontological [worldview] lens. I think students and the community expect that? I know I would. So, I'm just wondering, is that part of the strategic institutional barriers we face? Yeah, I think so. It's the strategy and design of a

colonial Western system that we all have to operate from. It's designed in a way where it continues to perpetuate and recycle that power. (YU)

So, who? Whose work is around shifting the system and critiquing the neo-colonial system? And I keep thinking that what we're experiencing in it [the university system], its being perpetuated into the schooling [primary, secondary] space. It's flowing into it, and all of that stuff is flowing back to us through initial teacher education. You know, because teachers are trained in university institutions and go into a school, then later come back with those deficit beliefs through their postgraduate studies, these dominant and privileged practices are maintained throughout the educational architectures of compulsory education. (DF)

Our battle – our tau – was evident not only in the way we were positioned in our institutions, but also through attempting to have our knowledges and ways of being legitimised and valued within educational spaces.

## Tau as Speaking Back/Between/With Cultural Practices

As previously discussed, the authors found that their cultural praxis (theory and practice) was used for the gain of the systemic status quo. The academic space is countercultural to the cultural space; there is no room for vā fealoaloa'i (space of respect).[54] It is one way, an individualistic, neoliberal way that is about 'I' and not 'we'. The authors understand this struggle as continuing to uphold systemic racism, where our cultural practices and ways of being are not valued in and by the institution, and thus we are disadvantaged in our interactions within and the changes we attempt to make to compulsory educational spaces. As Fetaui articulates below, our resistance to promoting ourselves and our collective drive underpinned by acts of service are practices which are important to us but which often work against us in educational spaces.

> *We both struggled to talk about ourselves and to put ourselves out there to get the promotion. But what we've also noticed is that when we went to go ask for help, the time we were given, it was just an email. But actually, as a collective, we normally sit, and we help each other.* (FI)

> *I know it's going to just come back to what [YU] said earlier. It's like the institution relies on our good will and on our Pasifika culture. Like they ride on our cultural values, backs for free. They entice us and then they use us to do all the relational stuff, all the invisible labour without the monetary returns. They use our ways, our cultural values, as weapons for their gains.* (FI)

While we have experienced institutional racism, we are not without our own agency. In the next section we explore how we, as Pacific academics, are battling and creating space for ourselves and others like us.

## Tau as Speaking Through Pacific Ethics: Creating Our Own Spaces

> *They use our ethnicity and our ways of being. They use it as a weapon against us, which then disadvantages us.* (JA)

The authors understand that while we are working within Western colonial institutions of education, we can disrupt these spaces in a range of ways. Jo Smith argues that the postcolonial context in Aotearoa New Zealand conditions the present and future of our nation, but our task is to break apart and open out 'the systems of representation that hold this society together'.[55] Therefore, this section highlights how our experiences of institutional racism have resulted in a range of movements and moments of disruption within the tertiary sector as well as within our vocations as Pacific educators. This example draws on our experience as guest editors for a Special Issue of *Ethnographic Edge* focused on privileging the voices of Pacific leaders in schools in Aotearoa New Zealand. As Yvonne describes, the Special Issue has grown out of our attempts to challenge Western notions of domination by doing what we believe is the right thing, even though we do not get 'paid' for it:

> *The culture that's prevalent . . . is a very Westernised notion of competition and individualism, whereas this process of that special journal is the opposite of that, right? Yeah. Yeah. Without pay, without – we're not doing it and paid research time, far out. We're trying to find time outside of our work time, you know, like even with your 40, 40, 20. And I know with my few days, I didn't get that ratio at my last place, we didn't even get that much time to do our own research, say, that a university would get. So, this is on top of that research, right? And it's because we know that it's the right thing to do. I was asked, 'don't you think you're doing too much?' So it goes back to those values, those core specific values of service, where I think that last workplace/institution has gotten away with taking advantage of our notion of service. But this is our way of saying, actually, no, we are self-determining in our service to our community and it's almost a political act, like an act of resistance, I think. Yeah.* (YU)

Fetaui wondered whether our attempts at convening a Special Issue were disruptive, as again, we were doing important work, but it was unpaid service work. She explained the negotiation happening in this space:

> *The Special Issue that we're doing at the moment is countercultural, the answer to the institutional racism*

*that is happening. Or is it? Working with these Pacific education leaders to get them published is a privilege. We won't get anything monetary from it because your service within the collective is reciprocal not in monetary terms but in respectful vā relations. So, it's almost like we are counteracting institutional racism by transforming our own spaces. I think I like the way you said counter-countercultural, because the culture and the institution is to hold power. And we all know that those who are in publishing, you know, the publishers there hold that power of telling stories . . . [I] think we feel uncomfortable and possibly repulsed. And that's why we're doing that special edition, because we see a cultural, relational vā gap. We are a collectivist people. Even the principals themselves are like, 'why are you doing this if you don't get paid?' We know the gap of institutional racism, and because we know, we are then collectively . . . called to change it. Well, put simply, we're trying our best to do things differently, right?* (FI)

Fetaui also drew attention to how we also challenge racism by writing about our experiences:

*There is something else that we do, and that is that we write about the racist experiences that have happened to us. We don't let people get away with it. We put it in writing. We've been able to publish it. Do you know what I mean? So, although our voices are not heard or acknowledged, and we feel we are the bitch of the institution because we get treated like one. We see it, feel it and take our agency to write the wrong . . . We literally fight because there's no other weapon that we've got, because the dominant have moved from not listening to being masters of pseudo-listening. We now get invites to the table, but only as eye-candy. We know this and feel this, so we, in turn, use the power of pen-ship and publishing as a means to fight back with the hope of genuine emancipation and transformation. It's so hard and tiring, fighting this invisible but potent block of systemic racism.* (FI)

The privileging of Pacific voices is a central way in which we challenge the dominance of the West. Drawing on Ngũgĩ wa Thiong'o's argument that literature, the written work, is one of the most enduring cultural processes that has worked to build a shared common vocabulary and tradition of domination, subordination but also resistance, we understand this practice as key.[56] Therefore, the publishing of a Special Issue that centres Pacific leadership, voices, experiences and ways of being contributes to literature that will disrupt and create space within our institutions. It is anticipated that the publication of our stories and Pacific voices will provide resources for initial teacher education, which will challenge and disrupt the White academic literary landscape that is often used within teacher education. Again, our challenging of structural racism is embedded within our cultural practices, which focus on service to others. Structural racism within tertiary institutions survives when we do nothing. Thus, it is our intention to talatalanoa our experiences to amplify continued work to disrupt and minimise harmful recruitment and HR practices.

### Recommendations for Change

Although we make no specific policy recommendations here, we have noted ways to disrupt structural racism as academics in higher education. The overarching structure of the education system in Aotearoa is Eurocentric and inequitable, and continues to drive our institutional experiences, highlighting the pervasive nature of racism from structural to institutional to personal. Through our tau talatalanoa, we illustrate recommendations for change that address the structural racism inherent in Aotearoa's compulsory education.

First, we must ensure that schools give parents the choice to select more than one ethnic identity. This recommendation reflects Yao and others' suggestion to change systemic practices that suppress multi-ethnic affiliation.[57] Further to this change must be schools' hierarchy of ethnic identities whereby Māori is first, followed by Pacific, then Asian. This current system is problematic because students are heterogeneous – that is, their ethnic identity is often multi-layered.[58] Student ethnicity is closely related to their racial–ethnic identity – so what does that mean for a student who might identify as Pacific or Asian over their Māori identity, or for students who might lean more to their Pākehā side?

Second, we recommend that higher education and tertiary institutions examine the ways in which their recruitment policies are aligned with equity strategies, with an assumption that such strategies exist. We posit that a tokenistic approach is insufficient. Rather, the academy needs to be progressive to ensure equitable representation of Pacific peoples, with an authentic design in HR for and by Pacific peoples at all levels. This may mean going beyond professional development for one-off cultural competency or cultural intelligence courses. Rather, we recommend a decolonised and Indigenised academy that demonstrates a commitment to Pacific lecturers in sufficient numbers with structured career pathways that normalise Indigenous language and knowledge systems and facilitate the transformation of institutional fragilities.[59]

## Conclusion

Racism in all its forms is a complex issue with damaging consequences for minorities, Indigenous and Pacific peoples. In this chapter, we have presented our experiences of institutional racism and the ways in which our Brownness has been weaponised by institutions and used against us. This violence enacted on us as Pacific people was described bluntly by Fetaui:

> *It's like a rewriting of our culture. Or being forced to re-write who we are as Pasifika. I know it's a really strong*

statement. I'm really sorry to use it, but it feels that way. It feels like the raping of that brown, exotic, other. It's like take, take, take, you know, and it's violent, it's racist, and it hurts in every way, seen and unseen. It's like the dusky maiden, right? People saw her and desired her to fill the gaps of their fantasy for their gain, and in the process violently demoralised her and every woman of the Pacific. Structural racism is violent. We are consistently advocating for our people – once upon a time it was considered a sacred duty – but after all the beatings, I'm struggling to see the sacredness when it is not reciprocated. When our cultural relational values and personhood are weaponised against us to enforce the dominant status quo. (FI)

While institutions are attempting to be more inclusive, we cannot help but feel that moves towards diversity and inclusion have merely become another tokenistic tick-box exercise. We really question how we move from inclusion and diversity to respect and value within our institutions and within our education system. As demonstrated in our chapter, we have attempted to use our experiences of racism to push back against systems of oppression and carve out safe space for us, our colleagues, and our students. It is an ongoing task, but we hope it is a task that will be completed soon so that the next generation does not have to continue this challenging work.

# MIGRATION—

# Time and Race
## Pacific Migration Journeys to Aotearoa

*Evalesi Tuʻinukuafe*

*I relish in moments of imagination both re-envisioning and believing that my ancestors skilfully navigated vast oceans towards new and familiar landscapes to trade foods, art, tools and knowledge without the need for a visa or a passport.*

## My Journey to Migration Studies

KO HOKU HINGOA KO EVALESI TUʻINUKUAFE, and my lineage traces back to Tonga, Sāmoa and Germany. I was born and raised in Glen Eden, West Auckland, in what they call 'the Astrology area' where the streets have names like Virgo, Pisces, Capricorn and Leo. My grandparents Hermann and Evalesi, along with my mum and her younger sister, migrated from Tonga in the early 1970s. Sadly, after a couple of years in New Zealand, my biological nana, Evalesi (my namesake), passed away. After my grandfather married his second wife, Irene, the nana I grew up with, they decided to buy a house on Leo Street in Glen Eden, which is still our family home where cousins, uncles, aunties and friends meet and talanoa about anything and everything.

I realise that my life would have been completely different if my grandfather hadn't followed his two older brothers to New Zealand shortly after they completed their master's degrees at the University of Auckland. Their scholarships from Tonga to New Zealand are the reason my family are here and have been here since. However, for other family members who migrated later, things were much tougher. For instance, I distinctly remember that during my teenage years, family members from Tonga would call my uncle Seko to be sponsored to stay in the country, while others needed some help with their immigration papers – but I was naive and did not really know what that meant nor what it required of my uncle and other elders in my family. My uncle Karl and aunty Naima helped many students, family members and friends during the Dawn Raids, risking not only their own safety but also the safety of their three children so that others could have a chance to start a new life in New Zealand. My uncle Edgar was known for his generosity and kindness in helping family and friends from throughout the Pacific to navigate tricky immigration processes as well as providing translation services. As an adult, I reflect on all these heroic actions with pride and admiration, and believe that it is now my turn to support our fāmili and kāinga/'āiga/whānau and others to tackle things like immigration processes, schemes and policies head-on.

My academic interest in migration studies began after I completed a Summer Research Scholarship at the University of Waikato in 2022 that explored the topic of racial preference and privilege in Immigration New Zealand. As an emerging migration scholar, I have come to see New Zealand's history within the Pacific region through a critical lens and have identified the extractive nature in which the New Zealand Government recruits Pacific migrant workers to support this country's economy under the false pretences of co-development, equal partnership, and mutual benevolence, to name a few. In reality, countries like New Zealand keep getting richer while Pacific countries are left with struggling economies and in some cases a brain drain.[1] New Zealand's relationship with the Pacific is toxic and highly problematic, to say the least. Pacific people like me who are part of the diaspora in New Zealand have a huge sense of responsibility towards Pacific people who wish to come to New Zealand not as disposable and temporary workers but through an equitable choice that offers them a way to bring their families, to receive a good education, and to be entitled to work in roles that they want to do and to be paid fairly. These intentions construct the migrant dream for most Pacific migrants, regardless of their visa status, and echoing the words of Karlo Mila from her poem 'For Sia Fiegel', many first-generation Pacific individuals carry heavy family expectations like these:

> *I am the seed of the migrant dream*
> *(ruia-mai-i-Rangiatea?)*
> *the daughter who is supposed to fill the promise*
> *hope heavy on my shoulders*
> *I stand on the broken back of physical labour*[2]

In a comparable way, I feel that I bear the responsibility of educating myself to understand how immigration policy is informed, designed and implemented so that I can challenge the homogeneity (very monocultural framework) that exists within the immigration sector and the migration studies space.[3] It is important that, 'With the migration of Samoan and other Pacific peoples to the Metropolitan centres of the world, the methodologies [of] our Indigenous knowledge and histories in these centres must similarly migrate'.[4] On that account, I endeavour to include Pacific methods and methodologies to co-create Pacific-focused immigration policies that align with Pacific aspirations for future generations to thrive in New Zealand.[5] Decolonising the immigration policies and schemes that have continued to privilege the inflow of White majority settler societies and European countries while simultaneously hindering other ethnic groups like Pacific peoples from pathways to residency is imperative. Interestingly, in some political spaces the Pacific region and its inhabitants are referred to as New Zealand's neighbours, friends and even family, depending on the political agenda in that moment. However, it is obvious that the very act of regulating Pacific migration movements is a direct product of racist structures that both shape and permeate settler-colonial New Zealand, like the perpetuation of racialised hierarchies that rank people based on their race.[6] This racism is manifested in the Pacific-targeted labour mobility schemes and quotas, and the racialisation of labour by funnelling Pacific migrant workers into low-skilled and low-paid jobs that non-Pacific New Zealand citizens are reluctant to do.[7]

### From Skilled Ocean Voyagers to 'Unskilled' Labourers

> *For the first time in history Pacific peoples are not dictating their own migration journeys. Worse yet, Pacific peoples who are traditionally poetic and articulate orators of their own histories and journeys have been back benched so that non-Pacific scholars may attempt to describe such experiences whilst excluding key cultural and 'relational elements'.*[8]

The New Zealand Government has been offering low-paid employment opportunities to Pacific peoples since the late 1950s under the guise of equal partnership and mutual benevolence, with New Zealand acting as a paternal figure.[9] However, this relationship between New Zealand and individual Pacific countries is very much a transactional arrangement based on supply and demand within New Zealand's primary industries.[10] It is important to note that the Pacific region has been, and still is, viewed by the New Zealand Government primarily as an affordable and reliable labour source coupled with a de facto 'non-citizenship'.[11] Collins describes non-citizenship as individuals not having 'the inherent right to remain permanently in New Zealand. The time limit stipulated in work visas guarantees that an individual can remain only up to the expiry date, and even that is subject to change in rare circumstances.'[12] Some may argue that visa expiry dates apply to all temporary work visas. However, not everyone is treated the same in this regard. Actions do speak louder than words, and past events have shown the fickleness of governmental prerogatives where Pacific migrants have been scapegoated ruthlessly and persecuted when their services or labour are no longer needed.[13] The Dawn Raids, which will be discussed at length later in this chapter and more explicitly in legal terms in the next chapter ('Climate Justice'), are a prime example of the unfair targeting of Pacific peoples by Immigration New Zealand. Some members of Pacific communities say that the Dawn Raids never stopped. An example that was made public occurred in May 2023 when a Tongan national was detained by police in the early hours of the morning for overstaying, only two years after the government's infamous Dawn Raids apology.

Currently, temporary migration for Pacific peoples is framed as a triple-win. The triple-win narrative is based on the idea that the migrant worker, the migrant worker's homeland, and the destination country benefit equally from temporary migration schemes like the Recognised Seasonal Employer (RSE) scheme.[14] Established back in 2007, this scheme has been New Zealand's leading labour mobility arrangement, offering seasonal work primarily to nine Pacific countries: Fiji, Kiribati, Nauru, Papua New Guinea, Sāmoa, Solomon Islands, Tonga, Tuvalu and Vanuatu.[15] To date, the horticulture and viticulture industries have been backboned by an estimated 103,821 Pacific seasonal workers, who have endured substandard living conditions, poor pay and 'denial of personal and cultural freedoms' as highlighted in the New Zealand Human Rights Commission's report, *The RSE Scheme in Aotearoa New Zealand: A Human Rights Review* from December 2022.[16] How is it that such gross levels of exploitation inflicted upon Pacific migrant workers keep occurring? Worse yet, how can so-called RSE experts turn a blind eye and say that exploitation discourse around the RSE scheme is uncalled for? This is especially hard to comprehend when one considers the above-mentioned report, which discusses how and why exploitation of RSE workers is so prevalent, noting that because of a 'lack of oversight, regulation, enforcement, and human rights protections within the RSE scheme . . . employers are able to exploit workers with few consequences if they wish'.[17]

Arguably, manifestations of racism exist within New Zealand's immigration system, encouraging mistreatment and exploitation even before Pacific RSE workers enter the country. Stipulations within the RSE Limited Visa are highly restrictive. For instance, workers must stay in accommodation provided by their employer; they are required to pay deductions for transport, food and more at their employer's discretion; they must pay for their medical insurance; and in some cases, RSE workers have been bonded to work for one employer.[18] Moreover, from the outset, Pacific migrant workers have been undervalued and assumed to be low-skilled and therefore suitable for manual duties like 'planting, maintaining, harvesting and packing crops'.[19] Clearly, racist framing and labelling of Pacific migrant workers aims to subjugate Pacific migrants and box them into racialised migrant categories that deem them 'undesirable migrant subjects in New Zealand',[20] when we know that Pacific peoples have endless potential in multiple employment sectors. Just think for a second: If your only reason for being here was to be an economic crutch for New Zealand and you could be sent back home on a whim, would you feel valued?

> We [Pacific migrant workers] were never invited because they liked us. We were invited because they need cheap labour.[21]

Supposedly, New Zealand's Pacific-focused immigration agendas have been based on the notion of co-development, which begs the question: At what stage of development is Tonga? Given that it has been one of the biggest Pacific participants in the RSE scheme since its inception, and so, it would be helpful to gauge Tonga's development progress. Bedford and Hugo conceptualised three levels of development, namely, 'fully furnished', which are countries that will 'have enough resources and economic potential to not rely on migration and remittances', 'partly furnished', which refers to countries that 'rely on remittances but have the potential to achieve higher domestic output if development aid and remittances are properly harnessed', and lastly, 'unfurnished', being countries 'with the resource constraints of small volcanic islands and atolls, [where] remittances are essential for their development'.[22] In the same report, Tonga and Western Sāmoa were categorised as 'partly furnished', and Bedford and Hugo suggest that the onus and potentiality of becoming 'fully furnished' lies in the hands of the Pacific countries, which must properly harness what remittances are given to them from countries like New Zealand.[23] Furthermore, countries like Tuvalu, Kiribati and Tokelau are categorised as 'unfurnished', meaning that 'migration is essential because of resource constraints and environmental change'.[24] Sadly, for those 'unfurnished' countries, when people leave their homelands to engage in temporary work it is not a choice but a means to survive.

> New Zealand's engagement in the Pacific is guided by the principles of understanding, friendship, mutual benefit, collective impact and sustainability.[25]

This bold statement from New Zealand's Ministry of Foreign Affairs and Trade assumes that a Pacific nation like Tonga is in equal partnership with New Zealand. Unfortunately, Tonga is believed to be 'the most heavily reliant country in the world on remittances (which comprise approximately 34% of the country's GDP)'.[26] At a glance, one may view New Zealand as a generous contributor to Tonga's GDP. However, Tonga's over-reliance on remittances has created a state of co-dependency, wherein around 4000 Tongan nationals travel to New Zealand annually as part of the RSE scheme.[27] Moreover, further increases in seasonal worker caps occurred in September 2023, and numbers are expected to rise by approximately 100 per cent over the next three to five years, from 19,500 Pacific RSE workers to an estimated 38,000.[28] When examining such data, I can't help but wonder: When will Tonga and other Pacific countries be free from selling workers to countries like New Zealand?

## There are Borders Within Borders

> *I believe that the immigration system is underpinned by racial hierarchies that aim to marginalise and control Pacific migrant mobility both to and within New Zealand's borders.*

The New Zealand immigration system operates through criteria-based visa applications that assess skill qualifications that most Pacific migrants are unlikely to possess owing to lack of access to tertiary education within the Pacific region.[29] This means that most Pacific migrants who wish to migrate to New Zealand are not qualified for the 205 preferred professions that are currently on the Green List.[30] This is a long list of professions that Immigration New Zealand values so much that applicants are offered two pathways to residency: through either Tier 1 (Straight to Residence Visa) or Tier 2 (Work to Residence Visa), which requires an applicant to work for two years in New Zealand in order to get residency.[31] Unsurprisingly, over 90 per cent of the Green List roles require an Australian and New Zealand Standard Classification of Occupations.[32] Now, compare this to the option to pick fruit for seven to eleven months at a time, only to be expected to leave and reapply to return for the next season. So then, if New Zealand genuinely wants to develop Pacific communities through the RSE scheme, shouldn't Pacific people be offered higher-paid roles, education pathways, and other employment opportunities that add to the long-term sustainability of their communities? In most Pacific countries, a goal shared by many high school students is to receive scholarships to study overseas in countries like New Zealand and Australia, so that they may graduate with a degree to help them qualify for better-paying jobs like those mentioned above (see also the Green List on Immigration New Zealand's website). Receiving a high-quality tertiary education is very much desired and respected in these communities.

> Tongan people and Pacific people want to come and live in New Zealand so that they can have a better life for themselves and their families. There are no universities in Tonga so parents want their children to come to university in New Zealand to have a better education that can lead to a better future.[33]

It is important to note that the Green List category is not formally capped, thus encouraging high intakes of highly qualified and skilled (mostly) non-Pacific migrants each year, and as of September 2023 an additional seventeen roles have been added to the list.[34] This process of exclusion by way of 'value'-based preference and skill, or lack thereof, can be likened to the gruelling process of being divided into teams at primary school (or any other school). To illustrate, when a captain or team leader (in this case Immigration New Zealand) hand-picked 'the best' team players (visa applicants for Green List roles) from a line-up, you were judged and compared to others based on your skills, what you looked like, relationships or connections you had with the team captain, and other so-called advantages you would bring to the team (in this case the New Zealand economy). We can compare this to the eligibility process for Green List roles and their streamlined access to residency. This shows that Pacific migrants are lacking the skill level that Immigration New Zealand deems valuable, and so they do not qualify to even apply for these Green List roles.

Unfortunately, most Pacific migrants are left with the less likely alternative of applying to become a permanent resident through Pacific quota schemes like the 2023 Pacific Access Category Resident Visa.[35] As of October 2023, The Pacific Access Category granted permanent residency to '500 Tongan and 500 Fijian citizens and 150 Kiribati and 150 Tuvaluan citizens . . . selected by ballot'.[36] The Samoan Quota Resident Visa currently offers 1650 Samoan nationals (previously 1100 since 1970) permanent residency to live, work or study in New Zealand.[37] To some, these numbers seem charitable on New Zealand's part. However, it is important to consider how many Pacific applicants pay for the chance to apply within this small quota system.

If we consider Tonga as a case study, we can see how inequitable this system is. Picture this: the average number of Tongan nationals that applied for residency between 2018 and 2023 was around 521 individuals per year; and between 2021 and 2022, for example, only 345 Tongans were granted their permanent residency (keeping in mind this includes the 250 of the Pacific Access Category at the time).[38] Moreover, Tongans are paying over NZ$1,385 per visa application, regardless of whether they acquire residency, which is a large amount of money considering the average monthly salary for a single person in Tonga is about 1,661 TOP (Tongan pa'anga) which equates to around NZ$1,157.95.[39] This is not only a financial burden to these applicants but also takes an emotional toll on individuals who are not granted a resident visa.[40] A metaphor that illustrates the unfair design of Pacific quotas along with their lofty prices is the infamous claw machine that can be found in most amusement arcades (can you tell I have an eight-year-old game-obsessed daughter?). The similarities are uncanny. Firstly, the claw machine is pre-programmed to pick up a prize only on a set number of plays; so too with the Pacific Access Category system, which has a set number of accepted applications or places (like the 500 Tongan citizens in 2023), thus limiting the number of people who will actually receive residency. This subsequently increases profit for the claw machine manufacturer – or New Zealand Immigration, in this case. Moreover, although the chances are slim for players and applicants in both cases, many still take financial risks in the hope that attempts will be rewarded. As simple as this comparison may appear, the fundamental truth is that in both situations, it is one's hope that drives one's actions to take a chance, and yet the outcome is controlled by a system, whether that be algorithmic or balloted.

(Thank you to my supportive partner Finn, who went down a rabbit hole researching the mechanics behind arcade claw machines. Your efforts are appreciated.)

## Historic and Contemporary Dawn Raids

*Before the fruit picking there was factory work. Same, same.*

A fierce display of racism towards Pacific migrants was seen during the 1974–76 Dawn Raids, when Immigration New Zealand officers teamed up with local police to initiate what was described by Dr Melani Anae as 'a racist beast let loose on Pacific people in full view'.[41] Fuelled by sheer racism, the Dawn Raids specifically targeted Pacific migrant people whose work visas had expired, even though the majority of illegal migrants at the time were of Pālagi descent.[42] It is estimated that in 1973 more than 80 per cent of temporary visa holders were from either the US, the UK or Australia, and yet the majority of deportees were Tongans (107 individuals) and Samoans (24 individuals).[43] The Dawn Raids palpably revealed the long entanglement between colonial structures and migrant racial preferences that (still) openly welcome European or White migrants.[44] In addition, since then, the racist framing and othering of Pacific migrants has consciously and subconsciously stuck to the psyche of many self-proclaimed Kiwis, whose view of New Zealand nationhood has a semblance of Whiteness that is linked 'with class and class mobility'.[45] This means that a non-Pacific migrant of European descent is deemed more likely to assimilate into New Zealand society as they are perceived as fitting 'the profile of the suitable migrant'.[46] Sadly, at the same time Pacific migrants are publicly labelled as undesirable migrants and undocumented overstayers.[47]

Interestingly, overstayers are defined by Immigration New Zealand as 'People who . . . regardless of nationality, must appreciate that if there are no special circumstances that call for the grant of a visa, they are expected to leave New Zealand, or face deportation'.[48] It would be interesting to know whether this definition was updated after the Dawn Raids to absolve the New Zealand Government of any allegations that the Dawn Raids deportees were arrested and detained based on race. This is important because groups like the Polynesian Panther Party publicly fought, campaigned and raised awareness about 'the core Panther ideology: that Pacific peoples' relationship with white New Zealanders was one of inequality and racism, with Polynesians represented as an underclass'.[49] Pacific peoples in New Zealand see no difference between the 1970s Dawn Raids and the recent 'out of hours immigration visit[s]' that occurred in April 2023 (as I mentioned earlier), especially when the target was a Tongan national.[50] This resulted in a review commissioned by the Ministry of Business, Innovation and Employment, which was carried out by Michael Heron KC, whose final report was released in June 2023.[51] Strategically framed as 'out of hours compliance activity', these visits only make up about 3 per cent of immigration check visits per year.[52] So then, this prompts some vital questions for us all to ponder: Is it even necessary to carry out these Dawn Raids today? And if so, what is the imminent threat to our society that condones these visits outside of office hours? Also, are these contemporary Dawn Raids a part of settler-colonial racial hierarchies portraying an external colonial relationship with the Pacific?

## Conclusion

For decades, racism within New Zealand's immigration system has impacted the mobility of Pacific migrants both to and within New Zealand. For far too long, Pacific migrants have been viewed as fit for only low-skilled and menial work that is often coupled with employment precarity and employee exploitation. Pacific migrants have been deemed 'reliable', 'happy', 'grateful' and 'hardworking' employees who sustain New Zealand's primary industries and then are expected to leave when they are no longer needed.[53]

As an emerging Pacific migration researcher, I have been told by non-Pacific migration experts that I am naive and don't fully understand how things work in government and in the immigration sector, but that doesn't dampen my hope for better Pacific migrant worker outcomes. Instead, it fuels me to hold space for Pacific voices to be an integral part of New Zealand–Pacific immigration conversations, because these discussions need to be with them and not only about them.

> *I relish in moments of visualisation of a time when Pacific peoples dictate their own journeys of migration to whenua, one that is informed and developed with our whanaungatanga and relationships to tangata whenua, not the settler-colonial nation state of New Zealand. I believe that this way of voyaging from homeland to Aotearoa will be a dignified experience and, in a way, a heartfelt reunion of ancient tupuna.* —Evalesi Tuʻinukuafe

## Recommendations for Change

Contrary to this colonial and capitalist framing of Pacific peoples, I know that Pacific peoples are intelligent, resourceful, diligent, creative and so much more. Their value is inherent in their languages, knowledge frameworks, family connections, traditions and vast migrations, both past and present. It is my hope that Pacific peoples will be offered more pathways to residency, through study and work options that will upskill them and enable them to apply for higher-paid roles (like those from the Green List) in the future. I believe that all Pacific RSE workers deserve to be treated with dignity and care and that their wages should be more than $25.47 per hour (the current threshold). I strongly believe that Pacific RSE workers should be offered alternative employment opportunities along with visa extensions if they wish to continue working in New Zealand after their seasonal contract ends, as this would increase their income and allow them to send larger remittances to their families back in their home countries. These Pacific migrant workers must be offered sustainable employment options that are not limited to menial jobs; if they are expected to leave their families and villages to work here, then they need to be offered work that can maximise their income. There has been talk from non-Pacific migration experts who really do believe that RSE workers are happy and that their families are grateful for the inflow of income. My question then remains the same: Who genuinely wants to pick fruit for more than 30 hours per week?

# CLIMATE JUSTICE

# There Can Be No (Climate) Justice on Stolen Land
## Pacific Peoples, Climate Change and the Law in New Zealand

*Dylan Asafo*

> It's over three years now that we've been here . . . we're vying for some recognition of being here, based on climate change . . . the mind would be more settled if indeed we are given PR [permanent resident] status.[1]

These are the words of Solofa,[2] a Tuvaluan elder, who left their home in Tuvalu to live in New Zealand (I use 'New Zealand' here to distinguish between New Zealand the settler-colonial state and Aotearoa the whenua or land on which the state has been imposed). Solofa is speaking to their struggles with cross-border climate-change-related displacement, which is when someone cannot live in their home country because the impacts of climate change (like rising sea levels and extreme weather events) and underlying socioeconomic factors (like poverty and unemployment) have made their homes uninhabitable.[3]

Cross-border climate-change-related displacement is a great injustice because most of the people experiencing it come from states that are least responsible for the climate crisis, like Tuvalu, but that tend to be the ones suffering the most from its impacts.[4] The injustice is made even worse when these climate-displaced peoples[5] try to migrate and resettle in some of the states most responsible for the climate crisis, like New Zealand, but are denied protection by those states without any acknowledgement of their role in displacing them in the first place.[6]

This is an injustice facing not only Indigenous peoples of Te Moana-nui-a-Kiwa (the Pacific Ocean) but many others around the world, where there are currently no laws in place to protect climate-displaced peoples by allowing them to resettle in other countries.[7] Legal experts have referred to this injustice as the protection deficit in the law.[8]

Because of the protection deficit, climate-displaced Pacific people like Solofa are now 'vying' to remain in New Zealand by applying for permanent resident (PR) status. These people first came to New Zealand under temporary visas, but if they cannot get PR status, they must then overstay these visas when they expire to live safely and with dignity.[9] Olivia Yates has done groundbreaking research into the lived experiences of climate-displaced Pacific people in New Zealand like Solofa and has argued that the New Zealand state is subjecting them to 'legal violence' by making them 'inhabit a space of invisibility . . . vulnerable to exploitation, stress and anxiety' and trapping them in 'a purgatorial state of "deportability"'.[10]

In this chapter, I want to further examine this 'legal violence' by examining the relevant laws involved, including the relevant policies made under these laws.[11] Rather than taking a standard legal approach to examining these laws, I take a racial justice approach that aims to call out the racial injustices perpetuated through the 'violence' of these laws and policies, and explore how we can eliminate these injustices. As noted by E. Tendayi Achiume, the former United Nations (UN) Special Rapporteur on contemporary forms of racism, racial discrimination, xenophobia and related intolerance, there is an urgent need for racial justice approaches to understanding and addressing the climate crisis:

> A racial justice approach to this crisis is both urgent and necessary, and yet within the global framework it

remains thoroughly marginalized . . . . The predominant global responses to environmental crises are characterized by the same forms of systemic racism that are driving these crises in the first place.[12]

My particular racial justice approach is inspired by the one Carmen Gonzalez has used to look at climate-change-related migration and displacement and the law more globally.[13] Gonzalez's approach focuses on the impact of racial capitalism, which refers to a 'world system' that transforms 'regional and cultural differences into racial forms of domination' and makes it so that 'racism is foundational to capitalism'.[14] In other words, racial capitalism is a system that makes it so that injustice in this world is not just about the divide between the rich and the poor but more about how people are racialised, as White people are more likely to be rich and powerful than people racialised as non-White, with people racialised as Black being most likely to be worse off.[15] To put this another way, the system of racial capitalism makes it so that the less White or more Black you are, the more poor and powerless you are likely to be. Racial capitalism has also been used to refer to what Nancy Leong describes as the process of 'deriving social and economic value from the racial identity of another'.[16] In other words, for those racialised as White to gain and maintain wealth and power, racial capitalism involves creating 'racial identities', which simply refers to the labels and stereotypes attached to or imposed on a racialised group based on racist ideas.

In taking this racial justice approach, my main argument is that the 'legal violence' inflicted on climate-displaced Pacific peoples seeking to live in New Zealand is driven by the law's commitment to upholding racial capitalism. In my view, the laws of New Zealand are firmly committed to racial capitalism because New Zealand is a settler-colonial state[17] that depends on the global system of racial capitalism to exist.[18] Specifically, the New Zealand state needs to create laws that protect the racial identity of 'conquerors' for non-Indigenous settlers (Tauiwi) most likely to be racialised as White to allow them to freely colonise and keep the state intact. At the same time, the state also needs to impose on Māori the racial identities of 'rebels', 'savages' and 'barbarians' to justify dispossessing them of their whenua as tangata whenua and denying them their rights to exercise tino rangatiratanga (Māori sovereignty and self-determination) as affirmed in te Tiriti o Waitangi (te Tiriti).[19]

But the work of racial capitalism in the Zealand state does not end there. The state must also impose specific racial identities on Tauiwi of colour, like Pacific peoples, to survive. These identities include the 'labourers', whose bodies can be exploited for profit to help fund the state, and the 'criminals', who cannot be exploited so are denied the legal right to remain in New Zealand and must then break the law to remain in the state and survive. This 'criminal' identity is imposed on climate-displaced Pacific peoples if they cannot get PR status, and so they are subject to the 'legal violence' of being 'trapped in a purgatorial state of "deportability"' as noted by Yates.[20]

Therefore, because racial capitalism is intertwined with settler-colonialism in New Zealand, climate-displaced Pacific peoples cannot begin to be free from this 'violence' as long as the settler-colonial state is in place and te Tiriti remains dishonoured. Simply put, there can be no justice, including climate justice, for Pacific peoples or any other group, on stolen land, and more broadly, in a world governed by the global system of racial capitalism.

To make this argument, this chapter has six parts. Part two is a brief positionality statement to position myself as a Samoan academic in the climate crisis and in Te Moana-nui-a-Kiwa. Part three provides some important context to the complicated issue of cross-border climate-change-related displacement before part four outlines the laws and policies creating the 'legal violence' climate-displaced Pacific peoples face when seeking to live in New Zealand. Then part five presents my main argument that we should understand this 'violence' as being a result of the New Zealand state's commitment to racial capitalism. Finally, part six proposes how we in Aotearoa can work towards a future free from this 'violence' by supporting Māori calls for honouring te Tiriti and dismantling racial capitalism more globally.

## Positionality

I write this chapter as a Samoan from the villages of Salani, Siumu, Satalo and Moata'a, who was born in Narmm in so-called Australia and raised in Tāmaki Makaurau in Aotearoa. While my villages in Sāmoa are increasingly impacted by the climate crisis, as a part of the Samoan diaspora, I have not personally experienced the displacing impacts of climate change. I am also largely sheltered from these impacts due to my privileges as a middle-class, able-bodied, cis-gendered male academic with New Zealand citizenship.

Acknowledging my privileges here is essential to highlight the limits of my knowledge and make space for Pacific peoples who have more direct lived experience with climate-change-related displacement and the impacts of the climate crisis more generally. These voices must be amplified and privileged when talking or writing about the climate crisis in Te Moana-nui-a-Kiwa. Therefore, all of my views here are open to criticism and rejection, particularly by Pacific peoples, Māori and Indigenous and negatively racialised peoples whose lived experiences and aspirations I aim to honour in this chapter.

## Providing Important Context to a Complicated Issue

I must also acknowledge at the outset that cross-border climate-change-related displacement is a deeply complicated issue. It is complicated in the sense that the climate crisis is forcing Pacific peoples and many other Indigenous and negatively racialised peoples around the world to face 'impossible choices' regarding cross-border climate-change-related displacement where they lose something significant no matter what 'choice' they make.[21] These 'choices' appear at different levels but are very much connected and informed by each other. Firstly, at the state government level, Pacific governments, particularly those of the most impacted nations like Kiribati and Tuvalu, are having to 'choose' between calling for the protection deficit to end to protect their citizens from displacement and keeping it intact due to the risks involved, including the risk that wealthy countries like New Zealand could use protection to evade their obligations to reduce their emissions and support effective adaptation measures in the Pacific.[22] Secondly, at more communal, familial and individual levels, many Pacific peoples have to 'choose' between remaining in their ancestral homelands, with which they have deep cultural and spiritual connections, or migrating to live in places like New Zealand in pursuit of safety and protection.[23] Thirdly, and also at communal, familial and individual levels, Pacific peoples who have already migrated to states like New Zealand are having to 'choose' between overstaying their visas on the one hand or going back to homes that have become uninhabitable and the dangerous if not fatal circumstances that follow.[24]

The reality is that different Pacific governments, communities, families and individuals do and will continue to navigate these 'impossible choices' differently depending on their particular circumstances and aspirations. So rather than passing judgment and foolishly suggesting that one choice is 'right' and the other is 'wrong', given the privileges I hold, I want to highlight the existence and deep injustice of these 'impossible choices' and suggest that the wealthy states most responsible for the climate crisis first and foremost bear the responsibility for any harm that might come from these 'choices'. Accordingly, I also want to emphasise that it is essential for these 'choices' to be discussed and addressed with nuance, care and the utmost regard for the lived experiences and aspirations of those facing them. It is with all of the above in mind that I examine this third 'choice' facing the climate-displaced Pacific peoples who have already migrated to New Zealand and are being subjected to 'legal violence' by the state.

## The 'Legal Violence' Climate-Displaced Pacific Peoples Face in New Zealand

When examining the 'legal violence' facing climate-displaced Pacific peoples in New Zealand, it is important to know that this 'violence' is not inflicted by laws and policies that explicitly state that they must be 'trapped in a purgatorial state' and live in fear of being deported, as Yates has noted.[25] Instead, various laws and policies that might seem fair and reasonable on the surface come together to inflict this 'violence' by making it extremely difficult for climate-displaced Pacific peoples to live safely and with dignity in New Zealand.[26] More specifically, these laws and policies establish pathways to living in New Zealand that are very hard, if not impossible, for climate-displaced Pacific peoples to access.

The two pathways that climate-displaced Pacific peoples seek out most are the Pacific Access Category (PAC) and the Samoan Quota Resident Visa. While these pathways provide PR status in New Zealand, not all citizens from the Pacific are eligible to apply. To be eligible, applicants must meet the following requirements: have a job offer that pays enough to support them and their family in New Zealand; be able to read, write and speak English in an interview; and be aged eighteen to forty-five years old.[27] To make things more difficult, applicants are not even guaranteed a visa if they meet all these requirements – they also have to be randomly selected from a lottery-like ballot. The current quotas are 150 Tuvaluan citizens, 150 I-Kiribati citizens, 500 Tongan citizens, and 500 Fijian citizens for PAC,[28] and 1650 Samoan citizens for the Samoan Quota Resident Visa.[29] The high stakes for climate-displaced Pacific peoples to be eligible and 'lucky' enough to be selected for this ballot are reflected in the following words of one Tuvaluan woman, Kalapu:[30]

> So dangerous to stay there, so scary . . . Because the island is so small, no mountains to go, no high buildings to go. So we make a plan to get a better life, and lucky we have a chance to come under this Tuvalu PAC.[31]

The other pathway that climate-displaced Pacific peoples seek out is the Skilled Migrant Category Resident Visa. Eligibility for this visa is based on a points system which requires applicants to have 160 points to be eligible for consideration. Points are awarded based on age (the younger you are, the more points awarded), whether you already have 'skilled' employment (with additional points given if you have high-paid work earning at least $53 per hour), qualifications (the higher your qualification, the more points you are awarded), your level of work experience, and whether you have an English-speaking partner who has skilled employment (with additional points given depending on the level of their qualifications).[32]

For climate-displaced Pacific peoples who cannot get 160 points and are unlucky with the PR visa lotteries, the next best pathway is a temporary visa, in the hope of getting PR status later on. While many different types of temporary visas are available, they all have very specific requirements. For example, partner visas require having a partner who is a citizen, PR, or temporary work visa holder, and study visas require enrolment in an educational institution.[33] One of the more accessible and inclusive temporary visas is the Accredited Employer Work Visa. This visa allows a stay of up to five years and requires an offer of employment at the median wage of $31.61, but there must be 'no New Zealanders available' to do the work offered.[34] Another temporary work visa specifically aimed at Pacific peoples is the Recognised Seasonal Employer (RSE) Limited Visa. This visa provides a limited stay to work in the horticultural and viticultural industries for seven months in any eleven-month period, with citizens from Tuvalu and Kiribati interestingly being allowed to remain an extra two months.[35] While these visas provide temporary protection, when they eventually expire, climate-displaced Pacific peoples are faced with an impossible 'choice': either return home to uninhabitable conditions or stay on as 'irregular migrants' – or even attempt to gain PR status while living 'undocumented'.[36] In other words, they must break the law to survive. Unsurprisingly then, some climate-displaced Pacific peoples remain home to avoid the harm and indignity of this 'legal violence' despite facing worsening, if not uninhabitable, living conditions.[37] Therefore, the experiences of climate-displaced Pacific peoples show us how laws and policies that seem fair and reasonable on the surface come together to inflict 'legal violence'.

## Understanding This 'Legal Violence' as Racial Capitalism in the Settler-colonial State

The question that arises now is: How can we understand the 'legal violence' facing climate-displaced Pacific peoples? In taking a racial justice approach to answer this question, I argue that this 'violence' should be understood as being a result of New Zealand's dependence on racial capitalism as a settler-colonial state. More specifically, to be able to exist in Aotearoa, the New Zealand state needs to uphold two sets of racialised identities through its many laws and policies – one set for desirable settlers and the other for undesirable settlers. The first set of racial identities for desirable settlers includes the 'conquerors' who are free to colonise to maintain the state and the 'labourers' whose bodies are exploited for profit by the 'conquerors'.

The 'conquerors' are most easily welcomed into the state through pathways like the Skilled Migrant Category Resident Visa. While some may say this visa's points system does not favour any particular ethnicity or group in society, its focus on employability, income, education level and English-language skills ensures that only specific groups of people can be conquerors – that is, people most likely to be racialised as White, from wealthy countries, rich, able-bodied, young and cis-gendered males. Therefore, people who are most likely to be racialised as Black or Brown, from less wealthy countries, poor, disabled, elderly, women, trans, and non-binary are largely and deliberately excluded from the conqueror identity.[38]

The other desirable settlers are the 'labourers'. They are also welcomed into the state, but only with carefully designed restrictions that make clear their desirability is limited and conditional. Importantly, there are two tiers of 'labourers' – the top tier having PR status and the bottom only having the right to stay in New Zealand temporarily. The top-tier 'labourers' are PAC and Samoan Quota Resident Visa recipients, who are given PR status, but only if they can assimilate into the state by having English-literacy skills and guaranteed employment, with the upper age limit of forty-five years ensuring that their bodies can be exploited for as long as possible. These PR visas also have quotas to ensure that there are not too many of these 'labourers' in the state taking opportunities and resources from the 'conquerors' to whom the state first and foremost belongs. As such, these 'labourers' face worse conditions than 'conquerors', where even those like Kalapu who were 'lucky' to have come under PAC visas faced low wages, high living costs, and tenuous housing arrangements 'no matter how tirelessly they worked'.[39]

The second tier of 'labourers' is for those who come under temporary visas like the Accredited Employer Work Visa and the RSE Visa. Despite being essential to the state's economy, the state makes clear that people on these visas cannot be a part of New Zealand and that their only value lies in their ability to provide labour on the 'conquerors'' terms. As Litia Tuiburelevu and Hugo Wagner-Hiliau have argued, labour-based initiatives like the RSE Visa must be understood as a continuation of New Zealand's long-standing practice of exploiting Pacific people's bodies for economic gain.[40] This practice spans from 'Blackbirding' in the nineteenth century to the luring of Pacific people to fill labour shortages in the post-World War II boom, followed by their systematic deportation in the infamous Dawn Raids.[41] The Dawn Raids also made clear that the desirable labourer identity is never guaranteed and can be taken away, when once sought-after Pacific migrants quickly became the state's scapegoats for the rampant unemployment of the early 1970s. This is just as Arcia Tecun, Anisha Sankar and Lana Lopesi have observed: 'Racialised migrants are accepted as long as they are compatible with the way that colonial capitalism operates, and they are excluded when they become antithetical to it in some way.'[42] Therefore, Pacific peoples can go from holding the desirable identity of 'labourers' one day to being relegated to the second set of racial identities for undesirable settlers the next on the whims of the state.

In the context of climate-change-related displacement, this second set of racial identities for undesirable settlers includes the three Elizabeth Stanley has listed and described as follows:

> First ... savages – those incapable of adapting or thriving under catastrophic environmental threats and who need to be saved by 'the West'. Secondly ... threats – the hordes who will threaten white civilization and who must be sorted, excluded, detained and deported. Thirdly ... 'non-ideal' victims – those undeserving of full legal protections but who may survive under hostile conditions in receiving states.[43]

While this list is spot on, in my view, another racial identity that should be added is the 'criminals'. This highlights how climate-displaced Pacific people who are 'undocumented' are made out to be unruly lawbreakers for overstaying their temporary visas when they cannot get PR status. This 'criminals' identity gains its power from the racist and popular belief that to maintain law and order the state must be 'tough on crime' by penalising people who break the law, regardless of whether their crimes or violations are largely driven by forces beyond their control, including colonisation and systemic racism.[44] It does not matter whether someone has to break the law to survive or even that they have been displaced from their homes due to no fault of their own. It also does not matter if some of these people were once seen as desirable to the state's economy as 'labourers' when they had temporary visas. The mere fact that they are breaking the law is enough to justify their deportation from the state, and the dangerous, if not fatal, consequences that come from that.

A question one might ask now is: How is it possible for New Zealand to have such racist immigration laws and policies when we have other laws that ensure the human rights of all people, especially the right to be free from discrimination based on race, colour, creed, age, gender and disability status? The answer to this question is unsurprising but still outrageous. Laws and policies around immigration and PR status can be racist because the state passed a special law allowing them to be. Specifically, section 392(2)(a) of the Immigration Act 2009 explicitly prohibits anyone from bringing a complaint of discrimination under the Human Rights Act 1993 against any immigration law, policy or decision.[45] Furthermore, the Human Rights Commission, which is meant to act as New Zealand's independent human rights watchdog, cannot bring proceedings to challenge any immigration law, policy or decision or even intervene, assist or take part in proceedings brought by any other individual or group.[46] Therefore, the immigration system was never designed to be fair and free from discrimination – the state has deliberately baked racism and intersectional discrimination into it.

The state's ability to pick and choose when and to whom human rights apply affirms a truth that Māori justice advocates have known for a long time – that human rights and freedoms belong only to those the state considers human. As Moana Jackson has explained, human rights and freedoms in New Zealand were never meant to be enjoyed by Māori, only by the conquerors who imposed the settler-colonial state on Māori and continue to do so:

> This country has always been reluctant to use the word 'freedom' to describe the efforts by Māori people to oppose colonisation and assert tino rangatiratanga ... the freedoms of liberal democracy were always adaptable, and included the freedom to declare war on our people, and the freedom to ignore the convention of majority rule and instead assume the power to govern ...[47]

To justify giving 'conquerors' the human rights and freedoms to colonise, the state needs to make Māori undeserving of their human rights and freedoms to exercise sovereignty on their own whenua. As Aikman has explained, to do this, the settler-colonial state needed, and still needs, the global system of racial capitalism to impose negative racial identities on Māori to make them out to be less than human, remarking:

> The racialisation of Māori as inferior was an essential component in the dispossession of Māori lands. This 'inferiorisation' rationalised the expropriation and exploitation of Māori lands for settler prosperity and supremacy . . . Māori became the 'rebel', the 'savage' and 'barbarous' other, unentitled to the civility of law and protection, and whose lands were dispossessed and exploited through a multiplicity of means.[48]

What does this mean for climate-displaced Pacific peoples and the 'legal violence' they are subjected to in trying to remain in New Zealand? Because the violence is driven by racial capitalism and the settler-colonial state it protects, freedom from this violence requires both the settler-colonial state and the global system of racial capitalism to be dismantled. To be clear, it is impossible for climate-displaced Pacific peoples to somehow be exempted from the racial identities imposed on them by racial capitalism, while the racial identities imposed on Māori that are used to justify the theft of their lands remain. After all, colonising 'conquerers' do not only need Indigenous peoples to be 'rebels', 'savages' and 'barbarians' in order to steal their land and deny their sovereignty; they also need non-Indigenous migrant 'labourers' and undesirable 'criminals' to make their conquests profitable, enjoyable and worthwhile.

This means we cannot work towards futures free from the violence inflicted on climate-displaced Pacific peoples within the settler-colonial state. We need to dream, imagine and fight for something new. Thankfully, Māori have been charting a brave new way forward towards a just Aotearoa for all other Tauiwi to follow. The next section proposes ways that we, as Pacific peoples, can begin doing that.

## Towards Futures Free from 'Legal Violence'

To dismantle the settler-colonial state and restore the ability of Māori to fully exercise tino rangatiratanga on their whenua, Māori are leading a movement towards Tiriti-based constitutional transformation. In a nutshell, constitutional transformation is about transforming how power is distributed in this country (in other words, the constitution) in a manner that 'settles colonisation, restores the balance between Māori as mana whenua (mana – power and authority derived from the gods, whenua – land; mana whenua is mana in the land) and predominantly European settlers, and allows the country to live in peace and harmony'.[49]

Some Pacific peoples might say that Tiriti-based constitutional transformation is too radical and unrealistic, so the right thing to do is to keep pushing for positive changes within the systems of the settler-colonial state. However, the reality is that the New Zealand state has proven time and time again that it is both incapable and unwilling to treat Pacific peoples as human beings deserving of dignity.[50] That is the unavoidable truth when it comes to every single injustice Pacific peoples face, including but not limited to poverty, poor access to housing, inequities in health and education, and injustice in the criminal legal system.

Unlike the state, Māori are capable of taking care of Pacific peoples and any Tauiwi, including when it comes to providing protection from climate-change-related displacement. This truth was articulated by Green Party co-leader Marama Davidson, when speaking to how Aotearoa should respond to climate-change-related displacement in Te Moana-nui-a-Kiwa, remarking: 'When it comes to welcoming any people here, tangata whenua should not only be at the decision-making tables of those plans, but can also take care, and welcome and resettle people better.'[51]

In terms of how exactly Tiriti-based constitutional transformation can allow Māori to take care of climate-displaced Pacific peoples, Tahu Kukutai and Arama Rata have called for the development of a 'Treaty-based model of Manaakitanga' for immigration in a Tiriti-based Aotearoa – manaakitanga being a core value in tikanga Māori that refers to 'the process of showing and receiving care, respect, kindness and hospitality'.[52] Kukutai and Rata note that, from a Māori perspective, this model would 'reflect [Māori] responsibilities to care for [Māori] neighbours across Te Moana-nui-a-Kiwa (the Pacific Ocean), a greater recognition of [Māori] whakapapa relationships, and the shifting needs of international communities'.[53]

The road to a 'Treaty-based model of Manaakitanga' can include some of the specific changes that climate-displaced Pacific peoples have called for to end the 'legal violence' inflicted on them. As Yates has noted, these changes include providing an amnesty to all 'irregular' and 'undocumented' migrants, resourcing communities to allow them to maintain their identities, languages and cultures, and making visa pathways like PAC more flexible.[54] However, we must take care to ensure these changes are not put forward as end goals that only end up maintaining and reinforcing the settler-colonial state. If these changes are to endure and lead to justice for all, they must be championed in ways that are consistent with or help work towards Tiriti-based constitutional transformation. This is because Western settler-colonial politics is defined by constant compromises and setbacks, which means that any positive change towards justice will not last or be effective in the state system.[55]

Moreover, we as Pacific peoples must understand that the need to champion Tiriti-based constitutional transformation is much deeper than securing our own freedom. As I have also argued elsewhere, we must actively support such transformation to remember and honour our relational responsibilities to Māori as tangata moana, a unique status for Pacific peoples in Aotearoa which recognises the various whakapapa (kin) links Pacific peoples share with Māori as our whanaunga (relations).[56]

We must also realise that Tiriti-based transformation will help us work towards other climate justice goals for Aotearoa and the wider Moana-nui-a-Kiwa, including securing meaningful reductions in emissions and effective adaptation measures.[57] This means that all Pacific peoples, including the state governments of Pacific nations, must realise that the New Zealand settler-colonial state will never make a genuine commitment to working towards climate justice. This will never change, even if we triple the number of Pacific judges and Members of Parliament or have a Pacific deputy prime minister or prime minister.

Of course, Pacific governments resisting settler-colonialism in New Zealand and supporting Tiriti-based constitutional transformation will be much easier said than done. There are deeply entrenched political and economic imbalances between the New Zealand state and Pacific governments which means that rejecting the legitimacy of the state in favour of tino rangatiratanga for Māori will be tricky – particularly in light of the various trade and aid arrangements with New Zealand and other wealthy states that Pacific Island nations have to rely on.[58] However, the unavoidable truth is that Pacific peoples must push our Pacific governments to be brave and resist these colonial pressures to honour our whakapapa with our Māori whanaunga and our other Pacific peoples living under settler-colonial rule. As the climate crisis continues to show us, the survival of our whenua, moana (ocean) and peoples depends on it.

But to achieve climate justice and rid ourselves of racial capitalism, our transformational work cannot be limited to Aotearoa or even Te Moana-nui-a-Kiwa. We must remember that racial capitalism is a global system that inflicts unjust violence worldwide, including through the global climate crisis. Therefore, it is impossible to dismantle racial capitalism within the confines of Aotearoa or Te Moana-nui-a-Kiwa while it rages on elsewhere. This reality requires us to work in solidarity with Indigenous and negatively racialised peoples around the world to dismantle racial capitalism and the international laws and institutions that uphold it.

This also means that we must challenge, if not reject, some of the solutions experts recommend if they do not explicitly and directly reject racial capitalism and settler-colonialism. An example of such a solution came from Ian Fry, the UN Special Rapporteur on the promotion and protection of human rights in the context of climate change. Fry has recommended that we solve the protection deficit by making changes to the Refugee Convention (the international agreement on the rights of people who are refugees) to provide protection for peoples experiencing climate-change-related displacement.[59] This recommendation is problematic because it ignores the reality that state governments, like New Zealand,[60] already inflict racially unjust violence against people who are refugees when applying the Refugee Convention through their domestic laws and policies,[61] so there is no reason to believe things would be any different when it comes to displaced peoples. As Gonzalez has noted, if the Convention were changed to fix the protection deficit, climate-displaced peoples would almost certainly still encounter violence through 'increasingly militarized borders, confinement in detention centres, lack of legal representation, and the impossible burden of demonstrating that their multifaceted and complex decision to migrate can be attributed solely to climate change'.[62]

Therefore, when thinking through global solutions to climate-change-related displacement and the climate crisis more broadly, we must take a racial justice approach to ensure that our solutions do not replicate or reinforce unjust systems like racial capitalism and settler-colonialism, but actively work towards dismantling them. While it is beyond the scope of this chapter to explore how racial capitalism might be dismantled globally, it is undeniable that to achieve climate justice, we must dream not only of a free Aotearoa and Te Moana-nui-a-Kiwa but also of a free world.

## Conclusion

This chapter has examined the 'legal violence' facing climate-displaced Pacific peoples and placed it not only within the wider domestic context of settler-colonialism in Aotearoa but also within the much wider global context of racial capitalism. Accordingly, it has made bold statements and suggested radical changes to our current reality that may be difficult for many to take seriously or imagine.

To close, I reiterate two powerful calls to action that we must always remember to help us dream bravely of freedom and fight tirelessly to turn these dreams into reality. Firstly, for us Pacific peoples needing to divest from the New Zealand state and support Tiriti-based constitutional transformation in Aotearoa, I reiterate the following beautiful invitation for Māori–Tauiwi solidarity from Kukutai and Rata:

> Māori and newer migrants have the opportunity to work together to create constitutional arrangements that are better suited to our diverse citizenry. During our own migration story, our ancestors were able to navigate to these shores due in no small part to their strength of vision. [Māori] navigators were able to see the distant islands of Aotearoa and pull them forth. This same ability to see beyond the horizon will enable us [to] pull forth a new constitution for this nation. The waka has been carved, and provisions are being loaded. Current political tides, treacherous though they may be, will not keep us from our destination: a fair, diverse and inclusive Aotearoa. Will you join us?[63]

Secondly, for all of us Indigenous peoples of Te Moana-nui-a-Kiwa pursuing climate justice, I reiterate the powerful words of Epeli Hau'ofa that remind us that it is not racial capitalism that binds and connects us; it is the sea and the ocean that is calling on us to fight for our freedom:

We are the sea, we are the ocean, we must wake up to this ancient truth and together use it to overturn all hegemonic views that aim ultimately to confine us again, physically and psychologically, in the tiny spaces which we have resisted accepting as our sole appointed place, and from which we have recently liberated ourselves....

We must not allow anyone to belittle us again, and take away our freedom.[64]

# HEALTH

## 'We Need to Get Real'
Structural Racism and the Wellbeing
of Pacific Peoples in Aotearoa

*Caleb Marsters*

> These [Pacific] inequities of quality of care and
> outcome represent a systemic failure of New Zealand
> citizen and human rights, and a national shame.[1]

THE QUOTE ABOVE IS FROM THE Health Quality and Safety Commission's *Bula Sautu* report, which investigated how the Aotearoa New Zealand (Aotearoa) health system is working (or not working) for Pacific peoples. 'Bula sautu' is a Fijian expression meaning prosperous living, good health, a life that is lived to its full potential, a life of abundance. In 2021, the *Bula Sautu* report highlighted that Pacific health outcomes on a population scale fail to live up to the promises of a 'good life'.[2] The report is one of the more recent explorations of the ongoing health disparities faced by Pacific peoples in Aotearoa and uses national data to show the complex contributing factors that impact on health for Pacific communities. As noted in the *Bula Sautu* report, some of the long-standing health inequities faced by Pacific peoples in Aotearoa are:

> Pacific peoples are dispensed mental health medication
> less than other populations.

Pacific peoples experience higher incidence and mortality rates of breast, lung and uterine cancers than other ethnicities.

Despite community initiatives that have helped to increase screening rates for breast cancer, Pacific peoples continue to have lower screening rates for many cancers, such as bowel cancer and cervical cancer, leading to later detection and shorter survival rates.

Pacific peoples bear a disproportionate burden of chronic health conditions such as cardiovascular disease, kidney disease, and diabetes, as well as greater hospitalisation rates due to these conditions.

Less than half (47 per cent) of pregnant Pacific women were registered with a lead maternity carer, compared with 81 per cent for non-Māori or non-Pacific women. This has led to consistently higher rates of mortality among Pacific mums and their pēpe (babies).

Pacific children experience a higher incidence of a range of conditions, including asthma, dental problems, and ear and skin infections, than children from other ethnic groups.

Pacific peoples live, on average, six years fewer than non-Māori non-Pacific peoples.[3]

And the list goes on . . .

Sir Collin Tukuitonga, a Niuean-born New Zealand doctor and public health expert, expressed considerable concern in response to this report; not because these findings are surprising or new, but because there has been mountains of evidence collected over the years that shows a clear need for systemic change in health.

Tukuitonga asserted that 'business as usual' would only spell more disparities:

> We'll have children continuing to miss out on vision and hearing tests and Well Child checks.... We'll have Pacific people with diabetes continuing to have blindness, amputations and kidney failure.[4]

In this chapter, I argue that structural change is urgently required to address the long-standing Pacific health inequities that we continue to see today. As Professor Damon Salesa, Pacific historian and Vice-Chancellor of AUT University, states, Aotearoa is getting more Pacific by the minute.[5] In health, if you cannot effectively engage and care for Pacific people, you are of limited use in three of the four largest district health boards (now regions) in Aotearoa. The Pacific future is now and has already happened in our biggest city, Auckland, where one in four children is Pacific.[6] The importance of supporting Pacific people's wellbeing will only grow and doing so will be a great asset for Aotearoa moving forward – that is, if we are wanting to move towards a society that serves and supports all. This goal requires more than just the token inclusion of a few Pacific individuals. Instead, it requires a fundamental shift in the vision and structural values that underpin our country – a country that has historically overlooked the structural racism, and accompanying privilege, entrenched in our society that impacts our daily lives, whether we would like to admit it or not. There is a Cook Islands tākiato (proverb) that goes 'E tu'a pukuruva'a nui' – the breadfruit must be distributed properly. Its wider implication, and what is particularly relevant to this discussion, is that when food and other resources are gathered, they should be shared strategically to ensure that everyone gets their fair share. From a Cook Islands perspective, when our values of aro'a (love) and 'akangāteitei (respect) are put into practice, those in the group who are struggling or vulnerable eat first, while those who are healthy and well-off eat last. If we are to get real about the health system in Aotearoa and our society, we must first accept that both historically and in present times, the distribution of resources and opportunities has privileged certain groups and discriminated against others. In the context of health, it means that certain groups are better equipped to carry the burden of ill-health than others. For example, our public institutions privilege a Pākehā way of knowing and being, and access to socioeconomic resources, which largely drive the health inequities we see today, has also been distributed in a way that has historically privileged European settlers and their descendants and exploited Māori, and discriminated against other ethnic groups such as Pacific peoples.

This is not a problem isolated to Aotearoa, however. From a health perspective, there is a phenomenon known as the inverse care law, which is present in almost every country in the world. The inverse care law contrasts the availability and accessibility of health services and resources for those most well-off financially against the inaccessibility of health services experienced by those least well-off, which leads to high levels of unmet health need, and, ultimately, health inequities (see Figure 1).[7] The presence of the inverse care law in almost every country in the world also highlights the significance of the broader capitalist structures and values that permeate our public institutions globally, which are leading to growing inequality within and between countries today.

If we are to have meaningful conversations around structural racism and health inequities in Aotearoa, then we must first strive to develop a greater collective conscience around race so that we can have more nuanced discourse on the ethnic disparities we allow to exist in our country. When I say 'we', I mean all of us living in Aotearoa – not just Pacific peoples. Such widespread inequity must be discussed as a collective, understood as a collective, and addressed as a collective. And of course, in this case, the discourse must be led by Pacific communities for change to be intentional, transformational and sustained. Part of undoing the structural racism that exists in our country is about acknowledging that there are many different ways to do things and that not all of these ways

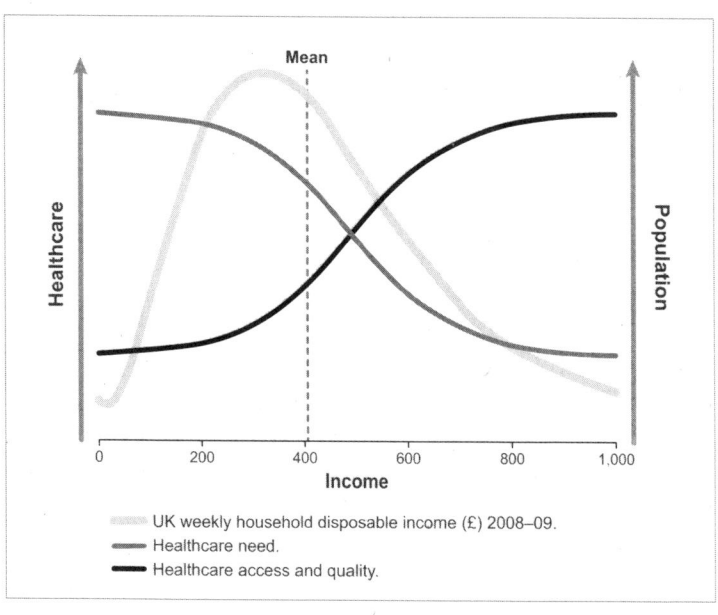

*Figure 1: Inverse Care Law*[8]

will align with colonial and/or capitalist norms; in this case, it is about establishing that those best positioned to support Pacific wellbeing – and thus those in whom we should invest the most – are Pacific communities themselves. As an added incentive, we know that when Pacific communities come up with innovative solutions to support wellbeing, those ideas have positive impacts on other communities when applied more broadly.[9] This should not be surprising, given the holistic approach to wellbeing that underpins most Pacific cultures and worldviews.[10]

### Defining Racism in Health

While this chapter is focused on structural racism, this section will briefly cover some of the different ways that racism operates in health. Interpersonal racism is the type of racism most people think of when they think of the term racism. Jones defines interpersonal racism as 'prejudice and discrimination, where prejudice means differential assumptions about the abilities, motives and intentions of others according to their race and discrimination means differential actions towards others according to their race'.[11] While Pacific examples of interpersonal racism in Aotearoa are endless, the most relevant examples here relate to racism and discrimination in the health setting, where Pacific families continue to report differential treatment, miscommunication, microaggressions and false assumptions. For example, Pacific families with children admitted for unintentional injuries report feeling vulnerable and unsure about how they will be viewed by hospital staff in light of the negative stereotyping of Pacific peoples in the media.[12] We also know that interpersonal racism has an impact on Pacific people's mental health and wellbeing, with perceived discrimination linked to higher psychological distress and lower self-esteem, lower subjective evaluation of health, and lower satisfaction with life.[13]

There is also the idea of internalised racism. Jones defines internalised racism as the process in which members of the stigmatised race begin to accept the racist views and stereotypes placed on their abilities, lifestyle and intrinsic worth.[14] It is evident in the way some Pacific students believe that school and academic careers are not for them, when Pacific people are anti-Pacific, when politics of respectability are encouraged, or when Pacific people defend the institutions that maintain the racially stratified status quo and blame our own people for not being 'good enough' to overcome the structural barriers in place. That is the power of racism – it can make a person feel contempt towards themselves, their own peoples, and their own culture. Personally, I don't like the term 'internalised racism' in the way it is used here, as it implies that there is a sense of blame placed on the person internalising the racism rather than on those people and systems enacting the racism. A more appropriate framework was shared with me by a Pacific community leader working in the education space. The terms he used were 'learned inferiority' and 'learned superiority'. This community leader developed these terms to frame the struggles of a group of Pacific secondary students attending a central Auckland public school who were forced to navigate structural racism and deal with racist microaggressions from teachers daily, which had a significant impact on their attendance, academic self-concept, and academic success. This community leader would often contrast this 'learned inferiority' with the 'learned superiority' of rich White students who attend private schools.

To add to this framework, I posit the use of more Aotearoa-friendly terminology – terminology that you can use with your racist family friends and family members to let them down lightly. The first is 'nice racism', where White people are unaware of their racism, firmly believing that they are not racist, when in fact, despite all their good intentions and smiling, their day-to-day actions perpetuate racism and are grounded in underlying racist views and assumptions that they are not even aware of. The second is 'straight-up racist' which refers to any discussion that is overtly and obviously racist and discriminatory. Where things get more challenging is when racism 'feels' racist to one party but is played off as not racist by another. For example, if a Pacific person interprets a comment as racist, is it racist? Or is it the intention of the speaker that counts? And who gets the final say? All too often allegations of racism are dismissed, downplayed or even defended. As an example, look at ACT leader David Seymour's refusal to apologise for a 'clearly not serious' 'joke' about blowing up the Ministry of Pacific Peoples.[15] This is where the power dynamics of Whiteness come in to play. The power to determine whether something is racist or not is often given to people and ideas that are in closest proximity to Whiteness and a British colonial worldview – illustrating how power and privilege are intertwined with Whiteness more broadly in Aotearoa.

In an attempt to provide a definition for structural racism, of which there are many, I choose to cite Dr Zinzi Bailey and others, who define structural racism as 'the totality of ways in which societies foster racial discrimination via mutually reinforcing and inequitable systems (in housing, education, employment, earnings, benefits, credit, media, health care, criminal justice, and so on) that in turn reinforce discriminatory beliefs, values, and distribution of resources'.[16] This discrimination is reflected in history, culture and interconnected institutions. Closely attached to structural racism is institutional racism, which refers specifically to discriminatory policies and practices carried out within public institutions.[17] The common misconception in Aotearoa is that racial power is something that is exclusive to individuals and not systemically threaded throughout society, culture or policies, or in the consequences of oppression and inequity. Many scholars argue the opposite – it is in fact structural racism and systems of oppression that inform and give power to everyday experiences of interpersonal racism.[18] The fact that we do not see any transformational or political urgency in response to the sustained and growing inequality in certain communities while the tax-free assets of the wealthiest people in the country are protected shows we have a long way to go to address the structural racism that underpins our society and sustains these stratified racialised outcomes. I always ask: If these statistics were flipped, how long do you think it would take for serious transformational change to be made?

Structural racism is difficult to address because the British institutions that have been in place since colonisation are treated as neutral and free from any cultural bias, despite being founded upon British values and structures that inherently privilege British communities and worldviews and marginalise non-British, especially Indigenous, ways of knowing and being. Furthermore, this seemingly neutral appearance makes it difficult to attempt structural change, as any alternatives are believed to 'privilege' the marginalised groups that change would support. The saying is true – to those accustomed to privilege, equality can feel like oppression. This is how the system of colonisation was designed, and the health inequities we see today are the embodiment of colonisation and colonial institutions that continue to view certain lives as superior and others as inferior. This is not merely academic theory – colonisation was and is a brutal and violent reality in Aotearoa. It was the methodical, barbaric and purposeful dispossession, genocide and exploitation of Indigenous peoples that has led to the disproportionate socioeconomic statistics and adversity experienced by Māori to this day. It is not some distant past – colonisation happened not too long ago here in Aotearoa and the wider Pacific region, and the continued impact of colonisation has not simply disappeared with time. Structural racism is colonisation and the colonising agenda working as planned, rather than the result of a one-off event or actions by an individual or rogue government. It is this racist grounding that must be addressed, dismantled and rectified for true transformational change to occur. This is why we need true partnership with and co-governance for Māori in Aotearoa. It is why we need policy related to free prescriptions. It is why we need policy that centres ethnicity as a factor in surgery waitlists. Imagine the barriers that Pacific people face just to get on the waitlist. In fact, I hope someone is supported to research how long it takes for patients to get the surgery or other treatment they require after experiencing their first symptoms – I am sure there will once more be a clear ethnic stratification in the results.

## Why Should We Care?

If empathy, morality and love are not enough of a motive, there are clear examples in Aotearoa and globally that demonstrate the negative impacts that inequality has on quality of life and social cohesion for everyone in society – not just those on the receiving end of adverse outcomes. The scale of income inequality, for example, has a powerful effect on how we relate to each other and the daily experiences we face. For example, in countries where the most income inequality exists, child wellbeing is at its lowest, not just for those living in poverty, but for all children (see Figure 2). As inequality grows, overall levels of subjective wellbeing decline – first for those at the lowest end of the spectrum, and then for those who are more financially well-off.[19]

We do not need any graphs or academic theory, however, to see that the breakdown of our society is happening before our eyes, especially in Tāmaki Makaurau Auckland, where numerous news media stories have covered the increasing number of Pacific people struggling to get by, living in cars, and relying heavily on social service providers for basic necessities such as food.[20] Yet, the social and political will to address socioeconomic inequality and promote transformational change remains on the margins, promoted by only a few staunch but minor political parties. For some, the state we are in today is the inevitable result of a country founded upon colonisation and a multitude of historical injustices. As Aotearoa has grown 'richer' off the back of stolen land, exploitation of the Pacific (see 'New Zealand and the Exploitation of Pacific Lands', p. 52), and the inequitable distribution of this growing wealth, many measures of wellbeing have declined, especially for those groups

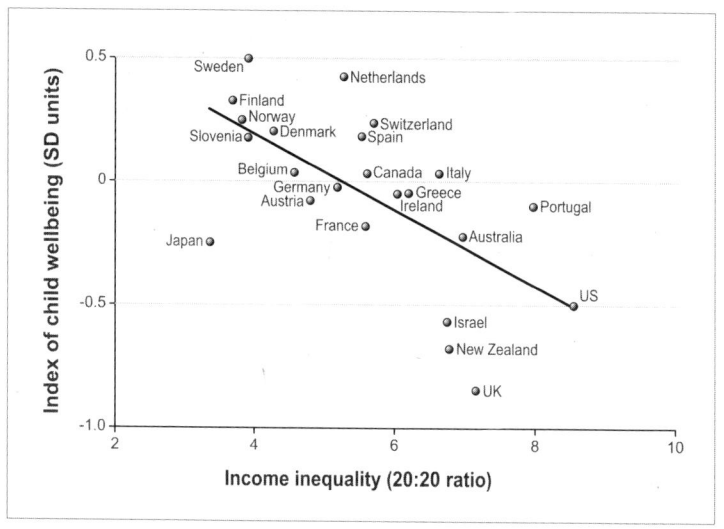

*Figure 2: Correlation between Income Inequality and the UNICEF Index of Child Wellbeing*[21]

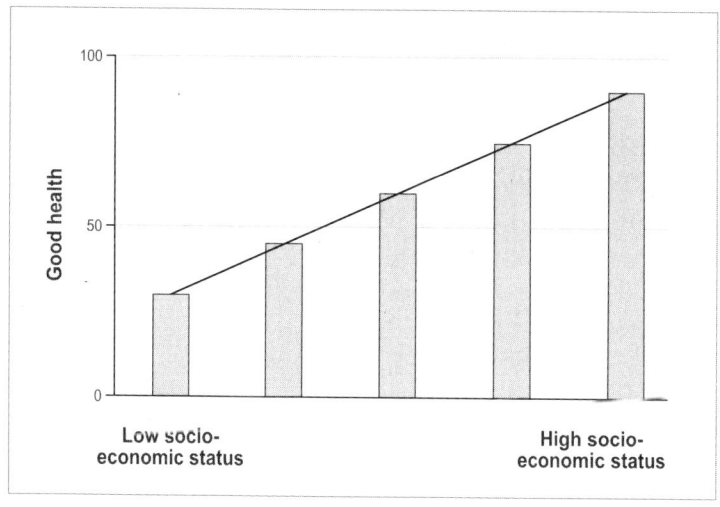

*Figure 3: Social Gradient in Health Outcomes*[22]

that have been left on the margins of this growing 'prosperity'. There have been increases in quality of life as a whole, but for marginalised groups, there have also been rising levels of anxiety, depression, drug addiction, and numerous other social challenges that have become intergenerational and almost normalised in our country.[23] This social gradient in health, wellbeing and social outcomes is, again, not isolated to Aotearoa. We see similar trends around the world, where those who are least well-off financially experience higher rates of adverse health and social outcomes as well as lower overall life expectancy (see Figure 3).[24]

As far as we like to think we have come as a society, there remains a clear ethnic stratification, or 'status quo', that we appear to be content with as a country. The ongoing structural racism underpinning our societal makeup and social institutions, albeit more covert nowadays, continues to sustain this status quo and is just as pervasive and harmful as ever. It is a tough predicament, however, to be one of the first generations to seriously face the challenge of addressing structural racism, privilege and discrimination. For starters, the mainstream discourse on race in Aotearoa is still very much in its infancy, with Māori communities historically leading the way in educating the country on what race is and what racism looks like. There is significant research capturing the structural and interpersonal racism faced by Pacific peoples in the health setting (see the Health and Safety Commission's *Bula Sautu* report). More importantly, Pacific people and families can tell you countless personal stories about the racism that they have experienced in health settings throughout Aotearoa. However, many of them may not speak up, out of respect, and the need to even make these accusations is seen as an additional burden for Pacific families, as they are going through often trying and painful times. It is obvious how these interactions can become a huge issue for Pacific people, impacting their engagement with the health system and the quality of care they and their families receive. As one New Zealand paediatrician puts it:

> Institutionalised racism is served up in many health services in and around NZ still. I think you have to be deaf, daft and blind not to spot it on a regular basis in our hospitals. It's all around us I'm afraid; it's rather endemic.[25]

Racism in health is a lot quieter, in some cases, but just as insidious and harmful as other forms of racism in society. It plays out in 'unconscious bias', negative stereotypes, and unfounded assumptions. It leads to assumptions that Pacific patients are 'non-compliant' and 'do not attend' their specialist appointments. It leads to Pacific pathways to care that are obstructed with barriers, which means many Pacific people access care at crisis point via the emergency room at their local hospital, making Middlemore Hospital simultaneously the most neglected hospital in the country and the busiest. It leads to years of life lost due to avoidable morbidity and mortality. Contrary to these assumptions, and with a bit more investigation and care, Pacific patients and their families are more than able to comply with health advice and attend their appointments given the appropriate support to overcome the additional barriers they face. Past experiences have shown that the barrier can be as simple as not having access to transport. In one case, a Pacific service user was missing their specialist appointments due to not having transport to North Shore Hospital from Glen Eden – a structural issue in itself, as Auckland Hospital would appear more accessible for those living in Glen Eden, given that there is a direct train from there to Grafton, where Auckland Hospital is located. Moreover, why are West Auckland residents expected to travel to North Shore Hospital, when North Shore residents are not asked to travel across the city to access their healthcare? In fact, that's how structural racism works – why do we expect certain communities, who generally have a lower socioeconomic status and face greater barriers to accessing healthcare, to make a cross-town journey for healthcare but not the more privileged demographic? Why is North Shore

Hospital better resourced than Waitakere Hospital? What would be the backlash if North Shore residents were suddenly expected to make the trip out west to Waitakere Hospital for their care? I think you get my point . . . structural racism works in an often-compounding manner.

This is why a greater focus on structural racism is required in Aotearoa, to understand how our everyday lives are closely intertwined with structural bias that privileges some and discriminates against others. Prioritising structural racism also enables us to acknowledge that these issues are bigger than any one individual or group or hospital. These stories and experiences of racism continue to emerge, despite a plethora of diversity training courses and cultural competency workshops. This is because there are deep-seated systemic factors underpinning these interactions, which continue to have very real consequences for the health and wellbeing of Pacific peoples today. While there is significant effort focused on addressing interpersonal racism, there appears to be little focus on the structural and institutional racism that gives power to these interpersonal experiences and leads to health inequities in the first place.

## Understanding Structural Racism's Contribution to Pacific Health Inequities

In exploring the impacts of racism on health, Camara Phyllis Jones, an African American physician, epidemiologist, and anti-racism activist who specialises in the effects of racism and social inequalities in health, provides a theoretical framework that breaks racism down into three forms: institutionalised racism, interpersonal racism, and internalised racism.[26] Institutionalised racism is defined in a similar vein to structural racism in that it refers to differential access to the resources, services and opportunities of society by race. Structural racism is exemplified by the over-representation of Pacific people living in the most deprived conditions, which sees

55.6 per cent of Pacific people living in areas of 'high deprivation' – even though many of us love our Pacific neighbourhoods and would not live anywhere else anyway.[27] Structural racism is exemplified by the unequal burden of risk factors that Pacific people must overcome and the inadequate health system responses that have been trialled and rolled out at the institutional level.[28] These structural and institutional disparities mean that Pacific communities experience a disproportionately high number of potentially avoidable deaths, with the number of deaths considered potentially avoidable twice as high for Pacific populations (47.3 per cent) compared to non-Māori non-Pacific populations (23.2 per cent).[29] Ultimately, these Pacific health inequities are the embodiment of structural racism and its associated systems of privilege and discrimination, which create a myriad of challenges and struggles for Pacific peoples in Aotearoa.

Jones goes on to theorise three main pathways through which structural racism contributes to ethnic inequities in health.[30] These include differential access to the determinants of health, differential access to healthcare, and differences in the quality of care received.[31] Let's first look at differential access to the determinants of health. 'Determinants of health' refers to the social and economic elements in our society that determine our quality of life and underpin the ethnic differences we see in health status. Key determinants of health include education, employment, income, access to quality health and social services, and housing. These determinants can make living a healthy life easy or hard based on one's access to protective factors such as nutritious food, quality housing, reliable transport, neighbourhood safety, and healthcare, as well as one's exposure to risk factors such as poverty, poor nutrition, cold and damp housing, unemployment, stressful life events, discrimination, and higher availability of drugs and alcohol. In Aotearoa, as in most countries, socioeconomic inequality (as a marker of structural racism) accounts for most of the inequities Pacific peoples experience in health. Differential access to the determinants of health means Pacific communities are exposed to additional and often-compounding risk factors for a plethora of illnesses and diseases. As Dave Letele explains:

> You only need to look around us. Our people are surrounded by bad choices. Everything bad for us is at arm's length. Not just bad food, but alcohol, addictions, pokies, the TAB. Everything bad is right here. And our people are up against it.
>
> I have parents working two to three jobs, and they're exhausted. Making healthy meals, even getting the right groceries, is the last thing on the list. Or not even on the list. And that affects the diet and health of the whole whānau.
>
> It's why we need a holistic approach. Our whānau need navigators, and people who've lived through their experiences. Our people don't come through our door alone, they come in with their kids, nieces, nephews, aunties and uncles. If we want to break the cycles, we've got to also educate the children, and the children have to see their parents working hard to achieve their results . . .
>
> Why not get rid of all the takeaway outlets around us if you really want to help? . . .
>
> Imagine if we're able to turn people around from being type-two [diabetics] altogether – because that's certainly something we've achieved many times before. Just think of the taxpayer savings in that . . .
>
> The system just needs to stop with the same old shit and actually empower us. We're already doing the mahi in our communities. We just need more funding and resources.[32]

Dahlgren and Whitehead's 'Rainbow Model' provides us with a reference point from which we can analyse how the different determinants of health are distributed in Aotearoa.[33] For each of these elements, Pacific communities face an inequitable and unfair burden of adverse outcomes – housing, education, employment, health, income, and access to quality health and social services. As illustrated by the 'Rainbow Model' (see Figure 4), the outcomes of individuals and communities are largely influenced by the social determinants of health and the wider socioeconomic, cultural and environmental conditions that influence their daily behaviours and life decisions.

Jones's second point is that structural racism leads to differential access to healthcare.[34] Common examples of this for Pacific communities include financial barriers, transport barriers, and language barriers that can make accessing care challenging.[35] Financial barriers disproportionately prevent Māori and Pacific people from accessing primary care and medication. Nearly a third of Pacific patients (29.3 per cent) responded that the cost of healthcare stopped them visiting a general practitioner (GP) or nurse, compared with 18.5 per cent of European patients.[36] Furthermore, Pacific adults were more than twice as likely as non-Pacific adults to not collect a prescription due to cost, after adjusting for age, gender and ethnicity.[37] Many Pacific people also face non-financial barriers to accessing healthcare. Pacific families, for example, were found to face increased barriers to accessing primary care for their children, despite healthcare being free for all New Zealand residents aged under 13 years of age.[38] The most common barriers included being unable to get an appointment in time, not having transport, and having a greater reliance on after-hours clinics.[39] Primary care services with cheaper GP fees generally have more patients enrolled, and thus, getting an appointment without waiting weeks can be a challenge. There are also challenges linked to employment and transport that can force Pacific people to rely more heavily on after-hours health services, which are often more expensive. For example, Pacific people are more likely to be

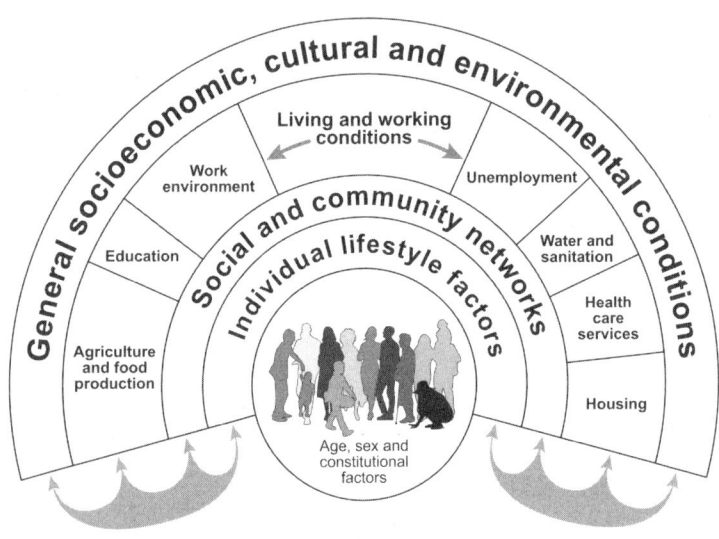

*Figure 4: Dahlgren and Whitehead's Rainbow Model of Health Determinants*[40]

employed in 'blue-collar' jobs that have less-flexible working hours and less job security, and they may have less sick leave or leave entitlements in general, which forces them to prioritise staying at work and getting a steady income over taking time off to attend to their health. There can also be barriers with transport, where a family may have to rely on public transport or only have one vehicle and have to wait for working family members to return.

Lastly, Jones's third point is focused on how racism can lead to differences in the quality of care that different ethnic groups receive.[41] Racism towards Pacific peoples has been reported throughout the health system and has been captured by several studies.[42] These studies have found that Pacific families report discrimination and judgement from health workers when their child has received an unintentional injury, delayed treatment for streptococcal throat – which leads to rheumatic fever – and miscommunication around the importance of ongoing secondary prophylaxis for rheumatic fever.[43] Moreover, Pacific families of children with cancer also experience differential care and treatment.[44] When we consider Pacific people's experiences of health and wellbeing through Jones's lens, it becomes undeniable that Pacific people and communities experience structural racism that undermines health outcomes and experiences within the health system.

## Racism and Health – It's Time to Get Real

The term 'racism' makes many people in Aotearoa uncomfortable. Most non-European communities in Aotearoa can openly discuss racism because almost every public interaction in our settler-colonial state has racial undertones. Whether it's attempting to appear 'non-threatening' when entering a predominantly White workspace, getting pulled over by the cops for no reason, struggling to find a house to rent, or being followed by security when out shopping, most people of colour have a myriad of well-meaning 'nice', 'ambiguous', and 'straight-up' racist encounters they can discuss. But when attention is drawn to White privilege and structural racism, Pākehā may respond with dismissal, anger and/or a refusal to engage in the discussion, because many people in positions of power find it hard to reconcile with the idea that their success is a product of privilege. This cognitive dissonance creates a feeling of discomfort and unease, which often leads to denial, rationalisation or other defence mechanisms to protect one's core belief(s).[45] When Taika Waititi expressed his view that New Zealand is 'racist as fuck', especially towards Polynesians, he sparked a similar cognitive dissonance among certain members of the population.[46] Waititi was met with waves of White fragility, defensiveness, dismissal, and even backlash from Pākehā in mainstream media and on social media sites. Obviously, this statement came as no shock to most non-White people who must navigate our racially stratified (read: racist) society every day. However, what this example demonstrates is just how covert structural racism is in Aotearoa, largely because the people it privileges are blind to its existence or see nothing to gain by addressing it. Nevertheless, there can be no true rectification and reconciliation without truth.

Colonisation imprinted Whiteness into the fabric of our contemporary nation state, which also naturally centred Pākehā ways of knowing and being at the expense and displacement of Māori peoples, land and tikanga.[47] In Aotearoa, it is this 'Whiteness' that underpins power, privilege and assumed superiority. It is important to note that this Whiteness is not necessarily bound to skin colour; rather it is connected to economic power and class. A major reason for why some Pacific families encouraged their children to forgo their mother tongue in order to get a Papa'a/Pālagi/Pākehā education once they migrated to Aotearoa – to be 'White', was to be 'successful' in the context of Aotearoa. The ascendancy of Whiteness in Aotearoa is directly reflected in the Pākehā-centric standards we accept as the 'norm' and dominant way of knowing, being and doing in Aotearoa.[48] These standards range from preferred aesthetics to cultural symbolism that attempts to ground Aotearoa within European and British heritages, English as the dominant language and as a criterion for citizenship, ways of living in relation to the environment (for instance, extractive capitalist agriculture), as well as education and health systems inherited from Britain. There are a number of examples to choose from, but what this brief historical analysis illustrates is that power in Aotearoa resides firmly in the hands of White settlers and their descendants. Through this analysis, we can see how Pacific people, cultures and communities become peripheral in the Eurocentric structures and institutions in Aotearoa, which inherently overlook the lived realities, needs and aspirations of Pacific people and communities. With so much focus on workshops and strategies to address interpersonal racism and unconscious bias in health these days, it can be easy to overlook the key underlying determinant that gives these acts power in the first place: structural racism. We like to believe we are not racist and live in a progressive country, but when it comes to discourse around race in this country, we are either naive or ignorant to the structural racism that has become deeply entrenched in public institutions like health.

The entrenching of health inequities and ethnic inequality in Aotearoa is real and racist. Health inequities, in particular, provide a practical opportunity to interrogate structural racism and the systems that have sustained ethnic inequities since the initial arrival of colonial settlers. The resulting colonial systems were built on colonial values that promoted colonial ideas of who is 'normal' and who is not; who is good and who is bad; what lives are valued and what lives are not; who is knowing and who is ignorant; and, ultimately, who is deserving and who is undeserving.[49] This system overlooked te ao Māori and tikanga Māori, and led to Māori as tangata whenua being marginalised, killed, displaced and discriminated against on their own lands.[50] However, these colonial systems were said to allow equal opportunity for all, in the same vein as the systems we have today. Thus, when disparities become apparent, it is asserted that the problem must lie with the individuals facing the disparities, not the system that is equal and fair to all. What we end up with is a system that promotes 'victim blaming' and places the burden of ill-health and all other challenges on those most discriminated against, overlooking the significant discrimination and privilege embedded within the systems that make up our society, despite the overarching evidence that structural racism and institutional inequities are rife. Scholars such as Papaarangi Reid and Moana Jackson suggest that a decolonial and/or equity focus may be the answer.[51] It forces us as a country to have the hard conversations around why we seem to just accept that certain groups live longer than others and analyse the reasons we use to justify doing nothing. But first, it requires us as a country to accept that structural racism exists in the first place – to accept that certain people are in the positions they are in because of privilege and others are where they are because of structural barriers and historic exploitation and injustices; to accept that our everyday experiences, life trajectories, and outcomes are attached to the structural racism, power and privilege that we continue to accept as the 'status quo' – a normalisation of racialised structures and ideas that give power and privilege to some groups and lead to discrimination and inequitable outcomes for others.

Ultimately, there are many differing understandings of ethnic health disparities, the causes behind them, and what we should do about them. There are two predominant theoretical positions that one can take. First, one can see the difference in health outcomes as the result of biological differences – that is, the genetic differences that exist between ethnic groups. Second, there is the theory that ethnic differences in health outcomes are the 'biological expression of racism' – or the embodiment of the structural racism and the wider societal disparities that underpin the socioeconomic and cultural environments that shape our everyday lives: the embodiment of cold and damp housing, the embodiment of an obesogenic environment, the embodiment of stress, the embodiment of putting that doctor or dentist visit off in order to put food on the table and pay rent, and the embodiment of both relative poverty – wherein access to health and social services is reduced – as well as absolute poverty – wherein people and families struggle to maintain basic living standards such as accessing food, shelter and housing. Prominent studies by Krieger and Reid and Robson provide overwhelming evidence supporting the latter.[52] While it is true that some ethnic groups are more genetically predisposed to certain illnesses than others, the same racial stratification present in almost all health and societal measures provides overwhelming evidence for the second theory – that Pacific health inequities are the embodiment of structural racism and its associated systems of privilege and discrimination that create a myriad of challenges and struggles for Pacific peoples in Aotearoa. This is why it is crucial to understand the underlying socioeconomic inequality discussed earlier.

Today, certain groups are better equipped to carry the burden of ill-health than others – we need to get real. Pacific health inequities in Aotearoa create significant direct and indirect costs to primarily Pacific communities, but also to the country as a whole. If we stick with the status quo, the 'cost of doing nothing' is predominantly borne by Pacific communities, but the net cost of Pacific health inequities to the government is substantially greater than the 'cost' of addressing the inequities that cause these disparities in the first place. The struggle is real. Despite these challenges, Pacific people achieve a lot, find a sense of fulfilment, and do life pretty well – forever grateful for whatever circumstances and lessons God provides.[53] Pacific communities are innovative in their responses to these challenges, but this chapter asks the question: Just because this is our narrative as Pacific peoples in Aotearoa, should this be the same narrative we pass down to the current and future generations of Pacific children and families? Our forefathers made sacrifices and paved the way for us to have the many opportunities we have today, and I would like to think we similarly want to further pave the pathways to prosperity for future generations to come. In this decolonising process, Pacific people, communities and cultures will – if they are empowered – be one of the great resources in Aotearoa.[54]

## Where Does Responsibility for Change Lie?

Despite the amazing community-led interventions and programmes doing the hard yards in our communities, I often find myself wondering if these grassroots solutions are the answer to the structural disparities and growing inequality we are seeing in Aotearoa. If these interventions are the ambulance at the bottom of the cliff, what can we do as a country to ensure these interventions are supported but do not become accepted as the solution to the wider structural and systemic issues driving the growing need for these services in the first place? There will always be a need for these interventions, but should the mammoth task of tackling the fallout of structural racism fall entirely on the shoulders of Pacific peoples themselves? Is it right to ask these Pacific community leaders and legends to sacrifice so much of their lives knowing that structural and policy change could ease the burden and, ultimately, lead to more effective change in the long term?[55] Where does responsibility for changing the health system lie? It is tough, because on the one hand these interventions represent self-determination in action – showing that Pacific communities can stand on their own, look after their own, and prosper. On the other hand, however, there is a fear that these amazing interventions will be seen as an equitable response to structural racism in health. I fear that the drain of structural racism becomes twofold for Pacific communities, in that the same communities impacted by these structural disparities will also bear the brunt of attempting to solve these issues. Ultimately, strategies to dismantle structural racism must prioritise addressing inequities in the distribution of the social determinants of health by ensuring economic security, housing security, educational opportunity, and equal treatment from the justice system, among others. Systems, structures and policies have created the inequities in health we see today, and it is these same systems, structures and policies that we can use to eliminate them.

There is, however, mounting opposition against structural change and pushback against policies that seek to prioritise equity and address structural racism. In line with National and ACT's mission to abolish 'race-based' equity policies, the University of Auckland's Māori and Pacific Admission Scheme (MAPAS) and its equivalent at the University of Otago, 'Te Kauae Parāoa', are set to undergo review – whatever that means. Although these programmes will never be scrapped, the notion of a review itself causes further unnecessary harm to the already hyper-visible and under-represented Māori and Pacific students enrolled in these programmes. As MAPAS graduate Dr Emma Wehipeihana (Ngāti Tukorehe, Ngāti Porou) explains:

> It doesn't matter that 'policies' are being targeted, or 'outcomes are being examined'. The positive outcomes from MAPAS and the Mirror on Society are well documented. The incoming government is being disingenuous in their characterisation here – they just want to incite prejudice. The real effect of this is that every trainee health professional coming through these programmes will feel that a 'you don't deserve to be here' target has been painted on their back. They will carry the hostility of this message into their exams, their assignments, onto the wards of our hospitals and into their homes. Have you ever tried to sit a medical school exam? Can you imagine how difficult they are? Then imagine that your right to exist in that exam room is being debated by our elected government who will absolutely encourage the media to participate in this attack while you're trying to remember the Krebs cycle or the anatomy of the brachial plexus.[56]

The purpose of these initiatives is straightforward – to train students of Māori and Pacific heritage, thereby increasing cultural representation in the health workforce and creating a workforce of doctors and health professionals that reflects Aotearoa's diverse reality. The current government's portrayal of these programmes as 'unfair privilege' is not only misleading but disingenuous, and is largely driven by ideological politics that ultimately aim to incite prejudice and outrage in the hopes of securing more votes. The current government's use of slogans like 'fairness' masks an agenda that seeks to sow division and distract the public from the historical injustices, persistent structural barriers, and growing economic inequality faced by these communities in Aotearoa.

The discourse surrounding, and prejudice against, equity programmes like MAPAS is not new, but given the well-documented and rapidly growing disparities Māori and Pacific communities are facing and the strong evidence base highlighting both the causes of and solutions to these inequities, it is especially disingenuous, ignorant and cruel. Furthermore, while these programmes have increased the number of Māori and Pacific doctors in the workforce, there is still significant work to be done to achieve true equity, with Māori doctors making up only 4.7 per cent of the workforce and Pacific people making up 2.3 per cent, up from 2.3 per cent and 1.1 per cent in 2000.

Perhaps most pertinent to the discussion of structural racism, however, is that our persistent need to 'justify' these equity programmes and policies, citing poor health outcomes, socioeconomic inequity, and historical traumas, highlights the structural racism entrenched in Aotearoa; and that any attempts to address the structural racism driving these ongoing disparities, which cause years of life lost and many more years of healthy life lost, are debated and targeted more than the inequities themselves – that any attempt to address structural racism is labelled as 'unfair privilege' and met with resistance, disdain and hate. Ultimately, having to continually argue for and justify these equity programmes only further hinders and distracts from making real progress towards greater equity and efficacy in the health system and Aotearoa as a whole. Structural racism is embodied in a government that is not only okay with Māori and Pacific communities suffering in perpetuity but actively seeks to deny and supress any attempts to address this suffering. Aue taue.

Like the health challenges facing Pacific communities, structural racism is complex, multifaceted and intense. It is embedded in government policy and founded upon colonisation, the doctrine of discovery, and historical injustices. Structural racism is insidious and enforced through institutional systems and policies that appear neutral, which has allowed it to be sustained for so long, despite progress in other areas of racial equality and human rights. Talavao Ngata, a Pacific housing researcher and advocate, provides an apt example of how seemingly neutral housing policy reforms in the 1990s led to the rapid decline in home ownership among Pacific families and a consequent decline in health and educational outcomes.[57] While these reforms appear neutral, a closer look at the historical context shows how structural privilege and discrimination play out in practice – as the 'Long-Term Insights Briefing' from the Ministry of Housing and Urban Development states:

> The New Zealand European population was in its prime child-bearing and rearing years in the 1950s, 1960s and 1970s. They benefited from a housing system, housing policy and government housing investment that stimulated the production of low-cost houses and helped young families into owner occupation. Both Māori and Pacific population structures have only recently had an age profile similar to the European population of the 1950s, 1960s and 1970s. However, the housing system does not invest in housing for young families in the way that it did between the 1950s and the housing reforms in the 1990s.[58]

It can be argued that structural racism is sustained by the racist attitudes of the majority who are motivated by economic self-interest and the desire to hold on to 'power'. While this could be true, it can also be argued that, today, structural racism is so entrenched in our society that many people and institutions are not even conscious of the role they play in upholding it – another example of 'nice racism' in action. It has become a central feature of the social, economic and political systems in which we all exist and which we have largely accepted as 'just the way things are'.[59] This line of thinking is both careless and dangerous, as it leads to the acceptance of racial disparities like the inequities we see in health as the natural, inevitable order of things. One thing most can agree on, however, is that our society privileges some and discriminates against others, so why is there an expectation that the same groups discriminated against by structural racism should also bear the burden of fixing the system? Moreover, why is there such a lack of focus on how those privileged by the system, however blameless, can contribute to creating a more fair and just system? And what motivations are there for those privileged by the status quo to change the system anyway? Some might ask: 'Why should we care?' If the arguments presented throughout this chapter are not enough to answer this question, consider that it is in our country's best interests to address structural racism and health inequities, as efforts to improve health outcomes for Pacific peoples will inevitably benefit other historically marginalised communities as well.

To effectively support Pacific wellbeing, we must think outside of the confines of the colonial institutions and systems that make up today's Aotearoa. These health inequities are complex, multifaceted, and often urgent; thus, we need to question the effectiveness of 'one-size-fits-all' approaches and give power to new, resourceful, ethnic-specific and creative ways of solving these pressing issues. Health is not a zero-sum game. While some groups will have to acknowledge their privilege and rectify historical wrongdoings, the many Māori and Pacific community-led health interventions out there provide us with a blueprint that we can use to address the structural racism that exists within our country and within institutions such as health and education. Programmes such as Dave Letele's Buttabean Motivation (BBM) have proven that providing connection, trust, love and care, as well as giving people the resources, time and space to work towards positive change for themselves, is an effective formula for sustainable improvements in physical health, mental health and overall quality of life, even in the face of a myriad of socioeconomic challenges originating at the wider structural and systemic level. Imagine a health system that is underpinned by the same values of love, service, connection and respect. Imagine the significant health gains for all communities if we made sure that the same love, service, connection and respect that sustain these Pacific community initiatives were pumped into redeveloping the structures, systems and institutions that make up our country. Imagine systems and institutions that centre the worldviews of Māori, Pacific and other historically marginalised communities. We can no longer plead ignorance, knowing the urgent need facing Pacific, Māori and other marginalised communities.

So, what are we going to do to put things right? We could celebrate Pacific communities by recognising the contributions of Pacific people in Aotearoa and the amazing cultural diversity we add to the country. We could run cultural safety workshops so clinicians can better engage with Pacific patients. We could subsidise school meals and provide equitable resources and ethnic-specific pathways to medical education as a Band-Aid to increase the health workforce and overcome the additional barriers that Pacific children face when attempting to attain quality education. These strategies might make Pacific communities feel better and open new opportunities for a few, but none of these approaches will do much to address the structural inequities and challenging conditions in which most Pacific communities live and which have the most powerful impact on health outcomes over the course of their lives. What we have to do, if we are to get real about addressing structural racism, is ensure that resources and opportunities, or the social determinants of health, are shared in an equitable way so that Pacific and other marginalised communities are able to live in a country that values their cultures, worldviews and ways of knowing and being just as much as European Pākehā cultures, worldviews and ways of knowing and being. This does not just mean equity in relation to material resources, but also equity in relation to our institutions, systems, laws, written or unwritten policies, and entrenched practices and beliefs. While today's generation may struggle to acknowledge structural racism and oppose such changes, future generations will prosper from a fairer and more just Aotearoa for all and will be unlikely to develop the same views. Ultimately, addressing racism at the structural level will also work to dismantle racism at the interpersonal level, or at least remove the power attached to this form of racism. This can only be achieved, however, if those with control over these systems, resources and power choose to make a difference.

## Conclusion

While cultural education and anti-racism programmes continue within the health sector, these exercises appear futile against the backdrop of mounting evidence that centres structural racism as the key driver of ethnic inequities in healthcare and health outcomes. As the system attempts to become more inclusive, rebranding as 'Te Whatu Ora' and taking on more equity-centred interventions, we must be mindful that these initiatives are not enough. The system as a whole must work towards a public-health-level approach that advocates for a more equitable and anti-racist distribution of the social determinants of health. In doing so, the system may contribute to the development of truly inclusive and self-determined approaches to health and wellbeing that respect and value the many differences that exist at the community, family and individual level, rather than discriminating against and alienating those who are unable to fit into the current colonial system. As discussed in this chapter, there are many examples of racism within healthcare at the structural, institutional and interpersonal levels. While there is significant effort focused on addressing interpersonal racism, there appears to be little focus on the structural and institutional forms of racism that give power to these interpersonal experiences and cause the health disparities within Pacific communities in the first place.

It is an ongoing task, but there is hope that continued discourse, collective reflection, and political action will change things so that future generations will not have to expend so much time, effort and energy on addressing this challenging task. As the esteemed Māori public health physician Professor Papaarangi Reid explains, it is not about finding out who is racist and who is not; it is about questioning how racism works in Aotearoa and how it can be addressed at its root.[60] This will be difficult and require many challenging and tough discussions. It will require us to lean into the cognitive dissonance we may feel when asked to explain why Pacific communities have fewer resources and reduced access to the social determinants of health; when we are asked to explain why only 25 per cent of Pacific youth leave school with the credits required to gain university entrance; when we are asked to explain why all wealth tax is 'off the table' but people are content with Pacific families paying exorbitant rent to live in garages and other makeshift accommodation or even living in cars. The answers to me are clear – structural racism means that our institutions, systems, policies and everyday actions (and inactions) create additional burdens for some and additional privileges for others. It's not just about addressing individual cases of racism; it is about addressing the structural racism that prevents certain groups from getting their fair share.

E tu'a pukuruva'a nui. Kia orana e kia manuia.

## Practical Recommendations
### Structural Problems Require Structural Solutions

Structural problems require structural solutions, and shifting to a Tiriti-centred and equitable Aotearoa would be a massive step towards greater health equity and collective prosperity moving forward. Despite the challenges, there are so many amazing initiatives doing effective work in the community. It's time to support these initiatives rather than attempt to tear them down (see MAPAS, Smokefree Aotearoa legislation, free prescriptions, etc.). There is an urgent need to reflect on whose lives, laws, structures and power are privileged here in New Zealand. There is an urgent need to reflect on and challenge the factors driving a resurgence in 'white grievance politics' in New Zealand that work against structural change and against 'race-based' initiatives that rightfully centre the communities in New Zealand that are most in need of additional support and opportunities.

## Say the Word

When thinking of practical recommendations, I thought to myself 'Where do you even start?' There are so many opportunities for us to do better as individuals and as a country – many simple and self-explanatory, but nonetheless challenging and requiring thorough self-reflection and open conversation. Say the word racism. Say it, acknowledge its existence, reflect on how you perpetuate racism, reflect on why you perpetuate racism, and reflect on what things you could do to challenge racism within yourself, your family, and your community.

## Vote with Equity and 'Anti-racism' in Mind

It's not rocket science. We've seen numerous examples of how policy and government actions can either increase or reduce inequality in our country. We want to ensure that health and social policy in Aotearoa makes the healthy choice the easy choice for our communities. Vote with equity and anti-racism in mind.

## Focus on Impact, Rather than Intention

'Nice racism' is common in healthcare. It is often subtle and can be unconscious, but it does have significant implications for outcomes, continuity of care, and quality of care. Despite overt forms of racism being depicted more in the media, racism does not necessarily have to be malicious – hence the term 'nice racism'. For example, Curtis and others state that health provider behaviour is enacted within a broader context of societal and structural racism and that clinicians must be mindful of how racism might impact on their perceptions, behaviour and clinical decision-making when working with Pacific patients.[61] When I tell health professionals that my wife is a GP, it has a profound effect on the care my son and I receive. Sadly, it is almost always required to ensure our needs and concerns as patients are heard and given legitimacy. Health professionals interact with the best of intentions, but research from Harris and others indicates that Māori, Asian and Pacific peoples experience significantly more incidents of racism in healthcare than European ethnic groups.[62] For clinicians, there is a need to constantly reflect on the bias and assumptions you bring into the care you provide. How might your worldview differ to the worldview of Pacific peoples? What does clear communication look like to you? What might clear communication look like to a Pacific family? Do you assume that a low level of health literacy requires a lower level of communication? Reflecting on your positionality and how it influences the way you care for Pacific patients is a good first step towards improving the quality of care you provide to Pacific peoples, which can act as an important buffer against the wider structural challenges facing Pacific peoples in health. Focus on impact, rather than intention.

### Listen to Pacific Peoples and Let Pacific Communities Lead Discussions, Interventions and Solutions

We cannot let unfounded assumptions inform the healthcare we provide and the health policy we develop, otherwise we will continue to see ethnic disparities in healthcare and health outcomes. Nobody knows the barriers to quality healthcare better than Pacific communities, and thus, nobody knows how to overcome these barriers better than Pacific communities themselves. Whether it is something as simple as language barriers and transport issues or as complicated as health literacy, Pacific communities know what works best for them, so the system must listen to these voices and share the power for change with these communities, even if their solutions do not align with traditional Western perceptions of health and healthcare. And that is what breaking down structural racism is about – changing the perspective through which we view issues and changing the frameworks we use to address these issues.

### Primary Care Improvements – Humanise the Gatekeepers of the System

Primary care providers are seen as the 'gatekeepers' of the health system in Aotearoa. For this reason, it is vital that this first port of call is approachable and engaging from a Pacific perspective. Improvements to primary care, from a Pacific perspective, must start first and foremost by investing in a strong Pacific primary care workforce – more Pacific nurses, GPs, psychologists, health support workers, bookers and receptionists. A deep understanding of Pacific values and relational protocol can make all the difference for Pacific patients struggling to access healthcare and navigate the health system. Further improvements could include longer appointment times, so that GPs can build rapport and better communicate with Pacific people and their families. There is also a need to better follow up with Did Not Attends (DNAs) to make sure there are no additional barriers facing Pacific patients and families. Whether it be transport, finances or other carer obligations, there is usually a reason why people DNA. Simply removing these people from the waitlist only further delays care.

## Shifting the Burden of Wellbeing from Individuals and Families to Community and Society

At the moment, certain groups are better equipped to carry the burden of ill-health than others. Pacific health inequities in Aotearoa create significant direct and indirect costs, primarily to Pacific communities but also to the country as a whole. Sticking with the status quo will lead to greater disparities in the future. While the 'cost of doing nothing' is predominantly borne by Pacific communities, the net cost of Pacific health inequities to the government and wider society is estimated to be substantially greater than the 'cost' of addressing the structural inequities that cause these health inequities in the first place.

# HIGHER EDUCATION

# The Pacific Pipeline
Structural Racism and Pacific Peoples in Higher Education

*Sereana Naepi*

WHEN I STARTED AS A HIGHER EDUCATION RESEARCHER, I had great hopes for how my work looking into promising practices would shape how we teach and engage with Pacific students at universities. I had been working with Māori and Pacific students for a number of years and thought that if we had research that showcased how to improve how we taught, then others would pick it up and things would change. A decade on, I am overwhelmed with just how often universities make that dream impossible. Instead, systemic structures prevent New Zealand's universities from making the shifts needed to better serve Pacific communities. As a result of this inability to make the changes necessary, not every Pacific student who walks through the doors of a higher education institution in the hope of a promised better future will make it across the graduation stage.

In higher education, we often talk of a pipeline to success.[1] Although there are problems with the analogy in that it suggests something passive as opposed to active,² it does help us to understand how structural racism excludes Pacific peoples. The pipeline often refers to a system where students enter higher education and then theoretically progress from recruitment to graduation and beyond to work or further study. However, across the globe, racialised bodies 'leak' out of the pipeline. For example, we might have a hundred Pacific students enter the higher education pipeline, but only sixty-nine will make it to the end.³ What follows is a detailed description of the Pacific higher education pipeline in New Zealand. I will detail how many Pacific people get into different levels of higher education, how many make it past their first year, and how many graduate. These numbers enable us to see where Pacific people 'leak' out of the pipeline in an overall image of the higher education sector that reveals the ramifications of the racism in its foundations and design.

Racism is one of those big words, a word that comes with accusation and defence. However, in higher education as a sector, I hope that we are prepared and willing to confront the figures in this chapter and recognise that these figures are not an accident. Instead, they reflect the historical and ongoing exclusion, marginalisation and underserving of Pacific peoples in New Zealand. Our sector is responsible for training the next generation of Pacific people, and right now, we are failing. Pacific people are this country's economic future; we are its youngest population and its future taxable workforce.⁴ If we miss this opportunity to grow a highly skilled next generation of workers, then there will be wider implications for the whole country – not just Pacific peoples.

## Terminology and Anchoring in this Chapter

Part of what can make engaging with data about the tertiary system difficult is that it requires a certain level of knowledge in order to understand what it is telling us. For example, a headcount of 1 is equal to a single student, no matter their level of enrolment, but

EFT refers to fulltime equivalent, where 1 is equal to the number of points required for a student to be enrolled fulltime. There are also different levels of qualification, signalling different levels of skill (and also impacting funding levels). Higher education refers to industry training organisations (ITOs), private training organisations, Te Pūkenga, tertiary providers, universities and wānanga.

This chapter is grounded in the idea that universities are designed to create the future workforce, with the pursuit of qualifications being centred around an investment and personal gain logic.[5] I want to be very clear from the outset that I stand by critiques of this logic – these critiques are important, and universities must be spaces where people can pursue ideas and skills that they enjoy. Not all learning needs to, or should, have an economic imperative. However, in order to fight a system, you sometimes need to use its own logic against it. This chapter is one of many opportunities to story and critique our system; it is not the only story to be told.

## So, What's Racism Got to Do with It?

Structural racism in higher education did not just happen overnight. Rather, it has been present in our institutions since the beginning. Sara Ahmed talks about structural racism as institutional habit. Institutional habits are the different ways that institutions choose to do things on a day-to-day basis that are a legacy of previous power dynamics.[6] These can be in simple things, like the gowns that are worn to graduation ceremonies, to more complex things, like how universities choose to deal with cheating within their examination system. The point Ahmed makes is that every single interaction, policy and physical space in a university is shaped by these institutional habits. Many of these habits were developed during a time when Pacific peoples did not have access to universities, which means that part of the challenge of being Pacific in today's higher education space is that we must also do the work of unpicking the different institutional habits that contribute to structural racism.[7]

The many ways in which colonialism and racism have been foundational to higher education globally and within New Zealand have been detailed extensively in the past.[8] The first university in New Zealand, the University of Otago, was established in 1869 and funded with 100,000 acres of pastoral land endowment.[9] The University of Otago is not an outlier here – our other universities were established through land confiscations.[10] My institution, the University of Auckland, was established through land confiscated in Whakatāne and the Waikato area.[11] These histories matter because, from the outset, our universities benefited from the colonial process while also being part of an education system designed to enforce the colonial process.[12] It is not just academics who have recognised racism within the higher education system. After international controversy, the University of Waikato instigated an independent report into allegations of racism within their university. The findings from the report led to the University of Waikato releasing a public statement acknowledging that 'because New Zealand's public institutions, including universities, are founded in our settlement history and adhere to Western university traditions and cultures, there is a case for structural, systemic, and casual discrimination at the University of Waikato'.[13]

The exclusion and underserving of Pacific peoples in New Zealand's university systems are well documented.[14] More recently, this critique has shown how Pacific staff are also excluded across the system,[15] in different fields,[16] and in specific disciplines.[17] In 2019, I recorded the lack of Pacific academics in our universities, with Pacific staff comprising only 1.7 per cent of academics, and found that the higher the academic rank, the fewer Pacific academics there are.[18] Data from 2021 showed that little had changed, with 2 per cent identifying as Pacific. The number of Pacific professors increased from five[19] in 2019 to ten in 2021.[20]

Furthermore, Pacific academics are underpaid and under-promoted. In 2020, Tara McAllister and others provided evidence that Māori and Pacific men and women were underpaid and underpromoted when controlling for excellence, age and field of study. Māori and Pacific women faced higher pay and progression gaps than Māori and Pacific men, resulting in a yearly income loss of $7,713.[21] Qualitative research with Pacific staff indicates that Pacific staff in universities experience bias and racism consistently.[22] Pacific women have outlined their experiences and how this impacts their ability to be successful within institutions that act to exclude them.[23] Pacific early career researchers have also recorded their experiences navigating universities, noting that while universities are committed to change, their lived experiences indicate there is significant progress yet to be made.[24] While solutions have been proposed,[25] interventions to address these issues are limited to what is possible within a colonial institution.[26]

Overall, both quantitative and qualitative data confirm the levels of racism that Pacific peoples face within the academy. This chapter uses quantitative data to highlight evidence that structural racism is still shaping our sector. It aims to describe the non-existent pipeline for Pacific peoples in higher education in New Zealand so that we can begin to make informed decisions and to drive change in our institutions, rather than simply waiting for change to take place.

## Higher Education, Pacific Peoples and Income

Universities in New Zealand are often described as playing a key role in the economy by training the next generations of professionals.[27] Higher education is sold as a solution to the economic inequity that is baked into our current system. Our government, and governments internationally, consider the different qualifications that can be attained to be a measurement of a population's 'human capital', or a population's skill and knowledge levels.[28] In short, having a tertiary education can lead to higher income levels than those who do not have a tertiary education.[29] If we look at the data in Table 1, we can see evidence of this in Aotearoa New Zealand.

| Highest qualification | 2013 | 2023 |
|---|---|---|
| No qualifications | $552 | $891 |
| School qualification | $566 | $1,040 |
| Level 1–3 tertiary certificate | $500 | $712 |
| Level 4–6 tertiary certificate or diploma | $622 | $1,212 |
| Bachelor's degree or higher | $921 | $1,458 |

Table 1: Median Weekly Income of Pacific People (Aged 25–64) by Highest Qualification (Source: Education Counts)[30]

For Pacific people, the highest median weekly income is attained by those who have a bachelor's degree or higher. Over the course of a year, the difference in income between having no qualifications and a bachelor's degree or higher was $29,484 in 2023. Over a working lifetime of forty years, this income difference expands to $1,179,360. This shows that tertiary education does provide us with the opportunity to increase our income levels, bringing more money into our households and contributing to our overall family and community wellness. However, Pacific peoples have inequitable access to higher education, lower completion rates, and different enrolment patterns, each of which impacts our ability to access this promise of a higher income after higher education.

We can look at past data to help us understand how many Pacific people will be currently accessing the additional income promised after completing higher education, and how this has changed over time. Table 2 indicates that between 1993 and 2021, Pacific people's highest qualifications have shifted from 58 per cent having no formal qualification in 1993 to only 29 per cent having no formal qualification in 2021. The highest shift in qualification levels is at bachelor's degree or higher, which increased from 3 per cent in 1993 to 16 per cent in 2021. However, the majority of the Pacific population still have a school qualification as their highest qualification, signalling that there remains a substantial loss of potential income within the Pacific community. Importantly, from 1993 to 2021, more than 50 per cent of the Pacific population had no tertiary qualification.[31]

| Highest qualification | 1993 | 2003 | 2013 | 2018[32] | 2021 |
|---|---|---|---|---|---|
| No qualification | 58% | 30% | 35% | 24% | 29% |
| School qualification | 20% | 36% | 26% | 32% | 30% |
| Tertiary certificate or diploma | 18% | 26% | 25% | 26% | 23% |
| Bachelor's degree or higher | 3% | 8% | 12% | 15% | 16% |

Table 2: Percentage of Pacific People (Aged 25-64) by Highest Qualification (Source: Education Counts)[33]

While Table 2 shows the percentage of the *entire* Pacific population's engagement across qualification levels, Table 3 shows more detail within the different qualification levels in higher education. Across almost two decades, we can see a decrease in enrolment across higher education. Perhaps we can have a small moment of joy for our high bachelor's and level 4 certificate enrolment, which lead to the highest income level (see Table 1).

| Level/type of study | 2003 | 2013 | 2018 | 2022 |
| --- | --- | --- | --- | --- |
| Certificate 1 | 2% | 2% | 0% | 0%[34] |
| Certificate 2 | 3% | 4% | 1% | 1% |
| Certificate 3 | 4% | 5% | 4% | 4% |
| Certificate 4 | 4% | 4% | 5% | 5% |
| Certificate/diploma 5–7 | 2% | 2% | 2% | 1% |
| Bachelor's degree 7 | 3% | 5% | 5% | 5% |
| Graduate certificate/diploma 7 | 0% | 0% | 0% | 0% |
| Honours degree/postgraduate certificate/diploma 8 | 0% | 0% | 1% | 1% |
| Master's degree 9 | 0% | 0% | 0% | 0% |
| Doctoral degree 10 | 0% | 0% | 0% | 0% |
| Total | 18% | 20% | 16% | 15% |

*Table 3: Pacific People's Education Participation Rates by Level and Type of Qualification (Source: Education Counts)[35]*

## Pacific Student Participation in Higher Education

In higher education, success is measured by recruitment, retention, and completion. These metrics reveal who enters (recruitment), who progresses beyond the first year and onwards (retention), and who completes their qualifications (completion). Together, they highlight the 'leaky pipeline', identifying where Pacific people may 'leak' out and where we should invest our resources for change: Is it that we never enter the higher education pipeline, is it that we do not progress past the first year, or is it that we do not make it to the end?

### Recruitment

Over time, Pacific enrolment has remained steady, with Pacific people making up 10 per cent of the entire student population from 2013 to 2023, and around 11 per cent of the Pacific community participating in higher education from 2018 to 2022.[36] At an initial glance, these numbers would suggest that the 'leak' within the pipeline is not at recruitment. However, it is important that we dig a little deeper than sector-wide enrolment, as this large data capture can hide inequities within the system.

We can consider different levels of qualifications and Pacific student enrolment to gain some insight into the level of Pacific student participation (Table 4). For example, if we compare 2013 to 2022, we can see that the percentages of Pacific students within the whole student population enrolled in certificate levels 1–4 and certificate and diploma levels 5–7 have decreased, while the percentage of Pacific students compared to the entire student body has increased in bachelor's, honours and postgraduate certificates and diplomas, and master's-level studies, and doubled in doctoral degrees. Pacific students are enrolling in higher-level qualifications across the sector, which is good when we consider the income difference between these qualification levels (see Table 1).

| Level/type of study | 2013 | 2017 | 2022 |
| --- | --- | --- | --- |
| Certificate 1 | 15% | 10% | 8% |
| Certificate 2 | 13% | 12% | 9% |
| Certificate 3 | 15% | 14% | 13% |
| Certificate 4 | 15% | 14% | 13% |
| Certificates/diploma 5–7 | 10% | 9% | 9% |
| Bachelor's degree 7 | 8% | 10% | 11% |
| Graduate certificate/diploma 7 | 6% | 6% | 6% |
| Honours degree/postgraduate certificate/diploma 8 | 4% | 5% | 6% |
| Master's degree 9 | 4% | 5% | 6% |
| Doctoral degree 10 | 3% | 4% | 6% |

Table 4: Percentage of Pacific Students in Total Student Population by Level and Type of Qualification (Source: Education Counts)[37]

Numbers are a funny thing, and even though many of us see numbers as truth, there are different ways of counting the student population. The data above shows us that, by EFT, the percentages of Pacific students compared to the overall student population have increased or remained stable at bachelor's level and higher. However, the Pacific student headcount participating in higher education has fallen from 24,110 in 2013 to 21,915 in 2022.[38] This drop is not surprising if we consider the COVID-19 lockdowns and subsequent job losses that impacted Pacific high school students in significant ways, creating a hole in the pipeline which some Pacific students have leaked out of.[39]

We can also look at this data in comparison to other ethnic groups to further our understanding of how inequity operates within the system (see Table 5). In 2022, we can see that 27 per cent of the Pacific student population was enrolled in certificate levels 1–3, which was associated with the lowest median annual income across the board (even lower than no qualification and school qualification; see Table 1). This means that more than a quarter of Pacific students are paying for a qualification from which they will earn less money than if they had not enrolled in any qualification. Further, we can see that just over half of all Pacific students are enrolled at a bachelor's level or higher, which leads to the highest median annual income (see Table 1). This data split reveals why it is important to understand where Pacific students are enrolled, and how this contributes to wider inequity within New Zealand through lower incomes for Pacific peoples.

|  |  | European | Māori | Pacific | Asian | Other |
|---|---|---|---|---|---|---|
| Levels 1–3 certificate | Headcount | 47,760 | 31,465 | 9335 | 10,915 | 4220 |
|  | Percentage of ethnic population enrolment | 22% | 44% | 27% | 12% | 20% |
| Bachelor's degree or higher | Headcount | 124,360 | 25,440 | 18,170 | 64,430 | 12,825 |
|  | Percentage of ethnic population enrolment | 57.44% | 35.78% | 52.10% | 70.79% | 60.35% |

*Table 5: 2022 Student Population by Ethnicity and Qualification Level (Source: Education Counts)*[40]

Overall, this enrolment data paints a picture of increased and steady participation in higher education by Pacific peoples. However, a more detailed analysis highlights that our participation rates are concentrated in particular areas of the sector, which has a corresponding effect on potential income levels. Importantly, I want to reiterate that more than a quarter of Pacific students are paying for qualifications that will result in a lower income than if they had left school without a qualification. This result is incredibly troubling, and we need to understand how and why Pacific students are being recruited into these programmes.

### Retention

Retention in TEIs measures how many students either complete their enrolment then move on to enrol in the next year, or finish their qualification and go on to further studies in the same area. Table 6 records the first-year retention rate of Pacific students in 2016 and 2021, enabling us to see how many Pacific students continued on to their second year after their first. In 2016, Te Pūkenga had the lowest total retention rate, replaced by Massey University in 2021. In 2016, the University of Otago had the highest retention rate, and they maintained this into 2021. The University of Auckland, the University of Waikato, and the University of Canterbury all had a decrease in first-year retention between 2016 and 2021. Higher education research identifies that the first year is crucial to ongoing student success.[41] Therefore, understanding whether Pacific students are 'leaking' out of the pipeline initially or as they go through their degree can help us to understand where to invest resources and when to intervene.

| Institution | First-year retention rate | | |
|---|---|---|---|
| | 2016 | 2018 | 2021 |
| University of Auckland | 79% | 80% | 78% |
| Auckland University of Technology | 69% | 69% | 72% |
| Massey University | 58% | 64% | 68% |
| University of Waikato | 75% | 70% | 71% |
| Victoria University of Wellington | 72% | 76% | 78% |
| Lincoln University | 67% | - | 80% |
| University of Canterbury | 78% | 65% | 71% |
| University of Otago | 85% | 79% | 83% |
| Total universities | 78% | 73% | 80% |
| Te Pūkenga | 44% | 60% | 69% |
| Total universities & Te Pūkenga | 45% | 71% | 72% |

Table 6: Pacific Students' First-Year Retention Rate in TEIs, Not Including Wānanga (Source: Tertiary Education Commission)[42]

## Completion

When tracking the impacts of structural racism in higher education, we can also look at completion rates. In Table 7, we can start to see significant discrepancies in completion rates beyond certificate level 4 and in the overall 'all levels' percentages. This data is important as it sheds light on how many of the recruited Pacific students are completing their qualifications. From this data, we can identify that in 2022, 31 per cent of all Pacific students enrolled in higher education did not complete their qualification. This outcome means that their investment in a better future will not be realised, and instead, they may find themselves burdened with debt that precludes this future from materialising.

| Level/type of study | European | Māori | Pacific | Asian | Other |
|---|---|---|---|---|---|
| Certificate 1 | 69% | 65% | 67% | 81% | 71% |
| Certificate 2 | 69% | 63% | 64% | 78% | 67% |
| Certificate 3 | 73% | 63% | 66% | 81% | 72% |
| Certificate 4 | 74% | 63% | 65% | 81% | 76% |
| Certificate/ diploma 5–7 | 80% | 72% | 65% | 78% | 75% |
| Bachelor's degree 7 | 88% | 80% | 71% | 86% | 83% |
| Graduate certificate/ diploma 7 | 90% | 83% | 77% | 90% | 86% |
| Honours degree/ postgraduate certificate/ diploma 8 | 92% | 86% | 79% | 91% | 88% |
| Master's degree 9 | 92% | 86% | 80% | 91% | 88% |
| All levels | 84% | 72% | 69% | 85% | 80% |

Table 7: 2022 Course Completion Rates by Ethnicity and Type and Level of Qualification (Source: Education Counts)[43]

By separating out the data by institution, we can see that in 2021, universities overall had a qualification completion rate of 65 per cent (see Table 8). The lowest completion rate was at Massey University, with only 31 per cent of Pacific students enrolled completing their qualification. The highest rate of completion was at the University of Otago. If we return to our pipeline analogy, these numbers mean that less than 50 per cent of Pacific students who took the university route in 2021 made it to the other end – and for those Pacific students who opted to study at Massey University, only 31 per cent made it there. By comparison, if you are not Māori or Pacific at Massey University, more than half of you, 56 per cent, will make it to the other end of the pipe.[44] This data is not an anomaly either – if we return to 2016 (the earliest available data), the numbers are similar, with only a few universities (University of Auckland, University of Waikato, Victoria University of Wellington, University of Otago) sitting above a 50 per cent course completion rate.

| Institution | Qualification completion rate | | |
|---|---|---|---|
| | 2016 | 2018 | 2021 |
| University of Auckland | 57% | 56% | 52% |
| Auckland University of Technology | 47% | 48% | 42% |
| Massey University | 26% | 30% | 31% |
| University of Waikato | 58% | 45% | 47% |
| Victoria University of Wellington | 51% | 54% | 53% |
| Lincoln University | 37% | 32% | 55% |
| University of Canterbury | 47% | 48% | 48% |
| University of Otago | 62% | 57% | 56% |
| Total universities | 63% | 49% | 65% |
| Te Pūkenga | 49% | 48% | 63% |
| Total universities & Te Pūkenga | 49% | 49% | 70% |

Table 8: Pacific Students' First Qualification Completion (Source: Tertiary Education Commission)[45]

## What are Pacific Students Studying?

Another aspect to consider here is what subject areas Pacific students are studying. Part of the reason for looking into this is that we know that qualifying in different areas leads to different income levels.[46] We also know that, as an economy, we need to ensure that we have the appropriate workforce to respond to global trends in science and technology. Right away, the numbers in Table 9 indicate to us that the future Pacific workforce will be focused on society and culture (32 per cent), management and commerce (16 per cent), and health (13 per cent). However, we can also see that we will continue to lack Pacific people qualified in agriculture (2 per cent), information technology (3 per cent) and natural and physical sciences (4 per cent).

| Field of study | Total Pacific across tertiary sector | |
|---|---|---|
| | EFT | % |
| Natural and physical sciences | 395 | 4% |
| Information technology | 280 | 3% |
| Engineering and related technologies | 765 | 8% |
| Architecture and building | 635 | 6% |
| Agriculture, environmental and related studies | 170 | 2% |
| Health | 1310 | 13% |
| Education | 600 | 6% |
| Management and commerce | 1555 | 16% |
| Society and culture | 3150 | 32% |
| Creative arts | 435 | 4% |
| Food, hospitality and personal services | 365 | 4% |
| Mixed-field programmes | 835 | 8% |

*Table 9: 2022 Enrolment of Pacific People by Broad Field of Study (Source: Education Counts)*[47]

We can dig even deeper into this data, looking at each overarching field of study to develop a deeper understanding, for instance, of our health field enrolments (see Table 10). This information very quickly reveals that the majority of Pacific students in health are enrolled in nursing and public health, meaning we are unlikely to address Pacific medical doctor shortages or grow our rates of Pacific pharmacists and dentists any time soon.[48]

| Field of study | Total Pacific across health | |
|---|---|---|
| | EFT | % |
| Medical studies | 65 | 5% |
| Nursing | 530 | 39% |
| Pharmacy | 35 | 3% |
| Dental studies | 20 | 1% |
| Optical science | 0 | 0% |
| Veterinary studies | 25 | 2% |
| Public health | 320 | 24% |
| Radiography | 10 | 1% |
| Rehabilitation therapies | 40 | 3% |
| Complementary therapies | 5 | 0% |
| Other health | 295 | 22% |

Table 10: 2022 Enrolment of Pacific Students by Health Field of Study (Source: Education Counts)[49]

Overall, the data shows us that there is significant work to do in getting Pacific students through to completion. There is no point in recruiting Pacific students into higher education when it does not have the foundational systems in place to support the success of our community. As things stand, we are simply recruiting Pacific students into a system where they incur debt but do not access promised higher incomes as a result.

## Unmaking the Pacific Pipeline

Overall, quantitative data shows us the impact of structural racism in the past, present and future. We can see that Pacific peoples' access to higher education has been limited in the past by structural racism and that this will be impacting our overall wealth statistics. Additionally, we can see that even though more Pacific people are accessing higher education, our universities continue to fail us, evidenced by markedly lower completion rates. Finally, by understanding our current enrolment patterns, we can envisage the future Pacific workforce, and know that a significant intervention is needed if it is going to be the workforce of the future.

These conclusions bring us back to the pipeline. The pipeline is of New Zealand's making – it was created through historical and contemporary policy, hiring, curriculum and pedagogical choices. The pipeline will not be fixed through quick patch-up jobs such as hiring a few Pacific academics, adding a Pacific lecture, or putting up a poster showing a smiling Pacific person. These patch-up jobs are not working. Instead, Pacific students face a system where, at some universities, only thirty-one students out of the initial hundred will make it through the pipeline to a 'better future'. The promise of higher education is not one that should be broken. If it is to be the solution to economic inequity, then it needs to address the structural racism that is evident in these numbers and in our stories.

*We can choose to unmake this pipeline.*

So, where to from here? There are a few things that can be done to address the structural racism that is built into New Zealand's higher education system.

## Easily Accessible and Informative Data for Pacific Communities

While there is accessible data across the sector, much of it is hidden behind confusing digital interfaces and significant knowledge barriers. If it were widely known that Massey University has had a qualification completion rate consistently below 35 per cent for nearly the last decade, it is unlikely that this pattern would have remained unchallenged for so long. Data needs to be easily locatable and informative, not just for researchers and public servants, but also for the public. This data also needs to be actively used for forward planning and investment in Pacific peoples in higher education – it should not be left to a higher education scholar to analyse and publicise this data: dedicated public servants should be doing this, so that the government and other organisations can make informed decisions about where to invest public and private resources in transparent and meaningful ways.

## Inquiry into Racism in the Sector

I echo calls made by Māori scholars for an inquiry into racism in our sector.[50] There is so much evidence, both qualitative and quantitative, that shows a significant need to understand how racism operates in the higher education sector so that it can be interrupted. We need to resource and instigate the change needed to create a system that is reflective of this whenua and moana.

## Build Our Understanding of Pacific Peoples' Participation in Certificate Levels 1–3

Many Pacific people study for a certificate at levels 1–3, which are also the qualification levels associated with the lowest weekly income, as shown in Table 1. If these Pacific people had instead carried no qualification (and therefore likely no student debt), they would be $9,308 better off per year.[51] This income gap is significant, so we need to understand why it is that Pacific people are predominantly completing these qualifications with low post-graduation value.

## Clear Impacts and Incentives for Supporting Pacific Students in Higher Education

The announced rethink of sector funding needs to ensure that there are clear incentives for serving Pacific communities well.[52] While there has been a rethink of Tertiary Education Commission equity funding,[53] half of our universities have had a lower than 50 per cent Pacific student qualification completion rate since 2016 (see Table 8). The rethink needs to be measured and readjusted soon, as it is not operating to change how Pacific students and communities access and complete higher education.

## Conclusion

Finally, I want to end this chapter with Tongan poet Karlo Mila's words from her poem 'Now that I am no longer one of us',[54] which I often reflect on when it comes to fixing this pipeline. I will never experience the luxury of just being an academic; instead, there remains an overwhelming pressure/desire/call to contribute in ways that will change things for Pacific peoples, because we cannot continue to be sold a dream that will not materialise.

> We are too busy
> wiping flat whites
> from the table

Too busy being told
to get rid of the black scuffs
from the floor.
Where is our space
for dreaming?

theorising
brainstorming
clarifying
conceptualising
articulating?

We're too busy
scrubbing away at the shit
and polishing with our spit
the mirrors in which you see yourself
so transparently
not even traces of our fingertips
are left behind
our elbow grease affords you
this clean pristine vision
and under the artificial light
you see yourself so sanitised
and never ever see
our dark faces
peering out of your shadows.

# JUSTICE SYSTEMS

# Recognising Stories of Suffering in Section 27 of the Sentencing Act 2002

## Barbara-Luhia Graham

*Fetu Talagi is 24 years old. He is Samoan, but was born and raised in New Zealand. Fetu was recently involved in the ram-raid of a small business in South Auckland. He has been charged with aggravated robbery under section 235 of the Crimes Act 1961.[1] Fetu was found guilty at trial, and now faces being sentenced to up to 14 years in prison. How did he get here?*

FETU IS A FICTIONAL CHARACTER CREATED for the purposes of this chapter.[2] Parts I and II of this chapter begin by telling his story of suffering, which refers to the way in which racism positions a person – politically, economically and socially – to ensure their early entry into the criminal justice system in New Zealand.[3] Part III of this chapter discusses how section 27 of the Sentencing Act 2002 enables sentencing judges to recognise such stories before the courts. The effectiveness of section 27 is analysed in Part IV. Finally, in concluding this chapter, I offer two endings to Fetu's story of suffering: *the choice of which is yours.*

## Positionality

I find myself situated at an intersection of identities – Tokelauan, Samoan and Pālagi/Pākehā. I was born and raised in Te Whanganui-a-Tara, but currently live in Tāmaki Makaurau, Aotearoa. I am, therefore, a descendant of migrants writing on whenua that belongs to Ngāti Whātua Ōrākei.

E mihi nei au ki te mana whenua o konei, ki a Ngāti Whātua Ōrākei.

## Part I

*We need more than science.*
*We need stories.*[4]

Everyone knows that suffering exists.[5] In colonised countries, suffering is seen in the way in which the most marginalised – Black and Brown bodies – feature in every indicator of inequality. In New Zealand, the most marginalised include Pacific peoples. The statistics speak for themselves:

- Approximately one in five Pacific children live in 'material hardship' (that is, going without six or more essential items). This is compared to one in ten Pākehā/Pālagi children.[6]
- Of the 4800 children and young people in state care, 11 per cent are both Māori and Pacific and 6 per cent are Pacific.[7]
- Pacific peoples make up 8 per cent of the general population, but account for 12 per cent of the prison population.[8]
- Pacific people have the highest rates of premature death from long-term health conditions. On average, Pacific people live six years fewer than Pākehā/Pālagi.[9]

These statistics are one manifestation of the suffering caused by centuries of colonisation. In my view, however, such suffering is not effectively conveyed by these statistics. As one of my most beloved authors once said, such statistics have become as 'banal as breakfast'.[10] They come in with the morning paper, consumed along with our bacon, eggs, and a cup of coffee.[11] 'It is the banality of this brutality that is truly troubling.'[12] Perhaps then, the texture of such suffering is best found within the stories behind the statistics.[13] Accordingly, I turn to Fetu.

In telling Fetu's story of suffering, I engage with 'story-telling': a core concept in critical race theory (CRT).[14] CRT is a scholarly movement that reckons with racism in the legal system and beyond.[15] Story-telling is a method of telling the stories of those people whose experiences are not often told because of their gender, race, class or other discriminatory distinctions.[16] Story-telling privileges experiences of racism and the resulting suffering that Black, Indigenous and people of colour (BIPOC) have endured as a legitimate form of knowledge.[17] In doing so, story-telling disrupts dominant discourses on race referred to as 'majoritarian stories'. Majoritarian stories privilege the dominant group – Whites, men, heterosexuals and the middle and/or upper class – by naming these social locations as natural or normative points of reference.[18] Majoritarian stories are grounded in White superiority, reinforcing racial hegemony by simultaneously silencing the experiences of BIPOC.[19]

CRT scholars call stories that disrupt majoritarian stories 'counter-stories'.[20] There are three types of counter-stories within CRT.[21] Fetu's story of suffering can be categorised as 'other people's stories'.[22] Other people's stories reveal experiences with racism in the third person.[23] This type of story offers biographical information about a person's experiences in relation to political, economic and social institutions in a sociohistorical context.[24]

In this chapter, Fetu's story of suffering is used as a counter-story to challenge the majoritarian stories that have been perpetuated about the criminal justice system in New Zealand. In particular, the majoritarian story that those in the criminal justice system have freely chosen their fate – that is, they have *chosen* to commit crime and, therefore, belong behind bars.[25] This majoritarian story about *choice* conceals the White supremacist belief that Brown bodies inherently belong in prison. This is consistent with the legal (specifically, sentencing) theory of free will, which encourages criminality as being the product of poor choices, rather than recognising the significance of structural racism.

Fetu's story of suffering reveals the way in which racism has positioned him – politically, economically and socially – to ensure his early entry into the criminal justice system. In the context of the United States, lawyer Michelle Alexander characterises this as follows:

> It is . . . more convenient to imagine that a majority of young [African American] men . . . freely chose a life of crime than to accept the real possibility that their lives were structured in a way that virtually guaranteed their early admission into a system from which they can never escape . . .[26]

Like these young African American men, Fetu's life has been structured in this way.

### Part II

> Suffering . . . is seldom divorced from the actions of the powerful.[27]

Fetu's story of suffering starts before he was born, with the colonial powers' expansion in the Pacific Islands from the late 1700s.[28] This colonisation saw the forced removal of Indigenous sovereignty in multiple Pacific Islands.[29] Sāmoa came under German rule at the end of the Second Samoan Civil War.[30]

Fetu's story of suffering then tells of two traumatic events that occurred in his community.

Firstly, at the beginning of World War I, the New Zealand Expeditionary Force landed at Apia and took control of Sāmoa from Germany. In 1918, the New Zealand Administration allowed a steamship (known as the *Talune*) carrying passengers infected with influenza to dock in Sāmoa.[31] This decision had catastrophic consequences, resulting in a pandemic with mass mortalities.[32] As communities were crippled, the New Zealand administrator, Robert Logan, described those grieving for their deceased as being 'like children . . . they will get over it if handled with care . . . they will later on remember all that has been done for them in the previous four years. . .'.[33] Fetu's great-grandmother was one of the many Samoans who died from the influenza in 1918. She was survived by her husband and three children who were fortunate to farewell her with a fa'alavelave.

Secondly, on 28 December 1929, members of the Mau movement (a non-violent movement for Samoan independence from colonial rule during the first half of the twentieth century) gathered in the streets of Apia.[34] New Zealand military police opened fire on the procession when Mau members attempted to prevent the arrest of the Mau secretary. Eleven Samoans were killed, including Mau leader Tupua Tamasese Lealofi III.[35] Fetu's great-grandfather attended the procession. He was left traumatised after witnessing the shootings because some of the victims were from his own village.

It is important to remember that these events are illustrative of two 'colonial encounters' in the Pacific.[36] Generally, these encounters were characterised by the dispossession of Indigenous political, economic and social structures, and possession of land and other natural resources that marked the beginnings of contemporary ethnic inequalities.[37]

Fetu's story of suffering then becomes one of migration to New Zealand. Prior to the 1950s, immigration was restricted on the grounds of race.[38] This changed following World War II, when the government encouraged Pacific people to migrate to New Zealand, albeit on the assumption that most of this migration would be temporary.[39] This migration was enabled through paternalistic legislation, policies and practices which positioned Pacific peoples as a temporary source of labour to be exploited to support the country's expanding primary and secondary industries.

Fetu's grandparents migrated to New Zealand in the early 1970s. They brought with them their three young children (including Fetu's father) and rented a house in Ponsonby. They found employment on the factory floors at the local freezing works.

Between 1973 and 1974, New Zealand fell into a recession following a global oil crisis.[40] The primary and secondary industries were significantly impacted, resulting in rising concern about immigration levels.[41] Pacific people were increasingly perceived as overstayers who took employment opportunities from New Zealanders.[42] This was the catalyst for the Dawn Raids, which began in 1974.

Described as an act of 'state-sanctioned racism', the raids were enabled by racist legislation – in particular, the Immigration Act 1964.[43] The Act had previously been ignored while the country's economy needed to be built, but an amendment to the Act in 1968 allowed for the deportation of migrants who had overstayed their work permits.[44] The Act also empowered police to ask migrants to produce a valid passport and permit to enter and remain in New Zealand.[45] This was disproportionately enforced against Pacific people.[46]

Fetu's grandparents were subjected to the relentless racism that characterised the Dawn Raids. In the first dew of dawn on 1 July 1975, their house was raided. At five years old, Fetu's father witnessed his own parents being placed in handcuffs by the police. They were charged with overstaying and held in prison cells for three nights before the charges were dropped.[47] Fetu's father's brother and sister looked after him while their parents were in prison. His brother, the oldest of the three siblings, had just turned twelve. While Fetu's grandparents were found to be living legally in the country, they had family and friends who were prosecuted.

Some of the children from these families had to be placed in state care because their parents were deported to Sāmoa.[48]

Between 1985 and 1986, Pacific people comprised approximately a third of overstayers but represented nearly 90 per cent of all prosecutions.[49] In comparison, migrants from the Western world also comprised approximately a third of overstayers, but represented only 5 per cent of all prosecutions.[50]

Following the Dawn Raids, Fetu's family experienced extreme financial hardship. The recession had halted large-scale migration and was followed by intense structural reform, with thousands of jobs lost in the primary and secondary industries.[51] Fetu's grandfather lost his job at the local freezing works. Fetu's grandmother subsequently became the sole provider for the family of five, who found themselves facing poverty.

At the same time, there was a revival of interest in inner-city living in Auckland by Pālagi/Pākehā. This marked the beginning of the gentrification of Tāmaki Makaurau. Pālagi/Pākehā began to move back to the inner-city, looking to buy and renovate or rent houses. This resulted in increased competition for what was already a relatively small housing market.[52] As a result, Fetu's grandparents' landlord increased their rent. Due to the financial pressure, they moved to Papakura. There they lived in a state house in a clustered community of low-income families who were also struggling to survive.

By this time, Fetu's father was fifteen. He was a fluent speaker of Samoan, but attended a secondary school where he was bullied by other students for speaking broken English. He felt both visible and invisible: visible to his bullies, but invisible to his teachers who had already assumed he would amount to nothing. Fetu's father began to misbehave in response to the racial bullying, forming friendships with other boys – bonded by their suffering. As a group, they would misbehave at school to attract the attention of their teachers who they perceived to be in positions of power. Over time, this misbehaviour escalated into wagging school and committing small crimes like stealing food from the local grocery store because they were hungry. It wasn't long before Fetu's father came to the attention of the police.

In 1988, Fetu's father came home from school. There were two social workers at the house, and his mother told him that they were going to take him shopping for some new clothes. Fetu's father went shopping with the social workers, but he was never taken home. Instead, he was taken to Weymouth Boys' Home.

During his time at Weymouth Boys' Home, Fetu's father was abused by those who were meant to be caring for him. He was, in every way, punished for being who he was. At 22 years old, Fetu's father was released from Weymouth Boys' Home. However, without the proper support systems in place, he soon found himself in prison.

Fetu's father cycled in and out of prison for eight years. In between these stints in prison, Fetu was born in 2000. As his mother looked out the window after giving birth, she noticed that the stars were shining, as if their ancestors had sensed their baby boy's arrival. 'Fetu,' she said, 'that is what we call you'. Fetu means star in Samoan.

At five years old, Fetu was taken into care by his grandparents, who still lived in Papakura. Like his father, he grew up in the same clustered community of low-income families. It seemed that suffering was a chronic condition for these families and that every day they dealt with different disadvantages which compounded – layer upon layer upon layer.

Fetu's story would replicate that of his father's by the time he reached secondary school. Like his father, he formed friendships with other boys – bonded by their suffering. They started to wag school and commit small crimes like shoplifting because, like the generation before them, they were often hungry.

In 2018, Fetu left school at the beginning of Year 12. He hadn't achieved university entrance, but was employed as an apprentice by his uncle. Over the next months, Fetu's uncle became the father figure he had never had. Fetu felt fully supported and loved by his uncle, and knew he had his best interests at heart when he gently guided him to part ways with his friends from school. However, this soon changed.

In 2023, Fetu's uncle died after being diagnosed with bowel cancer.[53] He had been feeling unwell for weeks, but was not comfortable visiting his doctor.[54] Overwhelmed with grief, Fetu sought support among his friends from school.

One night, Fetu's friends decided to ram-raid a local gas station. Fetu agreed, although he was apprehensive. Unknown to him, his friends had brought weapons with them. They beat the victim while Fetu watched without intervening. Suddenly, the police arrived, and they were all arrested at the scene.

When Fetu appeared in the District Court, the Judge called his name: 'Mr Fetu Talagi'. For the first time in his life, Fetu felt seen – someone in a position of power had finally recognised him.

*And they had even said his name.*

In sharing Fetu's story of suffering, I have challenged the majoritarian story outlined in Part I. Fetu's story reveals the way in which racism has positioned him – politically, economically and socially – to ensure his early entry into the criminal justice system in New Zealand. Justice Williams has characterised this as the way in which racism conspires to constrain an individual's agency.[55] For the purposes of this chapter, agency refers to an individual's power to choose from a full range of free choices in life. Agency is not fixed but fluid, and can be fettered or unfettered without entirely losing its character.[56] For BIPOC, our agency is fettered to different degrees depending on the extent to which racism – past and present – impacts our lives. To illustrate, I return to Fetu.

When Fetu, his friends, and other Pacific offenders appear before the courts, there is likely to be a malevolent monotony in their stories of suffering: racism has conspired to constrain their agency. That is not to deny their agency altogether: rather it is to recognise the circumstances of their lives.

Relevant to the circumstances of their lives is the fact that powerful people in our political, economic and social institutions have enacted legislation, policies and practices that have significantly reduced the range of choices available to them. These colonial instruments weave together like a web over time, compounding to create racial inequality. What becomes clear is that Fetu's agency (and the agency of others like him) was at risk of being fettered long before he was born because, as his story of suffering tells:

- *When the colonial powers colonised the Pacific Islands; powerful people were behind it.*
- *When the Talune was allowed to dock in Samoa; powerful people were behind it.*
- *When Tupua Tamasese Lealofi III and eleven other Samoans were murdered; powerful people were behind it.*
- *When Fetu's grandparents were enticed to migrate to New Zealand; powerful people were behind it.*
- *When Fetu's grandparents' house was raided on 1 July 1975; powerful people were behind it.*
- *When Fetu's grandparents' rent was raised and they were forced to relocate to Papakura; powerful people were behind it.*
- *When Fetu's father was placed in Weymouth Boys' Home; powerful people were behind it.*

Crucially, of the 655,000 children and young persons placed in state care (as reported by the Abuse in Care Royal Commission of Inquiry),[57] one in three went on to serve a prison sentence later in life.[58] Fetu's father was one of these children. Given that children with a parent in prison are eight to ten times more likely to end up in prison themselves (compared to children without a parent in prison),[59] what were Fetu's chances of leading a lawful life? Statistically, they were very low.

So, how will the criminal justice system recognise Fetu's story of suffering in sentencing him before the court? Part III discusses how section 27 of the Sentencing Act 2002 enables judges to recognise such stories in sentencing offenders.

## Part III

Sentencing hearings are governed by the Sentencing Act 2002.[60] The Act came into force on 30 June 2002 and represented a comprehensive reform of parts of the Criminal Justice Act 1985.[61] The Act sets out the purposes and principles of sentencing in sections 7 and 8, and the 'aggravating' and 'mitigating' factors associated with the offender and the circumstances of the offending in section 9.[62] Collectively, these sections assist sentencing judges in justifying their sentence selection.

Section 27 of the Act also assists sentencing judges in justifying their sentence selection. Section 27 allows an offender (regardless of their ethnicity) to request the court to hear a person or persons speak on their (the offender's) 'personal, family, whānau, community and cultural background'.[63] Section 27's predecessor was section 16 of the Criminal Justice Act, which required courts to hear from those who wished to speak for the offender about their 'background'.[64] Section 16 was enacted to address the over-representation of Māori offenders (particularly, young Māori offenders) in the prison population at the time.[65] Despite the potential in the statutory language to create a new path for how the criminal justice system sentenced offenders, section 16 remained stagnant for 30 years.[66] According to Justice Williams, the infrastructure to support its use was simply not there.[67]

Over the past five years, people working within the criminal justice system have breathed life into section 27.[68] This has been by way of section 27 reports – a personalised taxonomy of the offender – to be considered in conjunction with other relevant sections of the Act, including sections 7, 8 and 9.[69] These reports are more commonly known as 'cultural reports', but I will refer to them as 'section 27 reports'.

There are several ways in which section 27 reports influence sentencing, but mainstream media deliberately focus on discounts: where an offender receives a lesser sentence than they may have done without a report.[70] However, section 27 reports can also result in different kinds of sentences – community-based rather than imprisonment.[71] Even where prison is inevitable, due to the seriousness of the harm done, the information in a section 27 report can inform the placement of an offender in a particular prison unit (for example, drug treatment units).[72]

Section 27 is the vehicle that enables stories of suffering like Fetu's to come before the courts. This was recognised by Justice Whata in *Solicitor-General v Heta (Heta)*.[73] In articulating the logic behind section 27, Justice Whata acknowledged that colonisation had caused 'pervasive and persistent social disadvantage[s]' for Māori.[74] In the context of *Heta*, which involved a Māori offender, he referred to these collective 'pervasive and persistent social disadvantage[s]' as 'systemic Māori deprivation'.[75] He then discussed how section 27 (specifically, with reference to 'systemic Māori deprivation') can be used successfully in sentencing:

> There is no express requirement to have regard to systemic Māori deprivation in sentencing. However, the Court when fixing a sentence must consider 'any aggravating or mitigating factor the Court thinks fit'. Section 27, then, mandates consideration of the full social and cultural matrix of the offender and the offending. There is no obvious reason why this should exclude evidence of systemic Māori deprivation and how (if at all) this may have contributed to the offending.
>
> On the contrary, inclusion of all material background factors in the [sentencing] assessment . . . better serves the purposes and principles of sentencing to identify and respond to all potential causes of offending, including where relevant, systemic Māori deprivation.[76]

As Justice Whata finds, section 27 reports can – if well written – tell the stories of suffering of offenders (regardless of ethnicity). In telling such stories, they can convey the extent to which an offender's agency has been fettered and how this has contributed to their offending. However, not everyone has embraced *Heta* with enthusiasm.[77] This is seen in the case of *R v Carr*.[78] *R v Carr* involved the sentencing of a 'part-Māori' offender in the High Court. In responding to the section 27 report, Justice Downs observed:

> In any event, discounts in this context require care. Correlation and causation are not synonymous. Many people with disadvantaged backgrounds do not commit criminal offences let alone very serious ones like this, and many law-abiding people remain so despite difficult lives. Excessive discounts in this context risk undermining the criminal law's precepts of human agency and choice. This is not to deny the importance of upbringing or circumstance; it is to maintain perspective.[79]

Justice Williams agrees with that caution – in part. He warns that trauma does not guarantee that an individual will become an offender.[80] He provides the example of offender 'A'. The fact that people of a particular background (including 'A') have an 80 per cent likelihood of offending does not entitle anyone to automatically assume that 'A' was always going to offend.[81] In Justice Williams's view, this retrospective 'determinism' dispossesses 'A' of their agency:

> It is ... dehumanising to reduce an offender to victimhood and nothing more; it is to make them [the offender] a mere puppet of circumstance.[82]

Justice Williams is not suggesting that those who break the law bear no responsibility for their actions. This would deny their agency altogether and, therefore, disregard an essential element of their humanity. It would, in his words, deny their 'mana'.[83] As he concludes, 'proper rehearsals of these [offenders'] histories enable sentencing judges to calibrate as best they can the degree to which an individual's agency has been fettered by racism'.[84] He agrees that 'it is important to maintain perspective in assessing agency, however, without proper command of an offender's background, there can be no perspective – only myopia'.[85]

## Part IV

As discussed in Part III, section 27's predecessor, section 16, was enacted to address the over-representation of Māori offenders (particularly young Māori offenders) in the prison population in the 1980s. Has the number of Māori offenders (or Pacific offenders) declined since then? In short, no. Critics say that this is because sentencings are not the appropriate means of addressing over-representation.[86] In their view, section 27 is too little too late because it addresses the social factors that led to the offending *after* the fact.[87]

Despite these criticisms, it has been acknowledged that section 27 still has the potential to transform how offenders are sentenced, provided 'the system' can make it work.[88] Professor Khylee Quince proposes that the first step in realising section 27's potential is to increase family and community engagement with the courts.[89] This would give effect to the wording of the section which refers to a 'speaker or speakers' (rather than written reports), with the implication that this would be someone from the offender's family or community.[90] Quince observes that the practice of providing independently written reports emerged within Western paradigms of objectivity, providing comfort to those judges sceptical of speakers from offenders' families and communities.[91] The authors of the two-part report 'Pacific Peoples and the Criminal Justice System in Aotearoa, New Zealand' agree, and draw attention to the risks of over-reliance on independently written reports:

> ... overreliance on independently written s 27 reports risks turning the process into something of a sentencing

industrial complex, flattening complex lives into digestible synopses whilst disincentivising 'authentic voices' from being heard.[92]

Quince states that, in fact, the clear spirit and intent of the original provision (section 16) was to increase community engagement in the process, by empowering 'whānau to speak for themselves'.[93] 'Empowering whānau to speak for themselves is the gold standard, because there is innate power in telling our own stories.'[94] Our families and communities know, intimately, the catastrophic consequences racism has had – past and present. The full extent of this simply cannot be captured by independent report writers who only meet once or twice with offenders for the purpose of extracting extremely personal information to be presented before the court.

Moreover, when families and communities are empowered to speak for themselves, they are not sharing the offender's story in isolation: the offender's story is *their* story – and such stories are invitations to heal. Māmari Stephens observes that in her experience, section 27 reports are a form of rehabilitation for both the offender and the offender's family and community:

> It's not uncommon . . . for people who are having the reports written about them . . . to look at their own lives with different eyes . . . I think they can mark a turning point in a person's life, potentially.[95]

She further notes that:

> . . . they are most useful for the people in the whānau of the person who is being sentenced.[96]

So, how can 'the system' actively assist families and communities to engage in the sentencings of their loved ones? Quince suggests establishing culturally competent navigators who can work with families and communities to better bridge the gap between them and 'the system'.[97] Alternatively, she suggests the engagement of lay advocates (lay advocates appear in the Family Court in support of the child or young person who is subject to care and protection proceedings under the Oranga Tamariki Act 1989).[98]

In my view, either of these roles would serve offenders, their families and their communities, by bringing their stories before the courts in their *fullness*. Because, from stories of suffering emerge inseparable stories of overcoming extraordinary odds: stories about families and communities thriving, despite the cards they have been dealt by the coloniser's cruel hand. But it is these stories – stories about our beauty – which we have been led to believe are not worth telling. These stories honour the wholeness of who we are as a people, and it is these stories that must be excavated to reveal our truer selves. Section 27 could have assisted in achieving this, if only the cruel hand had let it.

## Conclusion

In concluding this chapter, I offer two endings to Fetu's story of suffering.

### Ending 1

In preparation for his sentencing, Fetu met with a section 27 report writer from 'Section 27 Reports NZ'.[99]

Fetu found that sharing his story of suffering with the report writer was a form of healing. At his sentencing, the Judge acknowledged aspects of his section 27 report and discounted his sentence by 25 per cent. Fetu's end sentence was one of home detention, ordered by the Judge to be served at his grandparents' house in Papakura. His grandparents had been at his sentencing and agreed to support him going forward. In handwritten notes on Fetu's file, the Judge wrote that 'Fetu held a special place in his grandparents' hearts' and that their support was characterised by their 'unconditional love' for him.

Fetu was approved to retain his employment as an apprentice, meaning he could remain a productive member of society. He was also ordered and approved to attend several rehabilitation programmes for young men in South Auckland. These programmes encouraged him to begin healing the intergenerational trauma in his family. When he talked to his grandparents about this healing, they held him closely and agreed to begin by facilitating some family meetings.

Their first family meeting is next week.

## Ending 2

Fetu was sentenced to a short term of imprisonment because no section 27 report was provided to the court. Following the general election in October 2023, legal aid funding for section 27 reports was removed under the Legal Services Amendment Bill introduced by the new National-led government.[100] As anticipated by opponents of the Bill, Fetu – like many other offenders – simply could not afford a report.[101]

On his release from prison, Fetu found himself relegated to the status of a second-class citizen. This is the power of a criminal conviction in New Zealand. A criminal conviction can result in different types of social discrimination that prevent a person from fully participating in society.[102]

Fetu struggled to find employment. For months, he stayed – unemployed – at his grandparents' house while they worked. He felt like he had fundamentally failed them.

On 28 December 2024, Fetu sat in his bedroom. He had come to believe the majoritarian story society had told him since birth: that his Brown body was nothing but a burden. Fetu decided to act accordingly – by ridding the world of this burden.

Fetu was found crumpled in the corner of his bedroom by his grandparents when they returned home from work. They held him closely as they cried, the three of them wrapped in a cold melancholy.

Fetu's death is remembered as the latest of a string of tragedies – linked together in a long line of lamentation. Given the suffering that racism causes in this country, it is no wonder that so many of our brothers and sisters wish to return to the warmth of their ancestors.

And when they do, they are welcomed by the words: '*We've been waiting for you.*'

# THE NEXT GENERATION

## To Weave Dreams of Liberation

*Chelsea Naepi*

> As the sea is an open and ever-flowing reality, so should our oceanic identity transcend all forms of insularity, to become one that is openly searching, inventive, and welcoming. In a metaphorical sense the ocean that has been our waterway to each other should also be our route to the rest of the world.[1]
>
> —Epeli Hauʻofa, 'The Ocean in Us'

> Freedom and love may be the most revolutionary ideas available to us, and yet as intellectuals we have failed miserably to grapple with their political and analytical importance.[2]
>
> Robin D. G. Kelley, *Freedom Dreams*

THE CONTRIBUTING AUTHORS OF THIS BOOK have illustrated the various forms of violence (which I define as an all-encompassing force of oppression from the interpersonal to the systemic) that

Pacific people have been subjected to and continue to live through. Having reached the final chapter of this book, we begin to develop an idea of just how catastrophic this violence is as a transformative force. Essentially, the lives of Pacific people have become flattened in Aotearoa New Zealand. We are denied a basic standard of living – a standard of *life* itself. The settler-colonial landscape that we have been placed into and subjected by continues to oppress and tear our relationships with one another and ourselves. With the three-headed coalition of National, ACT and New Zealand First settling in, anxieties rise as their legislative promises reflect a staunch agenda to unweave decades of reform, reaffirmation and resistance by many marginalised communities – especially Māori and Pacific peoples.

As mentioned in the first chapter of this book, many political commentators and community members have expressed their concerns about the implications of such changes for Māori and Pacific peoples, as most of the legislative changes bring significant impacts to the way we can navigate specific institutions, social support, and daily life. Repealing Fair Pay Agreements, smokefree laws, and equity-driven sections in the Oranga Tamariki Act and the Sentencing Act (see Barbara-Luhia Graham's extremely moving chapter on this) are just some of the first actions of a new government that will shift the way Pacific peoples are socially supported in the next three years. The removal of these policies confirms that movements of anti-racism and equality can quickly come to a halt once White liberalism becomes fed up with the demands of the oppressed. The liberal values of tolerance and (conditional) acceptance quickly spiral to reveal the true faces of White supremacy and colonial logics, proceeding to snatch back the smallest shreds of acknowledgement that have taken us generations to obtain. This new coalition's 'equality for all New Zealanders' rhetoric serves as a cruel co-option of all we have worked for as marginalised peoples. The promised land of milk and honey has now materialised into a vast expanse of dry soil, sparing us nothing as we continue to watch the fruits of our labour enjoyed by the colonial powers that brought us here. Tracing the arguments offered by the contributing authors of this book, we collectively find ourselves at this moment of stillness, asking each other: *Where do we possibly go from here?*

The opening epigraph of this afterword written by Fijian-Tongan academic and philosopher Epeli Hauʻofa serves as a foundation for the following thoughts I seek to lay out as a young Pacific woman who simultaneously mourns the past and hopes for better futures. These sporadic thoughts aim to speak to the visions offered by the authors of this book (and to you, dear reader) as we venture to dream and fight together for a society in which not just Pacific peoples, but all vulnerable and marginalised communities, may truly prosper. As we sit together and plot our next course of action, we must simultaneously reflect on our hopes for better and how these hopes will be placed within the wider struggles we witness unfolding before us – across both the motu and moana.

### Kinship Through Karanga: The Intimate Ties of Solidarity

The journey from Hawaiki to the shores of Aotearoa speaks to the endless resilience that the descendants of Oceania possess as master navigators of the winds, stars and sea. As tangata moana, we share these special ancestral ties with tangata whenua.

The incredible Indigenous scholar and lawyer Moana Jackson reminds us in *Imagining Decolonisation* of these intimate yet distant ties between Māori and Pacific peoples as descendants of Te Moana-nui-a-Kiwa.[3] Matua Jackson speaks tenderly of the radical force in remembering our ancestral pasts – affirming the necessity to remain in solidarity with tangata whenua as their Pacific kin. Dylan Asafo's chapter in this book and his separate article 'Freedom Dreaming of Abolition in Aotearoa New Zealand' echo such sentiments, expressing the importance of Pacific people's standing in solidarity with tangata whenua's struggles in calling for the Crown to honour te Tiriti o Waitangi.[4] Te Tiriti is indeed a tool of emancipation for Pacific peoples, acting as a taonga of Aotearoa New Zealand's constitutional foundations which must be honoured. I describe te Tiriti as a taonga because it serves as a large piece of the map we must use to chart a course towards the future. Te Tiriti is not just a legal document that represents the relationship between Māori, Tauiwi and the Crown. Te Tiriti serves as a radical affirmation of te ao Māori – reflecting the depth of Indigenous knowledge systems and Oceania as a whole, which cannot go ignored by the Western colonial world. Beyond being a legal document, te Tiriti serves as a physical representation of the paths of our inevitable future. The answers for beyond lie in Tiriti-based transformation, making space for radical visions in which Pacific prosperity may truly be actualised. Rahui Papa eloquently expresses the relevance and importance of supporting movements of Indigenous liberation for *all* descendants of Oceania, as sovereignty over our ancestral lands and oceans are a shared goal:

> Ko te tohe tonu o te mana motuhake ehara kē i te mea he tapu ki te Māori ko ia anake, engari e tuariari katoa atu ana ki runga ki ngā moutere, me ngā iwi o Te Moana nui a Kiwa whānui. Me te mea nei he whakapapa kei reira, he tātai whakaheke e tūhonohono mai ana rātou ki a tātou, tātou ki a rātou.

> The question of sovereignty isn't exclusive to Māori, it's a common debate across islands and peoples of the Pacific. Furthermore, we are bound by ancestry and lineage that connects us to them and them to us.[5]

It is through our bonds of solidarity with Māori that we may begin to finally see the path towards liberation materialise. This solidarity must be unwavering. It must be loud, proud and unapologetic, as it is within the liberation of Aotearoa's Indigenous peoples that we may truly achieve the visions of a new world for which we all yearn and dream at every moment. It feels timely to be speaking of our own experiences of racism, colonisation and systemic violence as Pacific peoples in the face of our new government and the harmful promises it brings. However, we must be emboldened to step beyond asking for policy reform, beyond institutional representation, and beyond holding difficult conversations around those sorts of topics (such as racism, colonialism and all the other -isms or -phobias that you can think of) within our social circles. Our next steps as a collective must be grounded in genuine solidarity with all those who experience the violent hand of oppression.

## Beyond the Shores of Te Moana-nui-a-Kiwa: Cartographies of Liberation Through Love

Following the call to stand in solidarity with all marginalised peoples across the moana, we may find inspiration for dreaming of the new world from the words of Black radical scholar Robin D. G. Kelley, who writes:

> The design and realization of such a space ought to be the product of a collective imagination shaped and reshaped by the very process of turning rubble and memory into the seeds of a new society.[6]

What remains to live in the rubble and memory of an empire? Aman Sium and Eric Ritskes discuss how within the process of imagining and creating Indigenous visions for the future, there is a tendency look to narratives of the past.[7] This rings true for Pacific peoples, as ancestral knowledge and heritage remain central to our passage into the future. What emerges from the rubble and memory of an empire requires us to walk backwards into the future, creating a rupture within time and space.[8] Beyond the colonial concept of linear time, we as Pacific peoples hold the ability to traverse both time and space through ancestral knowledge and genealogy.[9] Memory is our way into creation for the future.[10] The power of narrative and heritage is crucial to our survival as descendants of Oceania. I think of the words spoken by Haunani-Kay Trask, when she unapologetically states, 'our culture has to be the core of our existence, the core of our anger, the core of our mana'.[11] Our resistance can be found through the stories of our ancestors, the stories of our people and how they once lived and walked this Earth. While the colonial world tells their own stories of conquest and righteous domination to justify their presence on our (metaphorical and literal) islands, they lack the tender stories of belonging. Their efforts to soothe are rooted in the callous words and actions of theft and violence, haunted by the echoes of our ancestors as they watch us march and hear our demands for justice. As Moana Jackson states:

> These colonial stories may have helped explain the taking of power, but they could not give the colonisers the comfort of a place to stand. It was hard to feel at home when the descendants of those who had been killed were never far away and the smoke of the battlefield still lingered in the smoke of the forests that were being burned. In island stories, the intimacy of distance never lets memory entirely fade away.[12]

While I have no doubt the colonial world has no trouble sleeping at night over their actions, we cannot wait for them to awaken and realise such truths.[13] We simply do not have the possibility of waiting any longer, as our islands face the risk of returning to the ocean very soon. While we may have been dispossessed, displaced and disenfranchised, the colonial world cannot take away the strength we possess from our ancestors. The values our ancestors have passed down the generations to reach us are the forces we need in both ending and creating the world. They serve as a firm affirmation that indeed they were once here – their achievements and struggles serving as faint traces on an emerging map that we are now given the task to complete.

What can we chart on the map as Pacific peoples? What exactly do we bring to the table that is so transformative? I find the answer within our own worldviews and knowledge systems; I find it within the visceral and taboo. The radical values of love, empathy (mafana or aroha), relationality (fakafetuiaga or whakawhanaungatanga), and reciprocity (fakatautonu or utu) are just some of the many tools we possess in our daily lives that may bring visions of the future to life. These values we possess also echo true in other Indigenous worlds,[14] leading us to realise that colonisation has tried to sever our ties not only to ourselves[15] and Māori,[16] but to the rest of the oppressed world. Nigerian criminologist Biko Agozino masterfully articulates the power in connected love praxis (or action through love) in search of justice:

> Love praxis involves the compassionate search for reparative justice in recognition of the enduring legacies of centuries-old oppressive practices. The interconnectivity, self-similarity, recursiveness, fractional dimensions, infinity, and non-lineal geometry of humanity and nature call for such reparative justice to go beyond the human species and include the exploited nature that could only be ruined at the expense of humanity as a part of nature ... Part of what makes us human beings is that we are humane enough to care for other animal species that cannot advocate for themselves but also for all oppressed nationalities among humanity itself.[17]

As we reclaim visions of the future, we must do so through these values and in relation to each other. The world is simultaneously ordinary and extraordinary if we are to operate through the radical potential of relationality and love praxis. Understanding the experiences of other oppressed bodies across the moana creates another intimately distant tie in which we find commonality through shared memory. Robbie Shilliam expresses such ideas through the similarities of Maui and Legba, articulating the shared threads of commonality found within non-colonial cosmologies and worldviews that continue to be passed down through narrative.[18] While our worlds may be articulated differently, the feeling is all the same. We hold home in our hearts. We mourn, we love, we yearn, and we remember. These are the threads we must use to weave our visions of the future.

Thus, as the next generation, our task in carrying on this work put in front of us requires us to step into these unknowns and operate through the visceral again – to use love as a revolutionary tool of liberation for not just us but all marginalised peoples. While we have taken the time to map out the various forms of violence that racism has created in this world for us, we must now move to better understand where and how our experiences are placed in relation to the experiences lived by other marginalised communities. To speak of liberation on our shores requires us as Pacific people to recognise the similar wounds in others who are also carrying this pain, albeit in different ways.

We must continue to show solidarity with those whose struggle reaches the most violent depths of Western contempt. Beyond the struggles of our brothers and sisters in West Papua, Kanaky, Hawai'i, Kiribati, Tuvalu and Mā'ohi Nui who fight for their freedom, their integrity and their future, we must find our common threads with others who are also struggling under the oppressive forces of colonialism. The people of Palestine, Congo, Haiti, Sudan, Yemen, Kurdistan and Tigray (to mention only a few of the many struggles found within the Global South today) are experiencing the most egregious forms of colonial violence at this very moment. We must understand their struggle to better understand our own. Possessing all the knowledge we hold currently, there is no excuse to turn a blind eye to these atrocities unfolding before us in real time.

The most radical action of love for our ancestors and our descendants to come calls for us to step into such spaces – to critically question ourselves, the world, and to show up as best we can in efforts to cultivate a better harvest; so that everyone may eat together and feel the mafana (warmth, but also love or empathy) of the fire. The actions may be as small or large as we wish, but it starts with recognising the vastness of the ocean that extends all over the world. We must tap into our global consciousness and shed the restricted mindset of small islands in a vast sea. As described by Hauʻofa in the epigraph that opens this afterword, we must use the expansive nature of our moana as the extending force of love for our people into the beyond. To put it plainly, we must recognise that our experiences of racism as Pacific people are not created in isolation. This is going on *everywhere* across the globe, and we must inform ourselves of the struggles that other marginalised communities face to better understand our own. The world has come to be through colonial history and has not unfolded in a linear manner, despite their attempts to tell us so.[19] Our position right now as Pacific peoples is the result of many other stories of oppression, racial violence, extraction and forced assimilation. The roots of colonial history spread out beneath the soil through many branches, impacting different communities in several ways at the same time. This is something we need to recognise and hold close as Pacific peoples, as it is within this knowing that we may find our way home.

Just as our ancestors masterfully redirected their route upon challenges to discover the next island, we must continue to do the same. Pacific peoples must heed the call to collectivise and engage in transformative action to ensure the work of our ancestors does not dissipate into fading memory. Actions as small as learning about the struggles of other marginalised communities can be transformative in our role as globally conscious peoples. Like the ocean, may the fluidity of love and movement possess us to put thought into action.

I leave you with a chant that has been used these past eight months (when this afterword was written) as people have taken to the streets to demonstrate their unwavering support for the

Palestinian struggle. I feel it speaks directly to certainty of the future, reinforcing that the visions of liberation require the helping hands of all the oppressed. We the people must make waves and refuse to tolerate this violence a moment longer.

*We are the people*
*We won't be silenced*
*We are returning*
*Soon.*
*Soon.*
*Soon.*
*Soon!*

# NOTES

### ARTIST'S NOTE

1. Teresa Teaiwa, as quoted in Epeli Hauʻofa, 'The Ocean in Us', *The Contemporary Pacific*, vol. 10, no. 2, 1998, pp. 391–401: 392.

### RACISM – Why We Need to Talk About It

1. Satherley, Dan, 'Education Minister Chris Hipkins Not a Fan of the Phrase "White Privilege", but Acknowledges It Exists', *Newshub*, June 5, 2021, https://www.newshub.co.nz/home/politics/2021/06/education-minister-chris-hipkins-not-a-fan-of-the-phrase-white-privilege-but-acknowledges-it-exists.html
2. Throughout the book we use Aotearoa New Zealand to signal society and this whenua, and we use New Zealand to signal the settler state.
3. Mila, Karlo, 'Deconstructing the Big Brown Tails/Tales: Pasifika Peoples in Aotearoa New Zealand', in Avril Bell, Vivienne Elizabeth, Tracey McIntosh, and Matt Wynyard (eds), *A Land of Milk and Honey? Making Sense of Aotearoa New Zealand*, Auckland University Press, 2017, pp. 95–107: 95.
4. Harston, Gladys, 'No Pasifika MPs in Any National-led Government', *Tagata Pasifika*, November 4, 2023, https://tpplus.co.nz/politics/no-pasifika-mps-in-any-national-led-government/
5. McConnell, Glenn, 'Campaign Shift Gear – with Some Raising Concerns about "Dog Whistling" and "Racism"', *Stuff*, September 19, 2023, https://www.stuff.co.nz/national/politics/300979629/campaign-shifts-gear--with-some-raising-concerns-about-dog-whistling-and-racism
6. Neilson, Michael, 'David Seymour's Pacific Minister Guy Fawkes Comment: Calls Mount for Apology, PM Chris Hipkins Says Act leader "Should Be Ashamed of Himself"', *New Zealand Herald*, August 22, 2023, https://www.nzherald.co.nz/nz/politics/david-seymours-pacific-minister-guy-fawkes-comment-calls-mount-for-apology-pm-chris-hipkins-says-act-leader-should-be-ashamed-of-himself/2QLEE4XXWNBBRMF3WK2LV5EQIM/
7. ACT New Zealand, *ACT's Alternative Budget: End the Waste, Fix the Economy*, 2023, https://assets.nationbuilder.com/actnz/pages/12888/attachments/original/1695268559/ACT_Alternative_Budget_-_End_the_waste__fix_the_economy.pdf?1695268559
8. ACT New Zealand, 'Ending Divisive Race-based Policies', https://web.archive.org/web/20240304143456/https://www.act.org.nz/stopdivision; Hager, Nicky, 'Beware the Smooth Talker with a Forked Tongue', *E-Tangata*, October 8, 2023, https://e-tangata.co.nz/comment-and-analysis/nicky-hager-beware-the-smooth-talker-with-a-forked-tongue/?utm_source=twitter&utm_medium=social&utm_campaign=09Oct2023
9. Cochrane, Bill, and Gail Pacheco, *Empirical Analysis of Pacific, Māori, and Ethnic Pay Gaps in New Zealand*, NZ Work Research Institute,

July 2022, https://workresearch.aut.ac.nz/__data/assets/pdf_file/0004/672205/7e71e4dbee2432b576ef6fbc348f4d7109cdd073.pdf; Matada Research, *Pacific Pay Gap Inquiry Literature Review*, New Zealand Human Rights Commission, July 2022, https://hrc1-uat.sites.silverstripe.com/assets/Documents/Pacific-Pay-Gap-Inquiry-Literature-Review-v2.pdf; Ministry for Pacific Peoples, *Pacific Aotearoa Status Report: A Snapshot*, October 2021, https://www.mpp.govt.nz/assets/Reports/Pacific-Peoples-in-Aotearoa-Report.pdf; Stats NZ, *Pacific Housing: People, Place, and Wellbeing in Aotearoa New Zealand*, January 2023, https://www.stats.govt.nz/reports/pacific-housing-people-place-and-wellbeing-in-aotearoa-new-zealand/; Stats NZ, 'Pacific Peoples Ethnic Group', https://www.stats.govt.nz/reports/pacific-housing-people-place-and-wellbeing-in-aotearoa-new-zealand/#:~:text=The%202018%20Census%20recorded%20381%2C642,the%20total%20usually%20resident%20population; Tuiburelevu, Litia, Elizabeth Lotoa, Isabella Ieremia, Hugo Wagner-Hiliau, and Gabriella Coxon-Brayne, *Pacific Peoples and the Criminal Justice System in Aotearoa New Zealand*, July 2022, https://www.borrinfoundation.nz/wp-content/uploads/2023/10/PCJS_Report-1.pdf

10  Peters, Winston, 'We Must Deal to This Racism', Speech – New Zealand First, *Scoop*, August 20, 2023, https://pacific.scoop.co.nz/2023/08/we-must-deal-to-this-racism/

11  RNZ, 'Pasifika Community in for a "Rough Ride" under New Government – Academic', November 5, 2023, RNZ, https://www.rnz.co.nz/news/political/501734/pasifika-community-in-for-a-rough-ride-under-new-government-academic

12  New Zealand National Party and ACT New Zealand, *Coalition Agreement*, 2023, https://assets.nationbuilder.com/actnz/mailings/6945/attachments/original/National_ACT_Agreement.pdf?1700781466; New Zealand National Party and New Zealand First, *Coalition Agreement*, 2023, https://assets.nationbuilder.com/nzfirst/pages/4462/attachments/original/1700784896/National___NZF_Coalition_Agreement_signed_-_24_Nov_2023.pdf?1700784896

13  New Zealand Government, *Budget 2024: Summary of Initiatives*, 2024, https://budget.govt.nz/budget/pdfs/summary-initiatives/b24-sum-initiatives.pdf; New Zealand Government, *Vote Pacific Peoples*, 2024, https://www.treasury.govt.nz/publications/estimates/vote-pacific-peoples-social-services-and-community-sector-estimates-appropriations-2024-25

14  Fotheringham, Caleb, and Lydia Lewis, 'Budget 2024: NZ Govt Cuts Pacific funding by $26m in Budget', *RNZ*, May 31, 2024, https://www.rnz.co.nz/international/pacific-news/518321/budget-2024-nz-govt-cuts-pacific-funding-by-26m-in-budget; 'Pasifika Communities Will Bear Brunt of Cuts to Ministry for Pacific Peoples', *PSA*, May 10, 2024, https://www.psa.org.nz/our-voice/pasifika-communities-will-bear-brunt-of-cuts-to-ministry-for-pacific-peoples/

15  RNZ, 'Part-time workers could get less sick leave under law change, Workplace Relations Minister announces', *RNZ*, June 6, 2024, https://www.rnz.co.nz/news/political/518716/part-time-workers-could-get-less-sick-leave-under-law-change-workplace-relations-minister-announces

16  Foon, Eleisha, 'Sir Collin Tukuitonga Resigns from NZ Government Roles, Citing "No Confidence"', *RNZ*, December 11, 2023, https://www.rnz.co.nz/international/

pacific-news/504474/sir-collin-tukuitonga-resigns-from-nz-government-roles-citing-no-confidence
17 Foon, Eleisha, 'Pacific Leaders and Advocates Back Sir Collin Tukuitonga after Resignation', *RNZ*, December 12, 2023, https://www.rnz.co.nz/international/pacific-news/504536/pacific-leaders-and-advocates-back-sir-collin-tukuitonga-after-resignation
18 Foon, Eleisha, 'Pasifika "Standing with Māori", Govt Critic Says, as Reti Welcomes Pacific Peoples Role', *RNZ*, December 9, 2023, https://www.rnz.co.nz/international/pacific-news/504311/pasifika-standing-with-maori-govt-critic-says-as-reti-welcomes-pacific-peoples-role
19 Halpin, James, 'Efeso Collins Says His Skin Colour Cost Him 20,000 Votes in Auckland Mayoral Race', *RNZ*, November 3, 2022, https://rnz.co.nz/news/political/477993/efeso-collins-says-his-skin-colour-cost-him-20-000-votes-in-auckland-mayoral-race
20 'Model minority' refers to a person from a minority population who is docile and achieves at higher rates than the majority of their population.
21 A settler state is one where the colonial process has meant the settlers invaded, stayed, and set up their own governing state.
22 Bedford, Richard, 'Skilled Migration in and out of New Zealand: Immigrants, Workers, Students and Emigrants', in Bob Birell, Lesleyanne Hawthorne, and Sue Richardson (eds), *Evaluation of the General Skilled Migration Categories Report*, Commonwealth of Australia, 2006, pp. 221–25; Fraenkel, Jon, 'Pacific Islands and New Zealand – Immigration and Aid', *Te Ara – the Encyclopedia of New Zealand*, https://teara.govt.nz/mi/pacific-islands-and-new-zealand/print; Lay, Graeme, *Pacific New Zealand*, David Ling Publishing, 1996; Te Punga Somerville, Alice, *Once Were Pacific: Māori Connections to Oceania*, University of Minnesota Press, 2012.
23 Tecun, Arcia, Sankar, Anisha and Lana Lopesi (eds), *Towards a Grammar of Race in Aotearoa New Zealand*, Bridget Williams Books.
24 Ahmed, Sara, 'A Phenomenology of Whiteness', *Feminist Theory*, vol. 8, no. 2, 2007, pp. 149–68.
25 Mills, Charles W., *The Racial Contract*, Cornell University Press, 1997.
26 Ibid., p. 3.
27 Bonilla-Silva, Eduardo, 'Rethinking Racism: Toward a Structural Interpretation', *American Sociological Review*, vol. 63, no. 3, 1997, pp. 465–80: 469.
28 Myers, Lesli C., and Kara S. Finnigan, 'Using Data to Guide Difficult Conversations Around Structural Racism', *Voices in Urban Education*, vol. 48, 2018, pp. 38–45.
29 Henry, Frances, Enakshi Dua, Carl E. James, Audrey Kobayashi, Peter Li, Howard Ramos, and Malinda S. Smith, *The Equity Myth: Racialization and Indigeneity at Canadian Universities*, UBC Press, 2017.

## HISTORY – 'They Call Me a Bunga'
## Colonialism, History and Stereotypes in Aotearoa New Zealand

1 The Spinoff, 'Irrefutable Proof Taika Waititi Is Wrong and NZ Is Not Racist as Fuck', *The Spinoff*, April 9, 2018, https://thespinoff.co.nz/media/09-04-2018/irrefutable-proof-taika-waititi-is-wrong-and-nz-is-not-racist-as-fuck

2 While this comment is specific to Polynesians and not other Pacific peoples, the stereotypes in this chapter are common in reference to all Pacific peoples. In relation to Waititi's comments, Māori may also be included here as Polynesians. See: Te Punga Somerville, Alice, *Once Were Pacific: Māori Connections to Oceania*, University of Minnesota Press, 2012.
3 RNZ, 'Breach Upheld Over Kiwi Talkback Host Heather du Plessis-Allan's Pacific Leeches Comments', *RNZ*, April 4, 2019, https://www.rnz.co.nz/international/pacific-news/386314/breach-upheld-over-kiwi-talkback-host-heather-du-plessis-allan-s-pacific-leeches-comments
4 Latif, Justin, 'Amid Racism, Rumour and Fear Mongering, South Auckland Stands Up for Affected Family', *The Spinoff*, August 19, 2020, https://thespinoff.co.nz/auckland/19-08-2020/amid-racism-rumour-and-fear-mongering-south-auckland-stands-up-for-affected-family
5 Rawhiti-Connell, Anna, 'Dawn Raids Apology "Hollow" as Report Finds "Unusual" Lack of Follow-up', *The Spinoff*, July 11, 2023, https://thespinoff.co.nz/the-bulletin/11-07-2023/dawn-raids-apology-hollow-as-report-finds-unusual-lack-of-follow-up
6 Creak, Gabriel (@GabrielCreak), 'Stop? They Need to Return.', X, July 11, 2023, 9:10 a.m.; @jason_recliner (@jason_recliner), 'Apologising to the Dawn Raids Illegal Overstayers is Like Apologizing to Someone Who Got Arrested for Stealing Your Car', X, July 10, 2023, 4:42 p.m.
7 Neilson, Michael, 'David Seymour's Pacific Minister Guy Fawkes Comment: Calls Mount for Apology, PM Chris Hipkins Says Act leader "Should Be Ashamed of Himself"', *New Zealand Herald*, August 22, 2023, https://www.nzherald.co.nz/nz/politics/david-seymours-pacific-minister-guy-fawkes-comment-calls-mount-for-apology-pm-chris-hipkins-says-act-leader-should-be-ashamed-of-himself/2QLEE4XXWNBBRMF3WK2LV5EQIM/
8 Privilege for Pākehā in New Zealand society is often ignored, while those who do not have the same advantages are frequently seen as having some type of 'special' access to benefits. See: Borell, Belinda, Amanda Gregory, Tim McCreanor, Victoria Jensen, and Helen E. Moewaka Barnes, '"It's Hard at the Top but It's a Whole Lot Easier than Being at the Bottom": The Role of Privilege in Understanding Disparities in Aotearoa/New Zealand', *Race/Ethnicity: Multidisciplinary Global Contexts*, 2009, pp. 29–50.
9 Ahmed, Sara, 'A Phenomenology of Whiteness', *Feminist Theory*, vol. 8, no. 2, 2007, pp. 149–68: 154; see also: Fanon, Frantz, *Black Skin, White Masks*, Grove Press, 1967.
10 Skinner-Dorkenoo, Alison, Megan George, James Wages, Sirenia Sánchez, and Sylvia Perry, 'A Systemic Approach to the Psychology of Racial Bias within Individuals and Society', *Nature Reviews Psychology*, vol. 2, 2023, pp. 392–406.
11 Banaji, Mahzarin, Susan Fiske, and Douglas Massey, 'Systemic Racism: Individuals and Interactions, Institutions and Society', *Cognitive Research*, vol. 6, 2021, article no. 82.
12 The 'land of milk and honey' is a common reference to how our Pacific ancestors, as they moved to New Zealand, viewed their new life and opportunities: Māhina-Tuai, Kolokesa, 'A Land of Milk and Honey? Education

and Employment Migration Schemes in the Postwar Era', in Sean Mallon, Kolokesa Māhina-Tuai, and Damon Salesa (eds), *Tangata o le Moana: New Zealand and the People of the Pacific*, Te Papa Press, 2012, pp. 161–78.

13  Comedy often has the potential to make social commentary and invert expectations. Prior to *bro'Town*, 'Milburn Place' on the TV show *Skitz* also focused on stereotypes; Pearson, Sarina, 'Subversion and Ambivalence: Pacific Islanders on New Zealand Prime Time', *The Contemporary Pacific*, vol. 11, no. 2, 1999, pp. 361–88.

14  Teaiwa, Teresia, and Sean Mallon, 'Ambivalent Kinships? Pacific People in New Zealand', in James H. Liu, Tim McCreanor, Tracey McIntosh, and Teresia Teaiwa (eds), *New Zealand Identities: Departures and Destinations*, Victoria University Press, 2006, pp. 401–47; Anae, Melani, 'Put-Downs Turned Round – T-Shirts as Cultural History Canvases', in Mallon, Māhina-Tuai, and Salesa (eds), *Tangata o le Moana*, p. 237.

15  Anae, Melani, 'From Kava to Coffee: The "Browning" of Auckland', in Ian Carter, David Craig, and Steve Matthewman (eds), *Almighty Auckland?*, Dunmore Press, 2004, pp. 89–110.

16  Featuring Chris Alosio and cinematographer Bevan Crothers; Parata, Anahera (director), *Bunga* (television), New Zealand On Air, 2019.

17  SWIDT, *Bunga*, line 2.

18  Verner-Pula, Allyssa, 'They Call Me Bunga', *Craccum*, July 26, 2021.

19  One News, 'Hip Hop Group Swidt Highlight Pasifika Issues within NZ Culture, in New Single Bunga', *One News*, October 31, 2019, https://www.1news.co.nz/2019/10/30/hip-hop-group-swidt-highlight-pasifika-issues-within-nz-culture-in-new-single-bunga/

20  Ibid.

21  Leenen-Young, Marcia, '"Guardians" of Signatures? Future Directions in Pacific History from a Pacific Early Career Academic in Aotearoa', *Journal of New Zealand Studies*, vol. 33, 2021, pp. 36–54.

22  Ideally, the lyrics of *Bunga* would have been analysed line by line, but these stereotypes are repeated and so the citation of lyrics is not in order. However, I have referenced the song by line wherever possible.

23  Teaiwa and Mallon, 'Ambivalent Kinships?' The term 'historically disadvantaged populations' was coined by the United Nations in 1948: Estes, Richard, 'Disadvantaged Populations', in Alex C. Michalos (ed.), *Encyclopedia of Quality of Life and Well-Being Research*, Springer, 2014, pp. 1654–58.

24  Salesa, Damon, 'New Zealand's Pacific', in Giselle Byrnes (ed.), *The New Oxford History of New Zealand*, Oxford University Press, 2009, pp. 149–72.

25  Meihana, Peter, *Privilege in Perpetuity: Exploding a Pākehā Myth*, Bridget Williams Books, 2023.

26  New Zealand's colonial territories in the Pacific will be referred to as an empire in this chapter: Salesa, Damon, 'A Pacific Destiny: New Zealand's Overseas Empire, 1840–1945', in Mallon, Māhina-Tuai, and Salesa (eds), *Tangata o le Moana*, pp. 97–121.

27  Salesa, ibid.

28  HC Deb 17 June, 1845, vol. 81, pp. 669–70 (Charles Buller).

29   This is evident in the actions of the New Zealand leaders over this period: George Grey (Governor 1845–53; 1861–68; Premier 1877–79), Julius Vogel (Premier 1873–75; 1876), Robert Stout (Premier 1884; 1884–87); and Richard Seddon (Premier 1893–1900; Prime Minister 1900–1906).
30   Salesa, 'A Pacific Destiny', in Mallon, Māhina-Tuai, and Salesa (eds), *Tangata o le Moana*.
31   Arvin, Maile Renee, *Possessing Polynesians: The Science of Settler Colonial Whiteness in Hawai'i and Oceania*, Duke University Press, 2019.
32   Ausubel, David P., *The Fern and the Tiki: An American View of New Zealand National Character, Social Attitudes, and Race Relations*, Angus and Robertson, 1961.
33   'Thus it is now generally acknowledged that *The Fern and the Tiki* will be remembered as the provocative little book that played a limited but significant role – alongside Dame Whina Cooper's land march, the occupation of Bastion Point, and the Springbok Tour protests – in forever changing the social and political landscape of Aotearoa-New Zealand': Kersey, Harry A., 'Opening a Discourse on Race Relations in New Zealand: The Fern and the Tiki Revisited', *Journal of New Zealand Studies*, vol. 1, 2002, p. 16.
34   Ausubel, *The Fern and the Tiki*, pp. 149–50. For discussion on the belief that New Zealand is superior in race relations globally: Sinclair, Keith, 'Why Are Race Relations in New Zealand Better Than in South Africa, South Australia or South Dakota?', *New Zealand Journal of History*, vol. 5, no. 2, 1971, pp. 121–27; Belich, James, *The New Zealand Wars and the Victorian Interpretation of Racial Conflict*, Auckland University Press, 2013; Salesa, Damon, *Racial Crossings: Race, Intermarriage, and the Victorian British Empire*, Oxford University Press, 2011; Kidman, Joanna, Vincent O'Malley, Liana MacDonald, Tom Roa, and Keziah Wallis, *Fragments from a Contested Past: Remembrance, Denial and New Zealand History*, Bridget Williams Books, 2022.
35   Meihana, *Privilege in Perpetuity*.
36   Salesa, Damon, *Island Time: New Zealand's Pacific Futures*, Bridget Williams Books, 2017, p. 94.
37   Firth, Stewart, 'Colonial Administration and the Invention of the Native', in Donald Denoon and Stewart Firth (eds), *The Cambridge History of the Pacific Islanders*, Cambridge University Press, 1997, pp. 260–80.
38   Wendt, Albert, 'Towards a New Oceania', *Mana Review*, vol. 1, no. 1, pp. 49–60, republished in Guy Amirthanayagam (ed.), *Writers in East–West Encounter*, Palgrave Macmillan, 1987, p. 207.
39   Museum of New Zealand Te Papa Tongarewa, 'T-Shirts as Canvases', n.d., https://collections.tepapa.govt.nz/topic/1545#:~:text=Another%20derogatory%20 term%20used%20by,colour%2C%20especially%20a%20Pacific%20Islander; see also, Loto, Robert, Darrin Hodgetts, Kerry Chamberlain, Linda Waimarie Nikora, Rolinda Karapu, and Alison Barnett, 'Pasifika in the News: The Portrayal of Pacific Peoples in the New Zealand Press', *Journal of Community & Applied Social Psychology*, vol. 16, no. 2, 2006, pp. 100–118.
40   Lolohea, Alice, 'SWIDT Preview Brand New Album with the Release of BUNGA', *Tangata Pasifika*, October 24, 2019, https://tpplus.co.nz/entertainment/swidt-preview-brand-new-album-with-the-release-of-bunga/

41 Westcott, Kathryn, 'At last – an Explanation for "Bunga Bunga"', *BBC*, February 5, 2011, https://www.bbc.com/news/world-europe-12325796; Dunley, Richard, 'Bunga Bunga! The Great Edwardian Dreadnought Hoax', *The National Archives Blog*, October 16, 2017, https://blog.nationalarchives.gov.uk/bunga-bunga-great-edwardian-dreadnought-hoax/

42 The lyrics of *Bunga* quoted here and throughout this chapter are from: https://genius.com/Swidt-bunga-lyrics

43 Dunmore, John (ed.), *The Pacific Journal of Louis-Antoine de Bougainville, 1767–1768*, The Hakluyt Society, Series III, no. 9, 2002, p. 63.

44 Enlightenment thinker Jean-Jacques Rousseau is attributed with the development of the noble savage trope: men who were pure, primordial and child-like before they were corrupted by civilisation: Rousseau, Jean-Jacques, *A Discourse upon the Origins and Foundations of Inequality among Mankind*, anonymously translated, Lenox Hill Pub. & Dist. Co., [1761] 1971. European explorers often lamented the corruption of this pure state by contact with Europeans; see: Lee, Ida (ed.), *Captain Bligh's Second Voyage to the South Sea*, Longmans Green and Co., 1920, pp. 74, 87; Beaglehole, J. C. (ed.), *The Journals of Captain James Cook, I: The Voyage of the Endeavour 1768–1771*, Cambridge University Press, 1955, p. 99; *The Journals of Captain James Cook, II: The Voyage of the Resolution and Adventure 1772–1775*, Cambridge University Press, 1961, pp. 174–75; Cook, James, *A Voyage to the Pacific Ocean, II*, W. and A. Strahan, 1784, p. 136; Forster, George, *A Voyage Round the World*, University of Hawai'i Press, 2000, p. 121.

45 Dworkin, Gerald, 'Paternalism', in Edward N. Zalta (ed.), *The Stanford Encyclopedia of Philosophy* (Fall 2020 Edition), https://plato.stanford.edu/archives/fall2020/entries/paternalism/

46 This is a complex topic. See Vartije, Devin, 'Revisiting Enlightenment Racial Classification: Time and the Question of Human Diversity', *Intellectual History Review*, vol. 31, no. 4, 2021, pp. 603–25.

47 Durmont D'Urville, Jules, 'Sur les Îles du Grand Océan', *Bulletin de la Société de Géographie*, vol. 17, 1832, pp. 1–21.

48 Arvin, *Possessing Polynesians: The Science of Settler Colonial Whiteness in Hawai'i and Oceania*.

49 Anonymous, 'The Brain of the Native', *Pacific Islands Monthly*, February 21, 1938, p. 63.

50 Australian Department of Defence, Australian War Memorial, *Ex-German New Guinea Miscellaneous Reports January–February 1920*, March 14, 1919 (Governor Johnston to Secretary); see also Firth, 'Colonial Administration', 1997, p. 263.

51 Chairman McDonald to Rev. J. W. Burton, January 26, 1923, MM F; cited in MacNaught, Timothy J., *The Fijian Colonial Experience: A Study of the Neotraditional Order Under British Colonial Rule Prior to World War II*, ANU Press, 2016.

52 Cook Islands, *Cook and Other Islands Parliamentary Papers*, Appendices to the Journals of the House of Representatives, no. 214, Session II, 1906, A3, p. 102 (Walter Gudgeon).

53 An example of this is New Zealand Resident Commissioner Walter Gudgeon, who set up the first land court in the Cook Islands in 1903; see: Crocombe, Ron, *Land Tenure in the Cook Islands*, Oxford University Press, 1964.

54 Field, Michael, *Mau: Samoa's Struggle for Freedom*, Polynesian Press, 1991.
55 As seen in *Moby Dick* with the character Queequeg, the harpooner on board the *Pequod*.
56 Robertson, Christopher, 'Fiji Sugar Industry', *Economic Geography*, vol. 7, no. 4, 1931, pp. 400–11; Bartholomew, Duane, Richard Hawkins, and Johnny Lopez, 'Hawaii Pineapple: The Rise and Fall of an Industry', *HortScience*, vol. 47, no. 10, 2012, 1390–98.
57 There were, of course, exceptions, but this is the general pattern of life established with the rise of European industry in the Pacific.
58 This can be seen in the establishment of the scholarship scheme in the Pacific to educate a select few in the Western tradition: Leenen-Young, Marcia, and Sereana Naepi, 'Gathering Pandanus Leaves: Colonisation, Internationalisation, and the Pacific', *Journal of International Students*, vol. 11, no. S1, 2021, pp. 15–31.
59 Salesa, *Island Time*.
60 Smith, Stephenson Percy, *Niuē-fekai (or Savage) Island and Its People*, Whitcombe & Tombs, 1903.
61 Kidnapping was a typical tactic used by Cook: Beaglehole, John, 'The Death of Captain Cook', *Historical Studies Australia and New Zealand*, vol. 11, no. 43, 1964, pp. 289–305.
62 Macdonald, Barrie, 'Pacific Immigration and the Politicians', *Comment*, vol. 1, no. 1, 1977; see also: RNZ, *Untold Pacific History, Episode 1: The Dawn Raids*, https://www.youtube.com/watch?v=fueGYb822xQ
63 One News, 'Hip Hop Group Swidt Highlight Pasifika Issues'.

## ECONOMY – Is the Migrant Dream a Capitalist Dream?
Pacific Peoples and the Economy

1 New Zealand Treasury, *The New Zealand Pacific Economy*, November 2018, https://www.beehive.govt.nz/sites/default/files/2018-11/NZ%20Pacific%20 Economy%20Report%2013%20November%202018_0.pdf
2 Matada Research, *The $7 Cabbage Dilemma: Pacific Peoples and New Zealand's COVID-19 Response*, July 2022, https://matadaresearch.co.nz/wp-content/uploads/ The-7-cabbage-dilemma-Pacific-peoples-New-Zealands-COVID-19-response.pdf
3 Leenen-Young, Marcia, Sereana Naepi, Patrick Thomsen, David Taufui Mikato Faʻavae, Moeata Keil, and Jacoba Matapo, '"Pillars of the Colonial Institution Are Like a Knowledge Prison": The Significance of Decolonizing Knowledge and Pedagogical Practice for Pacific Early Career Academics in Higher Education', *Teaching in Higher Education*, vol. 26, nos. 7–8, 2021, pp. 986–1001; Naepi, Sereana, Tara McAllister, Patrick Thomsen, Marcia Leenen-Young, Leilani A. Walker, Anna L. McAllister, Reremoana Theodore, Joanna Kidman, and Tamasailau Suaaliia, 'The Pakaru "Pipeline": Māori and Pasifika Pathways within the Academy', *New Zealand Annual Review of Education*, vol. 24, 2019, pp. 142–59; Thomsen, Patrick, Marcia Leenen-Young, Sereana Naepi, Karamia Müller, Sam Manuela, Sisikula Sisifa, and Tim Baice, 'In Our Own Words: Pacific Early Career Academics (PECA) and Pacific Knowledges in Higher Education Pedagogical Praxis', *Higher Education Research & Development*, vol. 40, no. 1, 2021, pp. 49–62.

4   Crampton, Peter, Jo Baxter, and Zoe Bristowe, 'Selection of Māori Students into Medicine: Re-imagining Merit', *New Zealand Medical Journal*, vol. 134, no. 1543, 2021, pp. 59–68; Young, Iris Marion, 'Affirmative Action and the Myth of Merit', in Iris Marion Young and Danielle S. Allen (eds), *Justice and the Politics of Difference*, Princeton University Press, 2022, pp. 192–225.
5   Gonzalez, Carmen G., 'Climate Change, Race, and Migration', *Journal of Law and Political Economy*, vol. 1, no. 1, 2020, pp. 109–46: 112.
6   Marx, Karl, *Capital: A Critique of Political Economy* (vol. 1), Marx/Engels Internet Archive (marxists.org), 1995; Wallerstein, Immanuel, *The Capitalist World-Economy*, Cambridge University Press, 1979.
7   'Racialised bodies' refers to how a person's skin colour is given meaning over time. So, for example, to have brown skin in Aotearoa New Zealand can signify lazy, as explained in the 'History' chapter in this book. See Ahmed, Sara, 'Racialized Bodies', in Mary Evans and Ellie Lee (eds), *Real Bodies: A Sociological Introduction*, Palgrave, 2002, pp. 46–63.
8   Teaiwa, Katerina, 'Ruining Pacific Islands: Australia's Phosphate Imperialism', *Australian Historical Studies*, vol. 46, no. 3, 2015, pp. 374–91.
9   Mitchell, Claire, 'The Angry Sea Will Kill Us All', *Stuff*, October 2017, https://interactives.stuff.co.nz/2017/10/kiribati-the-angry-sea-will-kill-us-all/
10  Teaiwa, 'Ruining Pacific Islands', p. 387.
11  Teaiwa, Katerina, *Consuming Ocean Island: Stories of People and Phosphate from Banaba*, Indiana University Press, 2014.
12  Ibid.; Teaiwa, 'Ruining Pacific Islands'.
13  Shennan, Jennifer, 'The Banabans of Rabi', *New Zealand Geographic*, no. 80, July–August 2006, https://www.nzgeo.com/stories/the-banabans-of-rabi/
14  International Center for Advocates Against Discrimination, *The Displacement and Dispossession of Banaba: Justice for Rabi*, February 2, 2023, https://icaad.ngo/2023/02/27/the-displacement-and-dispossession-of-banaba-an-overview/
15  Ministry for Pacific Peoples, *Pacific Wellbeing Strategy*, 2022, https://www.mpp.govt.nz/programmes/all-of-government-pacific-wellbeing-strategy/
16  Tuiburelevu, Litia, and Hugo Wagner-Hiliau, 'Pick Your Own Damn Fruit', *E-Tangata*, November 1, 2020, https://e-tangata.co.nz/comment-and-analysis/pick-your-own-damn-fruit/
17  Leenen-Young, Marcia, and Sereana Naepi, 'Gathering Pandanus Leaves: Colonization, Internationalization, and the Pacific', *Journal of International Students*, vol. 11, no. S1, 2021, pp. 15–31.
18  New Zealand Human Rights Commission, 'Pacific Pay Gap Inquiry', New Zealand Human Rights Commission, 2022, https://pacificpaygap.hrc.co.nz
19  Ibid.
20  Stats NZ, 'Earnings for People in Paid Employment by Region, Sex, Age Groups and Ethnic Groups', https://nzdotstat.stats.govt.nz/wbos/Index.aspx
21  McAllister, Tara, Jesse Kokaua, Sereana Naepi, Joanna Kidman, and Reremoana Theodore, 'Glass Ceilings in New Zealand Universities: Inequities in Māori and Pacific Promotions and Earnings', *MAI Journal*, vol. 9, no. 3, 2020, pp. 91–102.
22  Fair Pay Agreements Act 2022.
23  Employment New Zealand, 'The Repeal of Fair Pay Agreements Legislation',

https://www.employment.govt.nz/about/news-and-updates/the-repeal-of-fair-pay-agreements-legislation/

## EDUCATION – Structural Racism and Education in Aotearoa

1. Fanon, Frantz, *Black Skin, White Masks*, Grove Press, 1967.
2. Hall, Stuart, *Representation: Cultural Representations and Signifying Practices*, Sage, 1997, p. 214.
3. Derrida, Jacques, *Positions*, University of Chicago Press, 1972.
4. Hall, *Representation*, p. 225 (emphasis in original).
5. Bhabha, Homi K., *The Location of Culture*, Routledge, 1994.
6. Hall, *Representation*, p. 230.
7. Allen, Jean M., and Melinda Webber, 'Stereotypes of Minorities and Education', in Steven Ratuva (ed.), *The Palgrave Handbook of Ethnicity*, Palgrave Macmillan, 2019, pp. 1–21.
8. Ibid., p. 3.
9. Fanon, *Black Skin, White Masks*; Hall, *Representation*; Helsby, Wendy, *Understanding Representation*, BFI, 2005; Wetherell, Margaret, *Mapping the Language of Racism: Discourse and the Legitimation of Exploitation*, Columbia University Press, 1993.
10. Wetherell, ibid.
11. Ibid., p. 84.
12. Liu, James H., Tim McCreanor, Tracey McIntosh, and Teresia Teaiwa, 'Introduction: Constructing New Zealand Identities', in James H. Liu, Tim McCreanor, Tracey McIntosh, and Teresia Teaiwa (eds), *New Zealand Identities: Departures and Destinations*, Victoria University Press, 2006, pp. 14–32.
13. Fanon, *Black Skin, White Masks*; Logan, Camille, 'Body Politics and the Experience of Blackness within the Field of Education', in George J. S. Dei and Marlon Simmons (eds), *Fanon & Education: Thinking Through Pedagogical Possibilities*, Peter Lang, 2010, pp. 11–20.
14. Hall, *Representation*, p. 233
15. Logan, 'Body Politics', in Dei and Simmons (eds), *Fanon & Education*.
16. Fanon, *Black Skin, White Masks*, p. 51.
17. Logan, 'Body Politics', in Dei and Simmons (eds), *Fanon & Education*.
18. Liu, James H., 'History and Identity: A System of Checks and Balances for Aotearoa/New Zealand', in Liu, McCreanor, McIntosh, and Teaiwa (eds), *New Zealand Identities*, pp. 69–89: 77.
19. O'Connor, Peter, 'A Suicide of the Soul: Neoliberalism, the Arts and Democracy', in Vicki Carpenter and Sue Osborne (eds), *Twelve Thousand Hours. Education and Poverty in Aotearoa New Zealand*, Dunmore, 2014, pp. 260–64.
20. Fanon, *Black Skin, White Masks*, p. vii.
21. Hodgetts, Darin, Bridgette Masters, and Neville Robertson, 'Media Coverage of "Decades of Disparity" in Ethnic Mortality in Aotearoa', *Journal of Community & Applied Social Psychology*, vol. 14, no. 6, 2004, pp. 455–72: 459.
22. United Nations General Assembly, *United Nations Declaration on the Rights of Indigenous Peoples*, 2007, https://www.un.org/development/desa/indigenouspeoples/wp-content/uploads/sites/19/2018/11/UNDRIP_E_web.pdf

23 Fanon, *Black Skin, White Masks*.
24 Ibid., p. 48.
25 Fepuleaʻi, Damon (director), *Dawn Raids* (television), Isola Productions, Auckland, New Zealand, 2005.
26 ʻOfa Kolo, Finau, 'An Incident in Otara: The Media and Pacific Island Communities', in Paul Spoonley and Walter Hirsh (eds), *Between the Lines: Racism and the New Zealand Media*, Heinemann Reed, 1990, pp. 120–22.
27 Ibid.
28 Ibid.; Fepuleaʻi, *Dawn Raids*.
29 Hodgetts, Masters, and Robertson, 'Media Coverage'.
30 Fanon, *Black Skin, White Masks*; Spoonley, Paul, 'Racism, Race Relations and the Media', in Spoonley and Hirsh (eds), *Between the Lines*, pp. 26–37.
31 Fanon, *Black Skin, White Masks*, p. 98.
32 Milne, Ann, *Coloring in the White Spaces: Reclaiming Cultural Identity in Whitestream Schools*, Peter Lang, 2017.
33 Codd, John, and Roger Openshaw, 'The Education System in Aotearoa New Zealand', in Paul Adams, Roger Openshaw, and Judith Hamer (eds), *Education and Society in Aotearoa New Zealand* (2nd ed.), Thomson, 2005, pp. 155–86.
34 Stephenson, Maxine, 'Thinking Historically: Māori and Settler Education', in Elizabeth Rata and Ros Sullivan (eds), *Introduction to the History of New Zealand Education*, Pearson, 2009, pp. 1–15.
35 Salesa, Damon, *Island Time: New Zealand's Pacific Futures*, Bridget Williams Books, 2017.
36 Yao, Esther S., Pat Bullen, Kane Meissel, Jemaima Tiatia, Theresa Fleming, and Terryann C. Clark, 'Effects of Ethnic Classification on Substantive Findings in Adolescent Mental Health Outcomes', *Journal of Youth and Adolescence*, vol. 51, no. 8, 2022, pp. 1581–96: 1582.
37 Education Counts, 'Ethnic Group Codes', December 2023, https://www.educationcounts.govt.nz/data-services/code-sets-and-classifications/ethnic_group_codes
38 Ibid.
39 Ibid.
40 Teaiwa, Teresia, and Sean Mallon, 'Ambivalent Kinships? Pacific People in New Zealand', in Liu, McCreanor, McIntosh, and Teaiwa (eds), *New Zealand Identities*, pp. 401–47: 409.
41 Zodgekar, Arvind, 'The Changing Face of New Zealand's Population and National Identity', in Liu, McCreanor, McIntosh, and Teaiwa (eds), *New Zealand Identities*, pp. 268–94: 268.
42 Hall, *Representation*, 1997.
43 Hosking, Mike, 'Don't Judge a School by Its Number', *New Zealand Herald*, November 13, 2014, https://www.nzherald.co.nz/nz/mike-hosking-dont-judge-a-school-by-its-number/DNMMR5QBHYEL2BUHPBVR32KLCA/
44 Churchward, Clerk M., *Tongan Dictionary: Tongan–English and English–Tongan* (Special Limited Edition), Government of Tonga, 2015.
45 Faʻavae, David T. M., Ruth Faleolo, 'Elisapesi Hepi Havea, Dion Enari, Tepora Wright, and Alvin Chand, 'E-Talanoa as an Online Research Method: Extending

Vā–Relations across Spaces', *AlterNative: An International Journal of Indigenous Peoples*, vol. 18, no. 3, 2022, pp. 391–401.

46  Iosefo, Fetaui, in discussion with the author, August 3, 2022.
47  Havea, 'Elisapesi Hepi, Farita T. Wright, and Alvin Chand, 'Going Back and Researching in the Pacific Community', *Waikato Journal of Education*, vol. 25, no. 1, 2020, pp. 131–43.
48  Kidman, Joanna, and Cherie Chu, '"We're Not the Hottest Ethnicity": Pacific Scholars and the Cultural Politics of New Zealand Universities', *Globalisation, Societies and Education*, vol. 17, no. 4, 2019, pp. 489–99: 489.
49  Ka'ili, Tevita O., *Marking Indigeneity: The Tongan Art of Sociospatial Relations*, University of Arizona Press, 2017.
50  Tertiary Education Commission, 'Performance-Based Research Fund', *Tertiary Education Commission*, November 30, 2023, https://www.tec.govt.nz/funding/funding-and-performance/funding/fund-finder/pbrf/
51  McAllister, Tara, Jesse Kokaua, Sereana Naepi, Joanna Kidman, and Reremoana Theodore, 'Glass Ceilings in New Zealand Universities: Inequities in Māori and Pacific Promotions and Earnings', *MAI Journal*, vol. 9, no. 3, 2020, pp. 91–102.
52  Ibid.
53  Smith, Graham Hingangaroa, and Linda Tuhiwai Smith, 'Doing Indigenous Work: Decolonising and Transforming the Academy', in Elizabeth. A. McKinley and L. T. Smith (eds), *Handbook of Indigenous Education*, Springer, 2018, pp. 1–27.
54  Tuagalu, I'uogafa, 'Heuristics of the Vā', *AlterNative: An International Journal of Indigenous Peoples*, vol. 4, no. 1, 2008, pp. 107–26.
55  Smith, Jo T., 'Postcolonial Affirmations: The Return of the Dusky Maiden in Sima Urale's *Velvet Dreams*', *Continuum*, vol. 22, no. 1, 2008, pp. 79–88: 82.
56  Thiong'o, Ngũgĩ wa, *Moving the Centre: The Struggle for Cultural Freedoms*, J. Currey, 1993.
57  Yao, Bullen, Meissel, Tiatia, Fleming, and Clark, 'Effects of Ethnic Classification'.
58  Ualesi, Yvonne, 'Culturally Responsive, Sustaining and Safe Youth Mentoring Practice in Aotearoa New Zealand – A Va Relational Approach', PhD thesis, University of Auckland, 2021.
59  Smith, Hinekura, Jade Le Grice, Sonia Fonua, and David T. Mayeda, 'Coloniality, Institutional Racism and White Fragility: A Wero to Higher Education', *The Australian Journal of Indigenous Education*, vol. 51, no. 2, 2022, pp. 1–18.

## MIGRATION – Time and Race
## Pacific Migration Journeys to Aotearoa

1  Underhill-Sem, Yvonne, and Evelyn Marsters, *Labour Mobility in the Pacific: A Systematic Literature Review of Development Impacts*, New Zealand Institute for Pacific Research, 2017, https://researchspace.auckland.ac.nz/bitstream/handle/2292/39560/labour-mobility-in-the-pacific-1gcb9qb.pdf?sequence=2&isAllowed=y
2  Mila, Karlo, *Dream Fish Floating*, Huia Publishers, 2005, p. 15.
3  Collins, Francis L., 'Geographies of Migration II: Decolonising Migration Studies', *Progress in Human Geography*, vol. 46, no. 5, 2022, pp. 1241–51.

4   Efi, Tui Atua Tupua Tamasese Taisi, 'Clutter in Indigenous Knowledge, Research and History: A Samoan Perspective', *Social Policy Journal of New Zealand*, vol. 25, 2005, pp. 61–69: 68.
5   Leenen-Young, Marcia, and Lisa Uperesa, 'Re-visioning Pacific Research Method/ologies', *Journal of the Polynesian Society*, vol. 132, no. 1–2, 2023, pp. 9–39.
6   Smith, Linda Tuhiwai, *Decolonizing Methodologies: Research and Indigenous Peoples* (3rd ed.), Zed Books, 2021.
7   Anae, Melani, *The Platform: The Radical Legacy of the Polynesian Panthers*, Bridget Williams Books, 2020; Nunns, Heather, Charlotte Bedford, and Richard Bedford, *RSE Impact Study: New Zealand Stream Report*, 2019, https://www.immigration.govt.nz/documents/statistics/rse-impact-study-new-zealand-stream-report.pdf; Spoonley, Paul, 'Economic Transformation and the Racialisation of Labour', *Australian and New Zealand Journal of Sociology*, vol. 28, no. 2, 1992, pp. 157–74.
8   Leenen-Young and Uperesa, 'Re-visioning', p. 20.
9   Collins, Francis L., 'Temporary Migration', in David Hall (ed.), *Fair Borders? Migration Policy in the Twenty-First Century*, Bridget William Books, 2017, pp. 46–68.
10  Bedford, Richard, and Graeme Hugo, *Population Movement in the Pacific: A Perspective on Future Prospects*, Department of Labour, 2012, https://www.mbie.govt.nz/dmsdocument/2750-population-movement-in-the-pacific-pdf
11  Collins, 'Temporary Migration', in Hall (ed.), *Fair Borders?*, p. 51.
12  Ibid., p. 52.
13  Anae, *The Platform*.
14  Battistella, Graziano, 'Migration in Asia: In Search of a Theoretical Framework', in Graziano Battistella (ed.), *Global and Asian Perspectives on International Migration*, Springer, 2014, pp. 1–25.
15  Bedford, Richard, and Charlotte Bedford, 'How Many Seasonal Workers from the Pacific Have Been Employed in New Zealand Since the RSE Scheme Began?', *New Zealand Geographer*, vol. 79, no. 1, 2023, pp. 39–45.
16  Ibid.; New Zealand Human Rights Commission, *The RSE Scheme in Aotearoa New Zealand: A Human Rights Review*, 2022, https://tikatangata.org.nz/our-work/the-rse-scheme-in-aotearoa-new-zealand-a-human-rights-review, p. 5.
17  New Zealand Human Rights Commission, ibid., p. 2.
18  Immigration New Zealand, 'Recognised Seasonal Employer (RSE) Scheme Research', https://www.immigration.govt.nz/about-us/research-and-statistics/research-reports/recognised-seasonal-employer-rse-scheme; Ministry of Business, Innovation and Employment, 'Recognised Seasonal Employer Policy Review – Options for Consultation: Summary', https://www.mbie.govt.nz/immigration-and-tourism/immigration/recognised-seasonal-employer-policy-review/recognised-seasonal-employer-policy-review-options-for-consultation/; New Zealand Human Rights Commission, *RSE Scheme*.
19  Hugo, Graeme, 'Best Practice in Temporary Labour Migration for Development: A Perspective from Asia and the Pacific', *International Migration*, vol. 47, no. 5, 2009, pp. 23–74: 35.
20  Simon-Kumar, Rachel, 'Neoliberalism and the New Race Politics of Migration Policy: Changing Profiles of the Desirable Migrant in New Zealand', *Journal of Ethnic and Migration Studies*, vol. 41, no. 7, 2015, pp. 1172–91: 1174.

21 See 'Economy' chapter in this book.
22 Bedford and Hugo, *Population Movement*, pp. 30–31.
23 Ibid., p. 31.
24 Ibid.
25 New Zealand Ministry of Foreign Affairs and Trade, 'Our Development Cooperation Partnerships in the Pacific', https://www.mfat.govt.nz/en/aid-and-development/our-development-cooperation-partnerships-in-the-pacific, para. 1.
26 Ministry of Foreign Affairs and Trade, *Tonga Four Year Plan*, 2021, https://www.mfat.govt.nz/assets/Aid/4YPs-2021-24/Tonga-4YP.pdf, p. 5.
27 Ministry of Foreign Affairs and Trade, *Tonga*.
28 Immigration New Zealand, 'Recognised Seasonal Employer (RSE) Scheme Research'.
29 Armstrong, Ann Cheryl, Seu'ula Johansson-Fua, and Derrick Armstrong, 'Reconceptualising Inclusive Education in the Pacific', *International Journal of Inclusive Education*, vol. 27, no. 11, 2023, pp. 1177–90.
30 Immigration New Zealand, 'Green List Roles', https://www.immigration.govt.nz/new-zealand-visas/preparing-a-visa-application/working-in-nz/qualifications-for-work/green-list-occupations
31 Ibid.
32 Immigration New Zealand, 'Check the ANZSCO List', https://www.immigration.govt.nz/new-zealand-visas/preparing-a-visa-application/working-in-nz/qualifications-for-work/check-anzsco-list
33 Tu'inukuafe, Naima (former Tongan interpreter at Immigration New Zealand), in discussion with the author, September 12, 2023.
34 Beehive, 'Immigration Settings Updates', https://www.beehive.govt.nz/release/immigration-settings-updates
35 Immigration New Zealand, 'Pacific Access Category Resident Visa: Visa Details', https://www.immigration.govt.nz/new-zealand-visas/visas/visa/pacific-access-category-resident-visa; Immigration New Zealand, 'Samoan Quota Resident Visa: Visa Details', https://www.immigration.govt.nz/new-zealand-visas/visas/visa/samoan-quota-scheme-resident-visa
36 Immigration New Zealand, 'The 2023 Pacific Access Category and Samoan Quota Ballots Open in August', https://www.immigration.govt.nz/about-us/media-centre/news-notifications/the-2023-pacific-access-category-and-samoan-quota-ballots-open-in-august, para. 2.
37 Beehive, 'Samoan Immigration Quota Change Announced', https://www.beehive.govt.nz/release/samoan-immigration-quota-change-announced; Immigration New Zealand, 'The 2023 Pacific Access Category and Samoan Quota Ballots Open in August'.
38 Figure.NZ, 'People from Tonga Granted Residence Visas for New Zealand', https://figure.nz/chart/VdkCtC3r2SRqmx9v; Tonga Statistics Department, 'Census Story', https://tongastats.gov.to/census-2/population-census-3/census-story/
39 World Salaries, 'Average Salary in Tonga for 2023', https://worldsalaries.com/average-salary-in-tonga/
40 Collins, 'Temporary Migration', in Hall (ed.), *Fair Borders?*
41 Anae, *The Platform*, p. 98.

42  Mallon, Sean, Kolokesa Māhina-Tuai, and Damon Salesa (eds), *Tangata o le Moana: New Zealand and the People of the Pacific*, Te Papa Press, 2012.
43  Anae, *The Platform*.
44  Ibid.; Collins, 'Geographies of Migration II'; Ward, Colleen, and En-Yi Lin, 'Immigration, Acculturation and National Identity in New Zealand', in James Liu, Tim McCreanor, Tracey McIntosh, and Teresia Teaiwa (eds), *New Zealand Identities: Departures and Destinations*, Victoria University Press, 2006, pp. 295–334.
45  Collins, 'Temporary Migration', in Hall (ed.), *Fair Borders?*; Simon-Kumar, 'Neoliberalism', p. 1186.
46  Simon-Kumar, ibid., p. 1174.
47  Anae, *The Platform*.
48  Immigration New Zealand, 'Overstaying a Visa Expiry', https://www.immigration.govt.nz/about-us/media-centre/common-topics/overstaying-a-visa-expiry, para. 1.
49  Anae, *The Platform*, p. 47.
50  RNZ, 'Dawn Raids Review Urges New Guidelines, Possible Law Change', *RNZ*, July 10, 2023, https://www.rnz.co.nz/news/political/493488/dawn-raids-review-urges-new-guidelines-possible-law-change, para. 3.
51  Ministry of Business, Innovation and Employment, 'Release of Independent Review into Out of Hours Immigration Visits', https://www.mbie.govt.nz/about/news/review-of-processes-and-procedures-around-out-of-hours-immigration-compliance-activity/
52  Heron, Michael, and Jane Barrow, *A Review of Processes and Procedures around Out of Hours Immigration Compliance Activity, and to Identify and Recommend Potential Changes to the Process Where Required.*, 2023, https://www.mbie.govt.nz/dmsdocument/26981-mhkc-inz-out-of-hours-final-report-29-june-2023, pp. 4–57: 4, 57.
53  Anae, *The Platform*.

## CLIMATE JUSTICE – There Can Be No (Climate) Justice on Stolen Land
Pacific Peoples, Climate Change and the Law in New Zealand

1  This quote comes from one of the Tuvaluan participants of Olivia Yates's empirical research for their doctoral thesis: Yates, Olivia, 'Stories of Neighbours and Navigators: Perceptions and Implications of Climate Mobility from Tuvalu and Kiribati to Aotearoa New Zealand', PhD thesis, University of Auckland, 2022, p. 119. This chapter owes great intellectual debt to Yates's thesis and the Tuvaluan and I-Kiribati communities who contributed to their research.
2  Solofa is a pseudonym given by Yates to protect the identity of this participant.
3  McAdam, Jane, 'Conceptualizing Climate Change-Related Movement', in Jane McAdam (ed.), *Climate Change, Forced Migration, and International Law*, Oxford University Press, 2012, pp. 15–38.
4  Crossen, Teall, *The Climate Dispossessed*, Bridget Williams Books, 2020.
5  I use the term 'climate-displaced peoples' here for simplicity and brevity, not to suggest that their displacement is caused by the impacts of climate change alone.

6 Rive, Vernon, 'Safe Harbours, Closed Borders? New Zealand Legal and Policy Responses to Climate Displacement in the South Pacific', in Paul Martin, Sadeq Z. Bigdeli, Trevor Daya-Winterbottom, Willemien du Plessis, and Amanda Kennedy (eds), *The Search for Environmental Justice*, Edward Elgar Publishing, 2015, pp. 221–38.
7 Ibid.
8 Ibid.
9 Yates, 'Stories of Neighbours and Navigators'.
10 Ibid., p. 120, drawing on Cecilia Menjívar and Leisy Abrego's articulation of 'legal violence'; see Menjívar, Cecilia, and Leisy J. Abrego, 'Legal Violence: Immigration Law and the Lives of Central American Immigrants', *American Journal of Sociology*, vol. 117, no. 5, 2012, pp. 1380–421.
11 Here, I refer to the policies, including the 'immigration instructions', that the Minister of Immigration is able to make under law, specifically the Immigration Act 2009, to create various types of residency and temporary visas. See Immigration Act 2009, ss 22–24.
12 Achiume, E. Tendayi, 'Report of the Special Rapporteur on Contemporary Forms of Racism, Racial Discrimination, Xenophobia and Related Intolerance', United Nations General Assembly, Seventy-seventh Session, Agenda Item 66(a), October 25, 2022, https://promiseinstitute.law.ucla.edu/wp-content/uploads/2022/10/A_77_2990_AdvanceUneditedVersion.pdf
13 Gonzalez, Carmen, 'Climate Change, Race, and Migration', *Journal of Law and Political Economy*, vol. 1, no. 1, 2020, pp. 109–46.
14 Ibid., p. 112.
15 As Gonzalez notes, 'racialised' or 'racialisation' refers to 'the process through which some bodies are privileged while others are classified as inferior or deficient on the basis of the distinct set of markers adopted in a particular region or nation at a particular time'; Gonzalez, ibid., p. 112.
16 Leong, Nancy, 'Racial Capitalism', *Harvard Law Review*, vol. 126, no. 8, 2013, pp. 2153–54: 2153. Here, I bring together Gonzalez's definition and this different but consistent conception of racial capitalism by Nancy Leong, thus proposing that within the 'world system' of racial capitalism that Gonzalez describes, there is the 'process' of racial capitalism that Leong describes.
17 Here I simply define a 'setter-colonial state' as a system of government that only has authority and power because it dispossesses Indigenous peoples of their land and denies them their sovereignty. See Aikman, Pounamu Jade William Emery, 'Tenants in Our Own Land? Racism, Settler Colonialism and Māori Home Ownership', in Arcia Tecun, Anisha Sankar, and Lana Lopesi (eds), *Towards a Grammar of Race in Aotearoa New Zealand*, Bridget Williams Books, 2022, pp. 49–60: 54; Wolfe, Patrick, *Traces of History: Elementary Structures of Race*, Verso, 2016.
18 Aikman, ibid.
19 Ibid.
20 Yates, 'Stories of Neighbours and Navigators', pp. 119–20.
21 Here, I adapt the title used by *The Guardian*'s multimedia series on the realities of climate-change-related displacement; see 'An Impossible Choice: The Pacific's

Climate Crisis', *The Guardian*, 2021–22, https://www.theguardian.com/world/series/an-impossible-choice-the-pacific-climate-crisis

22 Rive, 'Safe Harbours' in Martin, Bigdeli, Daya-Winterbottom, du Plessis, and Kennedy (eds), *The Search for Environmental Justice*.

23 Farbotko, Carol, 'Voluntary Immobility: Indigenous Voices in the Pacific', *Forced Migration Review*, vol. 57, 2018, pp. 81–83; McNamara, Karen, Robin Bronen, Fernando Nishara, and Silja Klepp, 'The Complex Decision-Making of Climate-Induced Relocation: Adaptation and Loss and Damage', *Climate Policy*, vol. 18, no. 1, 2018, pp. 111–17.

24 Yates, 'Stories of Neighbours and Navigators'.

25 Ibid., pp. 119–20.

26 Immigration Act 2009, ss 22–24.

27 Immigration New Zealand, 'Pacific Access Category Resident Visa', https://www.immigration.govt.nz/new-zealand-visas/visas/visa/pacific-access-category-resident-visa

28 Ibid.

29 Immigration New Zealand, 'Samoan Quota Resident Visa', https://www.immigration.govt.nz/new-zealand-visas/visas/visa/Samoan-quota-scheme-resident-visa

30 Kalapu is the pseudonym given to protect the identity of this participant.

31 Yates, 'Stories of Neighbours and Navigators', p. 120.

32 Immigration New Zealand, 'Skilled Migrant Category Resident Visa', https://www.immigration.govt.nz/new-zealand-visas/visas/visa/skilled-migrant-category-resident-visa#points

33 Immigration New Zealand, 'New Zealand Visas', https://www.immigration.govt.nz/new-zealand-visas

34 Immigration New Zealand, 'Accredited Employer Work Visa', https://www.immigration.govt.nz/new-zealand-visas/visas/visa/accredited-employer-work-visa

35 Immigration New Zealand, 'Regional Seasonal Employer Limited Visa', https://www.immigration.govt.nz/new-zealand-visas/visas/visa/recognised-seasonal-employer-limited-visa

36 Yates, 'Stories of Neighbours and Navigators', pp. 119–20.

37 Ibid., p. 130.

38 Simon-Kumar, Rachel, 'Neoliberalism and the New Race Politics of Migration Policy: Changing Profiles of the Desirable Migrant in New Zealand', *Journal of Ethnic and Migration Studies*, vol. 41, no. 7, 2015, pp. 1172–91.

39 Yates, 'Stories of Neighbours and Navigators', p. 120.

40 Tuiburelevu and Wagner-Hiliau, 'Pick Your Own Damn Fruit', *E-Tangata*, November 1, 2020, https://e-tangata.co.nz/comment-and-analysis/pick-your-own-damn-fruit/

41 Ibid.

42 Tecun, Arcia, Anisha Sankar, and Lana Lopesi, 'Colonisation and Race in New Zealand', in Arcia Tecun, Lana Lopesi, and Anisha Sankar (eds), *Towards a Grammar of Race in Aotearoa New Zealand*, Bridget Williams Books, 2022, pp. 27–37: 33.

43 Stanley, Elizabeth, 'Climate Crises and the Creation of "Undeserving" Victims', *Social Sciences*, vol. 10, no. 4, 2021, pp. 1–14: 1.

44 Borrows, Chester, '"Tough on Crime" Rhetoric Is Cheap, Easy and Terrifyingly Effective', *The Spinoff*, November 25, 2019, https://thespinoff.co.nz/politics/25-11-2019/tough-on-crime-rhetoric-cheap-easy-and-wildly-effective
45 Immigration Act 2009, s 392(2)(a).
46 Ibid., s 392(2)(b).
47 Jackson, Moana, 'Moana Jackson: No One's Exercise of Free Speech Should Make Another Feel Less Free', *E-Tangata*, May 6, 2018, https://e-tangata.co.nz/comment-and-analysis/moana-jackson-no-ones-exercise-of-free-speech-should-make-another-feel-less-free/, paras 21–22.
48 Aikman, 'Tenants in Our Own Land?', in Tecun, Sankar, and Lopesi (eds), *Towards a Grammar of Race in Aotearoa New Zealand*, pp. 49–60: 58–59.
49 Mutu, Margaret, '"To Honour the Treaty, We Must First Settle Colonisation" (Moana Jackson 2015): The Long Road from Colonial Devastation to Balance, Peace and Harmony', *Journal of the Royal Society of New Zealand*, 2019, vol. 49, pp. 4–18: 5.
50 Asafo, Dylan, 'Freedom Dreaming of Abolition in Aotearoa New Zealand: A Pacific Perspective on Tiriti-Based Abolition Constitutionalism', *Legalities*, vol. 2, no. 1, 2022, pp. 82–118: 94.
51 Marama Davidson, as quoted in Glasgow, Tim, 'Being Climate Change Refugees in NZ "A Last Resort" for Pacific People', *RNZ*, October 20, 2018, https://www.rnz.co.nz/international/pacific-news/369044/being-climate-change-refugees-in-nz-a-last-resort-for-pacific-people, para. 6.
52 Kukutai, Tahu, and Arama Rata, 'From Mainstream to Manaaki: Indigenising Our Approach to Immigration', in David Hall (ed.), *Fair Borders? Migration Policy in the Twenty-First Century*, Bridget Williams Books, 2017, pp. 36–45: 40.
53 Ibid., p. 41.
54 Yates, 'Stories of Neighbours and Navigators', p. 105.
55 Asafo, 'Freedom Dreaming'.
56 Ibid. Also, while this chapter refers to Māori and Pacific peoples as distinct groups, it is critical to note that there are many people who are both Māori and Pacific.
57 Awatere, Shaun, 'Confronting Climate Change Means Sharing Power', *E-Tangata*, July 22, 2022, https://e-tangata.co.nz/comment-and-analysis/confronting-climate-change-means-sharing-power/; Rive, 'Safe Harbours', in Martin, Bigdeli, Daya-Winterbottom, du Plessis, and Kennedy (eds), *The Search for Environmental Justice*.
58 Shrimpton, Sophie, 'Economic Neocolonialism and Free Trade in the Pacific', *Public Interest Law Journal of New Zealand*, 2021, vol. 8, pp. 81–103.
59 Office of the High Commissioner for Human Rights, *Providing Legal Options to Protect the Human Rights of Persons Displaced across International Borders Due to Climate Change: Report of the Special Rapporteur on the Promotion and Protection of Human Rights in the Context of Climate Change*, Office of the High Commissioner for Human Rights, United Nations, 2023, https://www.ohchr.org/en/documents/thematic-reports/ahrc5334-providing-legal-options-protect-human-rights-persons-displaced
60 Simon-Kumar, 'Neoliberalism'.

61 Achiume, E. Tendayi, 'Race, Refugees, and International Law', in Cathryn Costello, Michelle Foster, and Jane McAdam (eds), *The Oxford Handbook of International Refugee Law*, Oxford University Press, 2021, pp. 43–59.
62 Gonzalez, 'Climate Change', p. 120.
63 Kukutai and Rata, 'From Mainstream to Manaaki', in Hall (ed.), *Fair Borders?*, p. 44.
64 Hauʻofa, Epeli, 'Our Sea of Islands', in Eric Waddell, Vijay Naidu, and Epeli Hauʻofa (eds), *A New Oceania: Rediscovering Our Sea of Islands*, University of the South Pacific, 1993, pp. 2–16: 16.

## HEALTH – 'We Need to Get Real'
## Structural Racism and the Wellbeing of Pacific Peoples in Aotearoa

1 Health Quality and Safety Commission, *Bula Sautu: A Window on Quality 2021: Pacific Health in the Year of COVID-19*, 2021, https://www.hqsc.govt.nz/assets/Our-data/Publications-resources/BulaSautu_WEB.pdf, p. 11.
2 Ibid.
3 Ibid.
4 Sir Collin Tukuitonga, as quoted in Fagaiava-Muller, Mariner, 'Health System Systematically Racist Towards Pasifika – Report', *RNZ*, July 7, 2021, https://www.rnz.co.nz/international/pacific-news/446400/health-system-systemically-racist-towards-pasifika-report, paras 24–27.
5 Salesa, Damon, *Island Time: New Zealand's Pacific Futures*, Bridget Williams Books, 2017.
6 Statistics New Zealand, '2018 Census Population and Dwelling Counts', https://stats.govt.nz/information-releases/2018-census-population-and-dwelling-counts
7 Hart, Julian Tudor, 'The Inverse Care Law', *The Lancet*, vol. 297, no. 7696, 1971, pp. 405–12.
8 James, Jack E., 'Personalised Medicine, Disease Prevention, and the Inverse Care Law: More Harm than Benefit?', *European Journal of Epidemiology*, vol. 29, no. 6, 2014, pp. 383–90: 387.
9 Salesa, *Island Time*; Savila, Fa-asisila, Warwick Bagg, Boyd Swinburn, Bert van Der Werf, Dave Letele, Anele Bamber, Truely Harding, and Felicity Goodyear-Smith, 'Study Protocol for Evaluating Brown Buttabean Motivation (BBM): A Community-Based, Pacific-Driven Approach to Health', *BMC Public Health*, vol. 22, no. 1, 2022, pp. 1–9.
10 Marsters, Caleb, and Jemaima Tiatia-Seath, 'Young Pacific Male Rugby Players' Perceptions and Experiences of Mental Wellbeing', *Sports*, vol. 7, no. 4, 2019, pp. 1–19.
11 Jones, Camara Phyllis, 'Levels of Racism: A Theoretic Framework and a Gardener's Tale', *American Journal of Public Health*, vol. 90, no. 8, 2000, pp. 1212–15: 1212–13.
12 Ryan, Debbie, Corina Grey, and Brenden Mischewski, *Tofa Saili: A Review of Evidence about Health Equity for Pacific Peoples in New Zealand*, 2019, https://www.nzdoctor.co.nz/sites/default/files/2019-09/Tofa%20Saili-%20A%20review%20of%20evidence%20about%20health%20equity%20for%20Pacific%20Peoples%20in%20New%20Zealand.pdf

13 Kapeli, Sarah A., Sam Manuela, and Chris G. Sibley, 'Perceived Discrimination is Associated with Poorer Health and Well-being Outcomes Among Pacific Peoples in New Zealand', *Journal of Community & Applied Social Psychology*, vol. 30, no. 2, 2020, pp. 132–50.
14 Jones, 'Levels of Racism'.
15 David Seymour, as quoted in Iasona, Seni, 'ACT leader David Seymour Refuses to Apologise for "Clearly Not Serious" Guy Fawkes "Joke"', *Newshub*, August 18, 2023, https://www.newshub.co.nz/home/politics/2023/08/act-leader-david-seymour-refuses-to-apologise-for-clearly-not-serious-guy-fawkes-joke.html, para. 9.
16 Bailey, Zinzi D., Nancy Krieger, Madina Agénor, Jasime Graves, Natalia Linos, and Mary T. Bassett, 'Structural Racism and Health Inequities in the USA: Evidence and Interventions', *The Lancet*, vol. 389, no. 10077, 2017, pp. 1453–63: 1454.
17 Ibid.
18 Beagan, Brenda L., Stephanie R. Bizzeth, and Josephine Etowa, 'Interpersonal, Institutional, and Structural Racism in Canadian Nursing: A Culture of Silence', *Canadian Journal of Nursing Research*, vol. 55, no. 2, 2022, pp. 195–205; Paradies, Yin, Jehonathan Ben, Nida Denson, Amanuel Elias, Naomi Priest, Alex Pieterse, Arpana Gupta, Margaret Kelaher, and Gilbert Gee, 'Racism as a Determinant of Health: A Systematic Review and Meta-Analysis', *Public Library of Science*, vol. 10, no. 9, 2015, pp. 1–48; Reid, Papaarangi, and Bridget Robson, 'Understanding Health Inequities', in Bridget Robson and Ricci Harris (eds), *Hauora: Māori Standards of Health IV. A Study of the Years 2000–2005*, Te Rōpu Rangahau Hauora e Eru Pōmare, 2007, pp. 3–10; Talamaivao, Natalie, Ricci Harris, Donna Cormack, Sarah-Jane Paine, and Paula King, 'Racism and Health in Aotearoa New Zealand: A Systematic Review of Quantitative Studies', *New Zealand Medical Journal*, vol. 133, no. 1521, 2020, pp. 55–68; Williams, David R., and Selina A. Mohammed, 'Racism and Health I: Pathways and Scientific Evidence', *American Behavioral Scientist*, vol. 57, no. 8, 2013, pp. 1152–73.
19 UNICEF, *Worlds of Influence: Understanding What Shapes Child Well-being in Rich Countries*, 2020, https://www.unicef.org/reports/worlds-influence-what-shapes-child-well-being-rich-countries-2020
20 Martin, Hannah, '"Wake-up Call": Children Sleeping in Shelters, Cars, "Poor" Quality Homes – Study', *Stuff*, May 1, 2023, https://www.stuff.co.nz/national/health/300853733/wakeup-call-children-sleeping-in-shelters-cars-poor-quality-homes--study; RNZ, 'Food Parcels No Solution', RNZ, May 17, 2022, https://www.rnz.co.nz/international/pacific-news/467259/food-parcels-no-solution
21 Pickett, Kate E., and Richard G. Wilkinson, 'Child Wellbeing and Income Inequality in Rich Societies: Ecological Cross Sectional Study', *BMJ*, vol. 335, no. 7629, pp. 1080–85: 1085.
22 Marmot, Michael G., 'Understanding Social Inequalities in Health', *Perspectives in Biology and Medicine*, vol. 46, no. 3, 2003, pp. S9-S23.
23 Marriot, Lisa, and Dalice Sim, 'Indicators of Inequality for Māori and Pacific People', *Journal of New Zealand Studies*, no. 20, 2015, pp. 24–50; Nosa, Vili, Dwaine Faletanoai, Audrey Po'e-Tofaeono, and David Newcombe, 'A Perspective on Illicit Drug Use for Pacific People Living in New Zealand', *Journal of Pacific*

*Research*, vol. 21, no. 9, 2022, pp. 693–96; Statistics New Zealand, 'Wellbeing Statistics: 2021', https://www.stats.govt.nz/information-releases/wellbeing-statistics-2021/#mental; Sutcliffe, Kylie, Jude Ball, Terryann C. Clark, Dan Archer, Roshini Peiris-John, Sue Crengle, and Terry (Theresa) Fleming, 'Rapid and Unequal Decline in Adolescent Mental Health and Well-being 2012–2019: Findings from New Zealand Cross-Sectional Surveys', *Australian and New Zealand Journal of Psychiatry*, vol. 57, no. 2, 2022, pp. 264–82.

24 Marmot, 'Understanding Social Inequalities in Health'.

25 Anderson, Anneka, Briar Peat, Janine Ryland, Malakai Ofanoa, Hannah Burgess, Gemma Malungahu, Julie Wade, Julie Spry, and Leversha Alison, 'Mismatches Between Health Service Delivery and Community Expectations in the Provision of Secondary Prophylaxis for Rheumatic Fever in New Zealand', *Australian and New Zealand Journal of Public Health*, vol. 43, no. 3, 2019, pp. 294–99: 297.

26 Jones, 'Levels of Racism'.

27 Ryan, Grey, and Mischewski, *Tofa Saili*.

28 Ibid.

29 Walsh, Michael, and Corina Grey, 'The Contribution of Avoidable Mortality to the Life Expectancy Gap in Māori and Pacific Populations in New Zealand – A Decomposition Analysis', *New Zealand Medical Journal*, vol. 132, no. 1492, 2019, pp. 46–60.

30 Jones, Camara Phyllis, 'Invited Commentary: "Race," Racism, and the Practice of Epidemiology', *American Journal of Epidemiology*, vol. 154, no. 4, 2001, pp. 299–304.

31 Reid and Robson, 'Understanding Health Inequities', in Robson and Harris (eds), *Hauora: Māori Standards of Health IV*.

32 Dave Letele, interviewed in Fuatai, Teuila, 'South Auckland Deserves More than a "Short-Sighted, Short-Term Fix"', *E-Tangata*, May 7, 2023, https://e-tangata.co.nz/comment-and-analysis/south-auckland-deserves-more-than-a-short-sighted-short-term-fix/, paras 27–38.

33 Dahlgren, Göran, and Margaret Whitehead, *Policies and Strategies to Promote Social Equity in Health: Background Document to WHO – Strategy Paper for Europe*, 1991, https://www.iffs.se/publikationer/arbetsrapporter/policies-and-strategies-to-promote-social-equity-in-health/; Dahlgren, Göran, and Margaret Whitehead, 'The Dahlgren–Whitehead Model of Health Determinants: 30 Years On and Still Chasing Rainbows', *Public Health*, vol. 199, 2021, pp. 20–24.

34 Jones, 'Invited Commentary'.

35 Ryan, Grey, and Mischewski, *Tofa Saili*.

36 Health Quality and Safety Commission, *A Window on the Quality of New Zealand's Health Care: 2018*, 2018, https://www.hqsc.govt.nz/assets/Our-data/Publications-resources/Window-Jun-2018.pdf

37 Ministry for Pacific Peoples, *Pacific Aotearoa Status Report: A Snapshot: 2020*, 2020, https://www.mpp.govt.nz/assets/Reports/Pacific-Peoples-in-Aotearoa-Report.pdf

38 Ministry of Social Development, *Prevalence and Consequences of Barriers to Primary Health Care: March 2021*, 2021, https://www.msd.govt.nz/documents/about-msd-and-our-work/publications-resources/research/barriers-to-

primary health-care/prevalence-and-consequences-of-barriers-to-primary-health-care.pdf
39 Ibid.
40 Dahlgren and Whitehead, 'The Dahlgren-Whitehead Model', p. 22.
41 Jones, 'Invited Commentary'.
42 Anderson, Peat, Ryland, Ofanoa, Burgess, Malungahu, Wade, Spry, and Alison, 'Mismatches'; Ryan, Grey, and Mischewski, *Tofa Saili*.
43 Ibid.
44 Ibid.
45 Mcfalls, Elisabeth L., and Deirdre Cobb-Roberts, 'Reducing Resistance to Diversity Through Cognitive Dissonance Instruction: Implications for Teacher Education', *Journal of Teacher Education*, vol. 52, no. 2, 2001, pp. 164–72.
46 Taika Waititi as quoted in The Spinoff, 'Irrefutable Proof Taika Waititi Is Wrong and NZ is Not Racist as Fuck', *The Spinoff*, April 9, 2018, https://thespinoff.co.nz/media/09-04-2018/irrefutable-proof-taika-waititi-is-wrong-and-nz-is-not-racist-as-fuck, para. 3.
47 Thomsen, Patrick S., 'My Husband Is Sāmoan, So Talofa: The Erasive Racial Politics of Judith Collins', in Arcia Tecun, Lana Lopesi, and Anisha Sankar (eds), *Towards a Grammar of Race in Aotearoa New Zealand*, Bridget Williams Books, 2022, pp. 151–248.
48 Ibid.
49 Reid and Robson, 'Understanding Health Inequities', in Robson and Harris (eds), *Hauora: Māori Standards of Health IV*.
50 Reid, Papaarangi, Donna Cormack, and Sarah-Jane Paine, 'Colonial Histories, Racism and Health – The Experience of Māori and Indigenous Peoples', *Public Health*, vol. 172, 2019, pp. 119–24.
51 Moana Jackson, interviewed in Tutaki, Matthew, 'Moana Jackson: "I'm Absolutely Sure Transformation Is Coming"', *E-Tangata*, April 3, 2022, https://e-tangata.co.nz/korero/moana-jackson-im-absolutely-sure-transformation-is-coming/; Reid, Papaarangi, 'Structural Reform or a Cultural Reform? Moving the Health and Disability Sector to Be Pro-equity, Culturally Safe, Tiriti Compliant and Anti-racist', *New Zealand Medical Journal*, vol. 134, no. 1535, 2017, pp. 7–10.
52 Krieger, Nancy, 'Theories for Social Epidemiology in the 21st Century: An Ecosocial Perspective', *International Journal of Epidemiology*, vol. 30, no. 4, 2001, pp. 668–77; Reid and Robson, 'Understanding Health Inequities', in Robson and Harris (eds), *Hauora: Māori Standards of Health IV*.
53 Salesa, *Island Time*.
54 Ibid.
55 Braveman, Paula A., Elaine Arkin, Dwayne Proctor, Tina Kauh, and Nicole Holm, 'Systemic and Structural Racism: Definitions, Examples, Health Damages, and Approaches to Dismantling', *Health Equity*, vol. 41, no. 2, 2022, pp. 171–78; Liebow, Nabina K., and Travis N. Rieder, '"What Can I Possibly Do?": White Individual Responsibility for Addressing Racism as a Public Health Crisis', *Bioethics*, vol. 36, no. 3, 2022, pp. 274–82; Sullivan, Laura Specker, Dante Pelzer, Alexandra Rice, Yuri Karl Peterson, Robert M. Sade, Danyelle M. Townsend, Leigh Vaughan, Michelle Nichols, and Nancy Zisk, 'Responsibility for Structural

Racism in Medicine: Reflections and Recommendations from One Institution', *Narrative Inquiry in Bioethics*, vol. 11, no. 2, 2021, pp. 221–29.
56 Wehipeihana, Emma, 'We're Done with Being Asked to Justify Our "Privilege"', *The Spinoff*, November 29, 2023, https://thespinoff.co.nz/politics/29-11-2023/were-done-with-being-asked-to-justify-our-privilege
57 Ngata, Talavao, 'Pacific Futures in Housing: Cultural Capital, Economic Unease and Community Action', MA thesis, University of Auckland, 2023.
58 Ministry of Housing and Urban Development, *Long-Term Insights Briefing: Te hua o tō tātou taupori kaumātuatanga ki ngā anamata whanake whare, tāone anō hoki: The long-term implications of our ageing population for our housing and urban futures*, 2023, https://www.hud.govt.nz/assets/Uploads/Documents/Long-term-Insights-Briefing/Long-term-Insights-Briefing-2023-PDF-version.pdf, p. 14.
59 Ahmed, Sara, *On Being Included: Racism and Diversity in Institutional Life*, Duke University Press, 2012.
60 Reid, Papaarangi, 'Papaarangi Reid: "Aotearoa Is Built on Health Inequities"', *University of Auckland*, November 1, 2022, https://www.auckland.ac.nz/en/news/2022/11/01/papaarangi-reid-opinion-health-inequities.html
61 Curtis, Elena, Rhys Jones, David Tipene-Leach, Curtis Walker, Belinda Loring, Sarah-Jane Paine, and Papaarangi Reid, 'Why Cultural Safety Rather Than Cultural Competency is Required to Achieve Health Equity: A Literature Review and Recommended Definition', *International Journal for Equity in Health*, vol. 18, no. 1, 2019, pp. 1–17.
62 Harris, Ricci, Donna Cormack, Martin Tobias, Li-Chia Yeh, Natalie Talamaivao, Joanna Minster, and Roimata Timutimu, 'The Pervasive Effects of Racism: Experiences of Racial Discrimination in New Zealand Over Time and Associations with Multiple Health Domains', *Social Science & Medicine*, vol. 74, no. 3, 2012, pp. 408–15.

## HIGHER EDUCATION – The Pacific Pipeline
## Structural Racism and Pacific Peoples in Higher Education

1 Fradella, Henry F., 'Supporting Strategies for Equity, Diversity, and Inclusion in Higher Education Faculty Hiring', in SunHee Gertz, Betsy Huang, and Lauren Cyr (eds), *Diversity and Inclusion in Higher Education and Societal Contexts*, Palgrave Macmillan, 2018, pp. 119–51; Sethna, Beheruz N., 'Minorities in Higher Education: A Pipeline Problem?', *Research in Higher Education Journal*, vol. 13, 2011, pp. 1–11; Ysseldyk, Renate, Katharine H. Greenaway, Elena Hassinger, Sarah Zutrauen, Jana Lintz, Maya P. Bhatia, Margaret Frye, Else Starkenburg, and Vera Tai, 'A Leak in the Academic Pipeline: Identity and Health among Postdoctoral Women', *Frontiers in Psychology*, vol. 10, 2019, pp. 1–17; Zusi, Karen, 'Breaking Out of the Academic Pipeline', *Cell*, vol. 165, no. 7, 2016, pp. 1557–59.
2 Fradella, ibid.; Pihama, Leonie, Jenny Lee-Morgan, Sarah-Jane Tiakiwai, Linda Tuhiwai Smith, Tammy Tauroa, Desi Lonebear, Rangimarie Mahuika, and Joeliee Seed-Pihama, *Te Tātua o Kahukura: A National Project Report to Ako Aotearoa*, Ako Aotearoa, 2018, https://ako.ac.nz/assets/Knowledge-centre/NPF-15-009-He-Tatau-o-Kahukura/c89aadd7c5/REPORT-Te-Tatua-o-Kahukura.pdf

3 Education Counts, *Learners Summary*, August 2023, https://www.educationcounts.govt.nz/statistics/summary_tables
4 New Zealand Treasury, *The New Zealand Pacific Economy*, 13 November 2018, https://www.treasury.govt.nz/sites/default/files/2018-11/nz-pacific-economy-nov18.pdf
5 Ball, Stephen J., 'Performativity, Commodification and Commitment: An I-Spy Guide to the Neoliberal University', *British Journal of Educational Studies*, vol. 60, no. 1, 2012, pp. 17–28; Beban, Alice, and Nicolette Trueman, 'Student Workers: The Unequal Load of Paid and Unpaid Work in the Neoliberal University', *New Zealand Sociology*, vol. 33, no. 2, 2018, pp. 99–131; Giroux, Henry, *Neoliberalism's War on Higher Education*, Haymarket, 2014; Saunders, Daniel B, 'Neoliberal Ideology and Public Higher Education in the United States', *Journal for Critical Education Policy Studies*, vol. 8, no. 1, 2010, pp. 41–77; Shore, Cris, 'After Neoliberalism? The Reform of New Zealand's University System', in Susan B. Hyatt, Boone W. Shear, and Susan Wright (eds), *Learning Under Neoliberalism*, Berghahn Books, 2015, pp. 30–55.
6 Ahmed, Sara, *On Being Included: Racism and Diversity in Institutional Life*, Duke University Press, 2020.
7 Ibid.; Naepi, Sereana, 'Pacific Women's Experiences Working in Universities in Aotearoa New Zealand', *Higher Education Research & Development*, vol. 40, no. 1, 2021, pp. 63–74; Naepi, Sereana, 'Why isn't My Professor Pasifika?', *MAI Journal*, vol. 8, no. 2., 2019, pp. 219–34.
8 Carey, Kristi, 'On Cleaning: Student Activism in the Corporate and Imperial University', *Open Library of Humanities*, vol. 2, no. 2, e4; Kidman, Joanna, 'A People Torn in Twain: Colonial and Indigenous Contexts of University Education in New Zealand', *Interchange*, vol. 30, no. 1, 1999, pp. 73–91; Kidman, Joanna, 'Whither Decolonisation? Indigenous Scholars and the Problem of Inclusion in the Neoliberal University', *Journal of Sociology*, vol. 56, no. 2, 2022, pp. 247–62; Naepi, Sereana, and Marcia Leenen-Young, 'Gathering Pandanus Leaves: Colonization, Internationalization and the Pacific', *Journal of International Students*, vol. 11, no. S1, 2021, pp. 15–31; Smith, Avery, Hine Funaki, and Liana MacDonald, 'Living, Breathing Settler-Colonialism: The Reification of Settler Norms in a Common University Space', *Higher Education Research and Development*, vol. 40, no. 1, 2021, pp. 132–45; Stein, Sharon, *Unsettling the University*, Johns Hopkins University Press, 2022.
9 University of Otago, 'Our History', n.d., https://www.otago.ac.nz/about/history#:~:text=The%20University%20of%20Otago%2C%20founded,%2C%20Medicine%2C%20Law%20and%20Music
10 Smith, Funaki, and MacDonald, 'Living, Breathing Settler-Colonialism'.
11 Pihama, Leonie, 'Tīhei Mauri Ora: Honouring Our Voices: Mana Wahine as a Kaupapa Māori Theoretical Framework', PhD thesis, University of Auckland, 2001.
12 Pihama, Leonie, Jenny Lee-Morgan, Linda Tuhiwai Smith, Sarah-Jane Tiakiwai, and Joeliee Seed-Pihama, 'MAI Te Kupenga: Supporting Māori and Indigenous Doctoral Scholars within Higher Education', *AlterNative: An International Journal of Indigenous Peoples*, vol. 15, no. 1, 2019, pp. 52–61; Stein, *Unsettling the University*.

13. University of Waikato, 'Findings of the Independent Review into Public Claims of Racism at the University of Waikato – Released Today', September 25, 2020, https://www.waikato.ac.nz/news-opinion/media/2020/Findings-of-the-independent-review
14. Naepi, Sereana, Tara McAllister, Patrick Thomsen, Marcia Leenen-Young, Leilani A. Walker, Anna L. McAllister, Reremoana Theodore, Joanna Kidman, and Tamasailau Suaalii, 'The Pakaru "Pipeline": Māori and Pasifika Pathways within the Academy', *New Zealand Annual Review of Education*, vol. 24, 2019, pp. 142–59; Theodore, Reremoana, Mele Taumoepeau, Jesse Kokaua, Karen Tustin, Megan Gollop, Nicola Taylor, Jackie Hunter, Cynthia Kiro, and Richie Poulton, 'Equity in New Zealand University Graduate Outcomes: Māori and Pacific Graduates', *Higher Education Research & Development*, vol. 37, no. 1, 2018, pp. 206–21; Theodore, Reremoana, Mele Taumoepeau, Karen Tustin, Megan Gollop, Charlottes Unasa, Jesse Kokaua, Nicola Taylor, Sandhya Ramrakha, Jackie Hunter, and Richie Poulton, 'Pacific University Graduates in New Zealand: What Helps and Hinders Completion', *AlterNative: An International Journal of Indigenous Peoples*, vol. 14, no. 2, 2018, pp. 138–46.
15. McAllister, Tara, Jesse Kokaua, Sereana Naepi, Joanna Kidman, and Reremoana Theodore, 'Glass Ceilings in New Zealand Universities: Inequities in Māori and Pacific Promotions and Earnings', *MAI Journal*, vol. 9, no. 3, 2020, pp. 91–102; Naepi, 'Why Isn't My Professor Pasifika?'.
16. McAllister, Tara G., Sereana Naepi, Elizabeth Wilson, Daniel Hikuroa, and Leilani A. Walker, 'Under-represented and Overlooked: Māori and Pasifika Scientists in Aotearoa New Zealand's Universities and Crown Research Institutes', *Journal of the Royal Society of New Zealand*, vol. 52, no. 1, 2022, pp. 38–53; McAllister, Tara G., Sereana Naepi, Leilani Walker, Ashlea Gillon, Patricia Clark, Emma Lambert, . . . Theresa Alipia, 'Seen but Unheard: Navigating Turbulent Waters as Māori and Pacific Postgraduate Students in STEM', *Journal of the Royal Society of New Zealand*, vol. 52, no. sup1, 2022, pp. 116–34; Naepi, Sereana, Elizabeth Wilson, Samantha Lagos, Sam Manuela, Tara G. McAllister, Joanna Kidman, Reremoana Theodore, and Jesse Kokaua, 'Where Are We Now? Patterns of Māori and Pasifika Enrolment in the Natural and Physical Science and Society and Culture Fields in Aotearoa New Zealand', *Higher Education Research & Development*, vol. 40, no. 1, pp. 90–103.
17. Barber, Simon, and Sereana Naepi, 'Sociology in a Crisis: COVID-19 and the Colonial Politics of Knowledge Production in Aotearoa New Zealand', *Journal of Sociology*, vol. 56, no. 4, pp. 693–703.
18. Naepi, 'Why Isn't My Professor Pasifika?'.
19. Although it should be noted that the data is rounded up to five to protect privacy, so an increase to ten could signal an increase of between one and five.
20. Education Counts, *Human Resources 2022*, April 2023, https://www.educationcounts.govt.nz/statistics/resources
21. Barrett-Walker, Tessa, Franca Buelow, Lindsey Te Atu O Tu MacDonald, Ann Brower, and Alex James, 'Stochastic Modelling of Intersectional Pay Gaps in Universities', *Royal Society Open Science*, vol. 10, no. 10, 2023, pp. 1–14; McAllister, Kokaua, Naepi, Kidman, and Theodore, 'Glass Ceilings'.

22 Kidman, Joanna, and Cherie Chu, 'Scholar Outsiders in the Neoliberal University: Transgressive Academic Labour in the Whitestream', *New Zealand Journal of Educational Studies*, vol. 52, 2017, pp. 7–19; Kidman, Joanna, and Cherie Chu, '"We're Not the Hottest Ethnicity": Pacific Scholars and the Cultural Politics of New Zealand Universities', *Globalisation, Societies and Education*, vol. 17, no. 4, 2019, pp. 489–99.

23 Naepi, Sereana, '"I Didn't Come to Play": Pasifika Women in the Academy', in Taima Moeke-Pickering, Sheila Cote-Meek, and Ann Pegoraro (eds), *Critical Reflections and Politics on Advancing Women in the Academy*, IGI Global, 2020, pp. 52–69; Naepi, 'Pacific Women's Experiences Working in Universities in Aotearoa New Zealand'.

24 Baice, Tim, Sereana Naepi, Patrick Thomsen, Karamaia Muller, Marcia Leenen-Young, Sam Manuela, and Sisikula Sisifa, 'Developing Our Voices: Pacific Early Career Academics' Journeys in Aotearoa New Zealand', *Journal of New Zealand Studies*, vol. 33, 2021, pp. 10–24; Leenen-Young, Marcia, Sereana Naepi, Patrick Thomsen, David Taufui Mikato Fa'avae, Moeata Keil, and Jacoba Matapo, '"Pillars of the Colonial Institution are Like a Knowledge Prison": The Significance of Decolonising Knowledge and Pedagogical Practice for Pacific Early Career Academics in Higher Education', *Teaching in Higher Education*, vol. 26, nos, 7–8, 2021, pp. 986–1001; Thomsen, Patrick, Marcia Leenen-Young, Sereana Naepi, Karamia Müller, Sam Manuela, Sisikula Sisifa, and Tim Baice, 'In Our Own Words: Pacific Early Career Academics (PECA) and Pacific Knowledges in Higher Education Pedagogical Praxis', *Higher Education Research & Development*, vol. 40, no. 1, 2021, pp. 49–62; Pacific Early Career Researchers Collective, 'Relational and Collective Excellence: Unfolding the Potential of Pacific Early Career Researchers', *Journal of the Royal Society of New Zealand*, vol. 52, 2022, pp. 75–91.

25 Theodore, Reremoana, Joanna Kidman, Sereana Naepi, Jesse Kokaua, and Tara McAllister, 'Tackling Systemic Racism in Academic Promotion Processes', *MAI Journal*, vol. 10, no. 2, 2021, pp. 202–6.

26 Thomsen, Leenen-Young, Naepi, Müller, Manuela, Sisifa, and Baice, 'In Our Own Words'.

27 Universities New Zealand, 'About the University Sector', https://www.universitiesnz.ac.nz/about-university-sector#:~:text=The%20NZ%20university%20system&text=Universities%20help%20society%20by%20increasing,%2C%20teaching%2C%20accounting%20and%20engineering

28 Education Counts, *Educational Attainment in the Adult Population: Indicator Report*, October 2022, https://www.educationcounts.govt.nz/statistics/achievement-and-attainment

29 Education Counts, *The Income Benefits of Education*, July 2021, https://www.educationcounts.govt.nz/__data/assets/pdf_file/0011/208793/2020-The-income-benefits-of-education-Indicator-Report.pdf

30 Education Counts, *Education, Income and Earnings*, October 2023, https://www.educationcounts.govt.nz/statistics/beyond-study

31 Education Counts, *Educational Attainment*, p. 1.

32 The year 2018 is included in order to account for pre COVID-19 data and make it clear that the results are not a COVID-19 'blip'.

33 Education Counts, *Educational Attainment*, p. 1.
34 Zero per cent does not indicate that there are no Pacific students enrolled in this space, just that the percentage of the Pacific population enrolled at this level is below 1 per cent.
35 Education Counts, *Participation Rates*, August 2023, https://www.educationcounts.govt.nz/statistics/tertiary-participation
36 Education Counts, 'Tertiary Population Data – All Provider-Based Tertiary Education', https://www.educationcounts.govt.nz/statistics/population-data
37 Ibid.
38 Ibid.
39 Foon, Eleisha, 'Study or Work to Support Families, Pasifika Students Face Tough Choices', *RNZ*, May 14, 2022, https://www.rnz.co.nz/international/pacific-news/467075/study-or-work-to-support-families-pasifika-students-face-tough-choices; Stewart, Indira, 'High School Students Working All Night to Support Families', *One News*, June 18, 2023, https://www.1news.co.nz/2023/06/18/high-school-students-working-all-night-to-support-families; Tokalau, Torika, 'Covid-19: Pacific Teen Drops Out to Support Family, Years After Dad Did the Same', *Stuff*, January 13, 2022, https://www.stuff.co.nz/national/health/coronavirus/127276109/covid19-pacific-teen-drops-out-to-support-family-years-after-dad-did-the-same
40 Education Counts, *Learners Summary*.
41 Jansen, Ellen P. W. A., and Marjon Fokkens-Bruinsma, 'Explaining Achievement in Higher Education', *Educational Research and Evaluation*, vol. 11, no. 3, 2005, pp. 235–52; Krause, Kerri-Lee, and Hamish Coates, 'Students' Engagement in First Year University', *Assessment & Evaluation in Higher Education*, vol. 33, no. 5, 2008, pp. 493–505; Van Rooj, Else, Ellen P. W. A. Jansen, and Wim van de Grift, 'First-Year University Students' Academic Success: The Importance of Academic Adjustment', *European Journal of Psychology in Education*, vol. 33, 2018, pp. 749–67.
42 Tertiary Education Commission, 'View Educational Performance Using Interactive Charts', July 7, 2023, https://www.tec.govt.nz/funding/funding-and-performance/performance/teo/epi-reports/interactive-charts/#!/
43 Education Counts, *Learners Summary*.
44 Tertiary Education Commission, 'View Educational Performance'.
45 Ibid.
46 Education Counts, *Tertiary Graduate Earnings*, September 2018, https://www.educationcounts.govt.nz/statistics/beyond-study
47 Education Counts, *Field of Specialisation for Students Gaining Qualifications from Tertiary Education Providers*, June 2023, https://www.educationcounts.govt.nz/statistics/achievement-and-attainment
48 Curtis, Elana, Erena Wikaire, Kanews Stokes, and Papaarangi Reid, 'Addressing Indigenous Health Workforce Inequities: A Literature Review Exploring "Best" Practice for Recruitment into Tertiary Health Programmes', *International Journal for Equity in Health*, vol. 11, no. 1, 2012, pp. 1–15; Kawadawa, Karen, 'Health Workforce Crisis Needs Fresh Approach', *The Challenge*, September 6, 2022, https://www.auckland.ac.nz/en/news/2022/09/06/health-workforce-crisis-needs-fresh-approach.html
49 Education Counts, *Field of Specialisation*.

50 Gabel, Julia, 'Professors Call Out Racism as a "Major Issue" at Universities', *New Zealand Herald*, September 24, 2020, https://www.nzherald.co.nz/kahu/professors-call-out-racism-as-a-major-issue-at-universities/ZSQ2UDFJAMK2XHZEWDGTYLMXEA/; Walker, Leilani, and Sereana Naepi, 'Something is Broken in Our Universities', *E-Tangata*, August 21, 2022, https://e-tangata.co.nz/comment-and-analysis/something-is-broken-in-our-universities/
51 Education Counts, *Education, Income and Earnings*, 2023.
52 Ye, Jessica, 'What Do Students Want from a Higher Education Review?', *The Spinoff*, July 31, 2023, https://thespinoff.co.nz/society/31-07-2023/what-do-students-want-from-a-higher-education-review
53 Tertiary Education Commission, *Learner Success Plan Template for Investment in 2022*, https://www.tec.govt.nz/assets/Forms-templates-and-guides/Investment-toolkit-2021/Learner-Success-Plan-template
54 Mila, Karlo, *Dream Fish Floating*, Huia Publishers, 2005, p. 115.

## JUSTICE SYSTEMS – Recognising Stories of Suffering in Section 27 of the Sentencing Act 2002

1 Crimes Act 1961, s 235.
2 Based on my knowledge of people in New Zealand's criminal justice system.
3 'New Zealand' is used to describe the settler-colonial state that continues its illegitimate sovereign prerogative over Aotearoa.
4 Aguon, Julian, 'To Hell with Drowning', *The Atlantic*, November 1, 2021, https://www.theatlantic.com/culture/archive/2021/11/oceania-pacific-climate-change-stories/620570/
5 Farmer, Paul, 'On Suffering and Structural Violence: A View from Below', *Daedalus*, vol. 125, no. 1, 1996, pp. 261–83.
6 Child Poverty Action Group, 'Ministry of Social Development (MSD) Child Poverty Report 2022 Highlights Need to Support Struggling Families', https://www.cpag.org.nz/media-releases/ministry-of-social-development-msd-child-poverty-report-2022-highlights-need-to-support-struggling-families
7 Te Hiringa Mahara, 'Te Hiringa Mahara to Continue to Advocate for Young People after Oranga Tamariki Bill Passes Third Reading', https://www.mhwc.govt.nz/news-and-resources/te-hiringa-mahara-to-continue-to-advocate-for-young-people-after-oranga-tamariki-bill-passes-third-reading/
8 University of Auckland, 'Funding for Research into Pacific Experiences of the Criminal Justice System', https://www.auckland.ac.nz/en/news/2020/10/30/funding-for-research-into-pacific-experiences-of-the-criminal-ju.html#:~:text=%E2%80%9CIn%20the%20CJS%2C%20Pasifika%20peoples,prison%20population%2C%E2%80%9D%20she%20says
9 Health Quality and Safety Commission, *Bula Sautu: A Window on Quality 2021: Pacific Health in the Year of COVID-19*, 2021, https://www.hqsc.govt.nz/assets/Our-data/Publications-resources/BulaSautu_WEB.pdf, p. 11.
10 Aguon, Julian, *The Properties of Perpetual Light*, University of Guam Press, 2021, p. 76.
11 Ibid.

12 Ibid.
13 Farmer, 'On Suffering'.
14 Delgado, Richard, and Jean Stefancic, *Critical Race Theory: An Introduction*, New York University Press, 2017.
15 Asafo, Dylan, and Litia Tuiburelevu, 'Critical Race Theory and the Law in New Zealand', *Counterfutures*, vol. 12, 2016, pp. 95–133.
16 Solórzano, Daniel G., and Tara J. Yosso, 'Critical Race Methodology: Counter-Storytelling as an Analytical Framework for Education Research', *Qualitative Inquiry*, vol. 8, no. 1, 2022, pp. 23–44.
17 Delgado, Richard, and Jean Stefancic, 'Critical Race Theory: An Annotated Bibliography', *Virginia Law Review*, vol. 79, no. 2, 1993, pp. 461–516.
18 Merriweather Hunn, Lisa R., Talmadge C. Guy, and Elaine Mangliitz, 'Who Can Speak for Whom? Using Counter-Storytelling to Challenge Racial Hegemony', *Adult Education Research Conference*, 2006.
19 Ibid.
20 Ibid.
21 Ibid.
22 Solórzano and Yosso, 'Critical Race Methodology'.
23 Ibid.
24 Ibid.
25 Alexander, Michelle, *The New Jim Crow: Mass Incarceration in the Age of Colourblindness*, New York Press, 2010.
26 Ibid., p. 179.
27 Farmer, 'On Suffering', p. 274.
28 Mila, Karlo, 'Deconstructing the Big Brown Tails/Tales: Pasifika Peoples in Aotearoa New Zealand', in Avril Bell, Vivienne Elizabeth, Tracey McIntosh, and Matt Wynyard (eds), *A Land of Milk and Honey? Making Sense of Aotearoa New Zealand*, Auckland University Press, 2017, pp. 95–107.
29 Ibid.
30 Archives New Zealand, 'The Rise of the Mau and the Fall of Colonial Rule in Sāmoa', https://www.archives.govt.nz/discover-our-stories/the-rise-of-the-mau-and-the-fall-of-colonial-rule-in-samoa
31 Tomkins, Sandra M., 'The Influenza Epidemic of 1918–19 in Western Samoa', *Journal of Pacific History*, vol. 27, no. 2, 1992, pp. 181–97.
32 Ibid.
33 Laumea, Tuki, *1918: Samoa and the Ship of Death (Talune)*, 2018, https://www.nzonscreen.com/title/1918-samoa-and-ship-of-death-2018/quotes
34 NZ History, 'Black Saturday', https://nzhistory.govt.nz/politics/samoa/black-saturday
35 Ibid.
36 Mila, 'Deconstructing the Big Brown Tails/Tales', p. 70.
37 Ibid.
38 New Zealand Productivity Commission, *International Migration to New Zealand: Historical Themes & Trends*, 2021, https://www.treasury.govt.nz/sites/default/files/2024-05/pc-wp-international-migration-to-nz-historical-themes-and-trends.pdf

39  Ibid.
40  Mila, 'Deconstructing the Big Brown Tails/Tales'.
41  Hornblow, Andrew, and Sarah Wright, 'Emerging Needs, Evolving Services: The Health of Pacific Peoples in New Zealand', *Kōtuitui: New Zealand Journal of Social Sciences Online*, vol. 3, no. 1, 2008, pp. 21–33.
42  Krishnan, Vasantha, Penelope Schoeffel Meleisea, and Julia A. N. Warren, *The Challenge of Change: Pacific Island Communities in New Zealand, 1986–1993*, NZ Institute for Social Research and Development, 1994.
43  Anae, Melani, 'The Terror of the Dawn Raids', *E-Tangata*, October 18, 2020, https://e-tangata.co.nz/history/the-terror-of-the-dawn-raids/, para. 10.
44  Ibid.
45  Ibid.
46  Ibid.
47  Ness, Tigilau, 'Statement of Tigilau Ness for Tulou – Our Pacific Voices: Tatala e Pulonga (Pacific People's Experiences) Hearing', July 20, 2021, Abuse in Care Royal Commission of Inquiry, pp. 1–16, https://www.abuseincare.org.nz/our-progress/library/v/332/witness-statement-of-tigilau-ness-for-tulou-our-pacific-voices-tatala-e-pulonga-hearing
48  Luamanuvao, Dame Winnie Laban, 'Witness Statement of Luamanuvao Dame Winnie Laban', July 5, 2021, Abuse in Care Royal Commission of Inquiry, pp. 1–9, https://www.abuseincare.org.nz/assets/Uploads/Statement-of-Associate-Professor-Hon-Luamanuvao-Dame-Winnie-Laban-for-Tulou-Our-Pacific-Voices-Tatala-e-Pulonga-hearing.pdf
49  Prime Minister, 'Speech to Dawn Raids Apology', *Beehive*, https://www.beehive.govt.nz/speech/speech-dawn-raids-apology#:~:text=During%20the%20same%20period%2C%20overstayers,only%205%20percent%20of%20prosecutions.&text=While%20these%20events%20took%20place,on%20today%20in%20Pacific%20communities
50  Abuse in Care Royal Commission of Inquiry, 'The Journey for Pacific Peoples', https://www.abuseincare.org.nz/reports/from-redress-to-puretumu/from-redress-to-puretumu-4/1-1-introduction-2/1-1-introduction-2/
51  Mila, 'Deconstructing the Big Brown Tails/Tales'.
52  McGregor-Sumpter, Flynn, 'The Removal of the Pacific Community from Greater Ponsonby', *Auckland History Initiative*, https://ahi.auckland.ac.nz/2022/03/22/the-removal-of-the-pacific-community-from-greater-ponsonby/, pp. 1–5.
53  'Pacific, Māori More Likely to Die from Bowel Cancer', *Scimex*, June 8, 2018, https://bowelcancernz.org.nz/new/maori-pasifika-more-likely-to-die-from-bowel-cancer-study/
54  Rowe, Damian, '"Institutional Racism" Is Blocking Pacific and Māori Access to Health Care, Doctor Says', *Stuff*, June 16, 2019, https://www.stuff.co.nz/national/health/111727573/institutional-racism-is-blocking-pacific-and-mori-access-to-health-care-doctor-says
55  Williams, Sir Joe, 'Build a Bridge and Get Over It: The Role of Colonial Dispossession in Contemporary Indigenous Offending and What We Should Do About It', *New Zealand Journal of Public and International Law*, vol. 18, no. 1, 2020, pp. 3–27.

56 Ibid.
57 Abuse in Care Royal Commission of Inquiry, 'Part Three: What We Have Learned About Abuse in Care', https://www.abuseincare.org.nz/assets/Uploads/Abuse-in-Care-Volume-One-Large-Text.pdf
58 Scoop, 'Incarceration Rates and State Care Directly Linked According to New Research', *Scoop*, https://www.scoop.co.nz/stories/PO2208/S00169/incarceration-rates-and-state-care-directly-linked-according-to-new-research.htm
59 Lambie, Ian, 'The Prison Pipeline: Why Early Intervention Is the Best Solution', *International Journal of Birth and Parent Education*, vol. 9, no. 3, 2022, pp. 32–36.
60 Sentencing Act 2002.
61 Chhana, Rajesh, Philip Spier, Susan Roberts, and Chris Hurd, *The Sentencing Act 2002: Monitoring the First Year*, 2004, https://www.employmentcourt.govt.nz/assets/sentencing-act-year-1.pdf
62 Sentencing Act 2002, ss 7, 8 and 9.
63 Sentencing Act 2002, s 27.
64 Criminal Justice Act 1985, s 16.
65 (23 July 1985) 464 NZPD 5811, https://babel.hathitrust.org/cgi/pt?id=uc1.b3281415&view=1up&seq=1
66 Williams, 'Build a Bridge'.
67 Ibid.
68 Quince, Khylee, 'Authentic Voices Too Often Missing from Conversation', *Stuff*, April 3, 2021, https://www.stuff.co.nz/opinion/124724845/authentic-voices-too-often-missing-from-conversation
69 Tuiburelevu, Litia, 'Legally Brown: The Experiences of Pasifika Women in the Criminal Justice System', *New Zealand Women's Law Journal*, vol. 2, 2018, pp. 78–106.
70 Quince, 'Authentic Voices'.
71 Ibid.
72 Ibid.
73 *Solicitor-General v Heta* [2018] NZHC 2453, http://www.nzlii.org/cgi-bin/sinodisp/nz/cases/NZHC/2018/2453.html?query=title(Solicitor%20General%20near%20heta)
74 Ibid., at [40].
75 Ibid.
76 Ibid., at [41].
77 Williams, 'Build a Bridge'.
78 *R v Carr* [2019] NZHC 2335, http://www.nzlii.org/nz/cases/NZHC/2019/2335.pdf
79 Ibid., at [61].
80 Williams, 'Build a Bridge'.
81 Ibid.
82 Ibid., p. 20.
83 Ibid.
84 Ibid.
85 Ibid.
86 Stenning, P, and Julian V. Roberts, 'Empty Promises: Parliament, The Supreme Court, and the Sentencing of Aboriginal Offenders', *Saskatchewan Law Review*, vol. 64, no. 1, 2001, pp. 158–65.

87 Oakley, T. J., 'A Critical Analysis of Section 27 of the Sentencing Act (2002)', MSocSci thesis, University of Waikato, 2020.
88 Quince, 'Authentic Voices'.
89 Ibid.
90 Ibid.
91 Ibid.
92 Tuiburelevu, Litia, Elizabeth Lotoa, Isabella Ieremia, Hugo Wagner-Hiliau, and Gabriella Coxon-Brayne, 'Pacific Peoples and the Criminal Justice System in Aotearoa New Zealand', Michael and Suzanne Borrin Foundation, October 2023, p. 179, https://www.borrinfoundation.nz/pacific-peoples-and-the-criminal-justice-system-in-aotearoa-new-zealand/
93 Quince, 'Authentic Voices'.
94 Ibid.
95 Māmari Stephens, as quoted in 'Cultural Reports Help in Rehabilitation – Law Lecturer', *RNZ*, March 10, 2021, https://www.rnz.co.nz/news/te-manu-korihi/438102/cultural-reports-help-in-rehabilitation-law-lecturer, para. 6.
96 Ibid., para. 8.
97 Quince, 'Authentic Voices'.
98 Ibid.
99 Section 27 Reports NZ is a fictional company. There are a number of private companies that contract out for section 27 report writing in New Zealand.
100 RNZ, 'Legislation Scrapping Funding for Section 27 Cultural Sentencing Reports Passes under Urgency', *RNZ*, March 6, 2024, https://www.rnz.co.nz/news/political/510971/legislation-scrapping-funding-for-section-27-cultural-sentencing-reports-passes-under-urgency
101 Bhamidipati, Soumya, 'Axeing of Cultural Reports Funding Will Hurt Poorer Sections of Society, Experts Say', *RNZ*, February 8, 2024, https://www.rnz.co.nz/news/national/508705/axeing-of-cultural-reports-funding-will-hurt-poorer-sections-of-society-experts-say
102 Community Law, 'Prisoner's Rights', https://communitylaw.org.nz/community-law-manual/test/release-from-prison/preparing-for-release/#:~:text=Getting%20your%20Steps%20to%20Freedom,Income%20when%20you're%20released&text=This%20is%20a%20lump%2Dsum,remand%20or%20after%20being%20sentenced.

### THE NEXT GENERATION – To Weave Dreams of Liberation

1 Hau'ofa, Epeli, 'The Ocean in Us', *The Contemporary Pacific*, vol. 10, no. 2, 1998, pp. 391–401: 397.
2 Robin, Kelley D. G., *Freedom Dreams: The Black Radical Imagination*, Beacon Press, 2002, p. 12.
3 Jackson, Moana, 'Where to Next? Decolonisation and the Stories in the Land', in Bianca Elkington, Moana Jackson, Rebecca Kiddle, Ocean Ripeka Mercier, Mike Ross, Jennie Smeaton, and Amanda Thomas (eds), *Imagining Decolonisation*, Bridget Williams Books, 2020, pp. 133–55.

4   Asafo, Dylan, 'Freedom Dreaming of Abolition in Aotearoa New Zealand: A Pacific Perspective on Tiriti-Based Abolition Constitutionalism', *Legalities*, vol. 2, no. 1, 2022, pp. 82–118.
5   Papa, Rahui, 'Indigenous Kanak Call on Māori for Help: "We Are the Same People"', *Re:*, 2024. https://www.renews.co.nz/indigenous-kanak-call-on-maori-for-help-we-are-the-same-people/?fbclid=IwAR2svkLSmcYj5PIBSQQsDoNIEoh oe_FDMWaS8wFc_xmorvd48R-RM4vTTzU_aem_V77aEYYTTAUBjnyrq-3n0g
6   Kelley, *Freedom Dreams*, p. 197.
7   Sium, Aman, and Eric Ritskes, 'Speaking Truth to Power: Indigenous Storytelling as an Act of Living Resistance', *Decolonization: Indigeneity, Education & Society*, vol. 2, no. 1, 2013, pp. I–X.
8   Sankar, Anisha, Daniel Hernandez, and Kassie Hartendorp, 'Imagining Elsewhere: A Critically Romanticized Conversation on Indigenous Futures', in Anna-Maria Murtola and Shannon Walsh (eds), *Whose Futures?*, Economic and Social Research Aotearoa, 2020, pp. 15–31.
9   Māhina, Hūfanga 'Okusitino, 'Tā, Vā, and Moana: Temporality, Spatiality, and Indigeneity', *Pacific Studies*, vol. 33, nos 2/3, 2010, pp. 168–202.
10  Tecun, Arcia, 'Knew World Undercurrents', in Arcia Tecun, Lana Lopesi, and Anisha Sankar (eds), *Towards a Grammar of Race in Aotearoa New Zealand*, Bridget Williams Books, 2022.
11  Trask, Haunani-Kay, 'Journey to Justice: A Conversation with Dr. Haunani-Kay Trask', *Vimeo*, https://vimeo.com/39644495
12  Jackson, 'Where to Next?', in Elkington, Jackson, Kiddle, Mercier, Ross, Smeaton, and Thomas (eds), *Imagining Decolonisation*, pp. 145–46.
13  Sartre, Jean-Paul, 'Preface', in Frantz Fanon (author), *The Wretched of the Earth*, translated by Constance Farrington, Penguin Books, 2001, pp. 7–26.
14  Armah, Ayi Kwei, *Two Thousand Seasons*, Heinemann Educational Publishers, 1973; Barghouti, Mourid, *I Saw Ramallah*, Bloomsbury Publishing, 2005; Friedland, Hadley, *The 'Wetiko' Legal Principles: Cree and Anishinabek Responses to Violence and Victimization*, University of Toronto Press, 2018; Kimmerer, Robin Wall, and Monique Gray Smith, *Braiding Sweetgrass for Young Adults: Indigenous Wisdom, Scientific Knowledge, and the Teachings of Plants*, Zest Books TM, 2022; McMaster, Gerald, and Nina Vincent, *Artic/Amazon: Networks of Global Indigeneity*, Goose Lane Editions, 2023.
15  Hauʻofa, Epeli, 'Our Sea of Islands', *The Contemporary Pacific*, vol. 6, no. 1, 1994, pp. 148–61.
16  Jackson, 'Where to Next', in Elkington, Jackson, Kiddle, Mercier, Ross, Smeaton, and Thomas (eds), *Imagining Decolonisation*; Te Punga Somerville, Alice, *Once Were Pacific: Māori Connections to Oceania*, University of Minnesota Press, 2012.
17  Agozino, Biko, 'Fuck the Law: Decolonizing Nomophilitis with the Discourse of Love', *Globalizations*, vol. 17, no. 7, pp. 1091–103: 1096.
18  Shilliam, Robbie, *The Black Pacific: Anti-Colonial Struggles and Oceanic Connections*, Bloomsbury Publishing, 2015.
19  Sankar, Anisha, 'The Intimacies of Four Continents – and a Sea of Islands', in Arcia Tecun, Lana Lopesi, and Anisha Sankar (eds), *Towards a Grammar of Race in Aotearoa New Zealand*, pp. 61–75.

# CONTRIBUTORS

## Editor

*Sereana Naepi* (Fijian, Pākehā) is an associate professor in sociology at Waipapa Taumata Rau, the University of Auckland. With a research focus on equity in higher education, Indigenous research methodologies, and the experiences of Pacific peoples, Māori and early career researchers in academia, she is committed to addressing systemic barriers to success in universities and advocating for institutional change. Her work explores the impact of neoliberalism on education and the need for Indigenous knowledge systems to be recognised within academic spaces. Sereana has co-authored research on decolonising universities and improving pathways for underrepresented scholars. She is a recipient of the Rutherford Discovery Fellowship and Spencer Education grants. Through her scholarship and advocacy, she contributes to rethinking how education serves diverse communities, challenging traditional structures to create more just and inclusive learning environments for future generations.

## Authors

*Ashlea Gillon Aramoana* (Ngāti Awa, Ngāpuhi, Ngāiterangi) is a kaupapa Māori transdisciplinary researcher and lecturer at Waipapa Taumata Rau.

*Barbara-Luhia Graham* (Tokelauan, Samoan, Pālagi/Pākehā) is a professional teaching fellow in law at the Faculty of Law at Waipapa Taumata Rau. She also oversees the Moana-Oceania Academic Initiative (MAI) programme at the Auckland Law School.

*Caleb Marsters* (Cook Islands Māori – Takitumu, Rarotonga and Palmerston) is a lecturer at Te Wānanga o Waipapa, School of Māori Studies and Pacific Studies at Waipapa Taumata Rau. He has a background in community and public health. His research focuses on Pacific wellbeing, male mental health, positive youth development, Pacific education and sports in the Pacific.

*Chelsea Naepi* (Niuean, Filipina, Persian) is a professional teaching fellow in law at the Faculty of Law at Waipapa Taumata Rau. As a student and educator, her research interests focus on critical theory, violence, colonialism and Oceanic perspectives on global relationalities and justice.

*David Taufui Mikato Faʻavae* (Tongan, Samoan) is an associate professor at Te Kura Toi Tangata School of Education, Te Whare Wānanga o Waikato, the University of Waikato. David is the son of Sio Milemoti and Fatai Onevai Faʻavae . His research focuses on Pacific education, leadership and Indigenous methodologies, with a particular emphasis on Tongan and broader Oceanic contexts. David has co-authored works such as 'Grounding our Collective Talanoa: Enabling Open Conversations' and 'Empowering Emerging Academics and Educators in Oceania: Why the Rethinking Pacific Education Initiative?'. His scholarship often explores concepts such as vā and talanoa and aims to decolonise educational practices and centre Pacific voices in academia. Through his work, David contributes to the empowerment of Pacific communities and the reimagining of educational landscapes in Oceania.

*Dylan Asafo* (Samoan) is a senior lecturer in the Faculty of Law at Waipapa Taumata Rau. Dylan's main academic interests encompass race and legal frameworks, climate justice in the Pacific region, constitutional and human rights law within Pacific contexts, and criminal justice and abolition.

*Evalesi Tuʻinukuafe* (Tongan, Samoan, German) is a Pacific community developer, sociologist and linguist based at Waipapa Taumata Rau.

*Fetaui Iosefo* (Samoan) is a doctoral candidate specialising in critical studies in education at Waipapa Taumata Rau. Additionally, she serves as a teaching fellow. Her research focuses on wayfinding with āiga (family) through an ethical lens using critical autoethnography, vā, and references to Samoan Indigenous perspectives concerning diaspora identity.

*Jean M. Uasike Allen* (Tongan, Pākehā) is a senior lecturer in the School of Curriculum and Pedagogy in the Faculty of Arts and Education at Waipapa Taumata Rau. Her academic contributions focus on Pacific de-coloniality, especially in the fields of health education, online gaming, and wellbeing.

*Lisa Meto Fox* (Samoan, Pākehā) is an Auckland-based equity activator with over twenty years of experience in community organising and advocacy. Lisa brings a unique perspective to her work, focusing on equity and systemic change. A former lawyer and emerging governor, she is dedicated to working towards a world where marginalised communities can thrive.

*Marcia Leenen-Young* (Samoan, Pālagi) is a senior lecturer and historian specialising in Pacific Studies at Te Wānanga o Waipapa, School of Māori Studies and Pacific Studies at Waipapa Taumata Rau. She has a diverse academic background, encompassing the history of ancient Rome and New Zealand's colonisation in the Pacific, as well as the learning and teaching of Pacific students.

*Toleafoa Yvonne Ualesi* (Samoan, Tokelauan and Fijian) is a senior lecturer in the School of Education at Auckland University of Technology (AUT). Her research interests include the application of Indigenous knowledge systems both in adolescent development and initial teacher education. Her contributions include vā relationality in the diaspora of Aotearoa New Zealand, and culturally responsive multimethods.

*Vasemaca (FKA Ema) Tavola* (Fijian) is an artist-curator based in South Auckland. Vasemaca's practice is aligned with the politics of decolonisation and Indigenous feminisms, motherhood, and histories of BIPOC art and activism in the Global South.

# INDEX

A page number followed by 'f' indicates a figure. A page number followed by 't' indicates a table. An endnote is indicated by a page number followed by 'n' and the note number.

Abuse in Care Royal Commission of Inquiry, 184
Achiume, E. Tendayi, 98
ACT party, 2, 10, 124
Agozino, Biko, 201
Ahmed, Sara, 4, 11, 155
Aikman, Pounamu Jade, 109
Alexander, Michelle, 178
Alosio, Chris, 13
Anae, Melani, 12, 91
ancestors
 ancestral knowledge and values, 49, 69, 199–201
 navigation by, 81, 114, 197
 and Pacific–Māori relationships, 93, 111–12, 197–98
Aotearoa New Zealand society
 lack of understanding of history, 10, 14–15, 40
 Māori deprivation, 100, 109, 125, 137, 186
 Māori self-determination struggles, 58–59, 110, 128, 171, 198
 Māori and Pacific ancestral relationships, 93, 111–12, 197–98
 Pacific peoples in, 12, 17–18, 35, 37, 60, 91
 Pākehā norms in, 58, 60, 120, 136 37
 structural racism in, 1–2, 119, 124–25, 128, 136–38, 144
 suburban segregation, 30, 64, 131, 181
 *see also* New Zealand settler state; socioeconomic inequities
Asafo, Dylan, 197
assimilation, 55, 57, 60–61, 69

Auckland
   hospital accessibility, 129–30
   Pacific children in, 119, 123
   socioeconomic inequality in, 30, 126, 181
Ausubel, David, 16

Bailey, Zinzi, 124
Banaba, 40–41
Bedford, Richard, 86–87
binary oppositions, 19, 53–54
Bonilla-Silva, Eduardo, 5
Bougainville, Louis-Antoine de, 21, 25
'Brain of the Native, The', 22
British Phosphate Commission, 41
*bro'Town*, 12
*Bula Sautu* report (Health Quality and Safety Commission), 117
Buller, Charles, 15
*Bunga* (short film)
   lyrics, 20, 24, 27, 30–31, 35
   meaning and origin of 'bunga', 19–20
   refuting stereotypes, 12–14

Campbell, John, 13
capitalism
   exploitation of labour, 38–39, 42–45, 106, 180
   exploitation of lands, 26, 38–39, 40–41
   and increasing inequality, 120, 124, 126
   the myth of meritocracy, 38, 44–45
   racial capitalism, 99–100, 105–7, 109, 112–13, 221n16
   *see also* New Zealand economy
Chu, Cherie, 67
climate-change-related displacement, 97, 98–99, 102, 111, 113–14
climate-displaced peoples
   access to visas, 98, 103–4
   definitions of, 97–98, 220n5
   and a future free of 'legal violence', 110–14
   and impossible choices, 101–2
   'legal violence' and, 98, 99–100, 104–5, 109, 111, 113
   Māori attitudes to, 110–11
   racial identities and, 99–100, 105, 107, 109
Collins, Fa'anānā Efeso, 3
Collins, Francis L., 84
'colonial gaze', 53–54
colonial period
   categorisation of Pacific peoples, 16, 22
   concept of European superiority, 11, 22, 56, 125, 136–37

exploitation in the Pacific, 27–28, 42, 126, 179
and Indigenous sovereignty, 100, 109, 178–79, 198, 200, 221n17
and the 'Native' stereotypes, 18–19, 21–23, 25, 212n44
New Zealand as a colonial power, 14–17, 21, 26, 179
paternalistic benevolence and, 17, 21–22, 32
plantation agriculture in the Pacific, 25–26, 28, 32
Colonial Sugar Refining Company, 28
colonisation
    impacts of, 126, 176–77, 186
    ongoing processes of, 58–59, 60–61, 125, 137, 202–3
    social structures and systems, 11–12, 22, 34, 125, 137–38
    *see also* New Zealand settler state
compulsory education
    assimilation and, 55, 60–61, 69
    decile ratings, 64
    difficulties faced by immigrants, 63, 181
    enrolment forms for, 62–64
    ethnicity-based funding, 63
    impacts of racism in, 58–60, 123
    Māori perspectives and language in, 58
    Pacific students' credits, 147
    Pākehā knowledge and, 53, 58
    reporting by ethnicity, 63
    and students' ethnic identities, 62–64, 78
    and white flight, 64
    *see also* education
constitutional transformation, 110–12, 114, 125, 147, 198
Cook, James, 22, 31
Cook Islands, 15, 18, 119
counter-stories, 177–83
Criminal Justice Act 1985 s 16, 185, 188, 189
criminality
    individual agency vs. racism, 178, 183–84, 187–88
    state care and, 184
    *see also* sentencing
critical race theory (CRT), 177
cultural reports (s 27 reports), 190–91
Curtis, Elena, 149

Dahlgren, Göran, 133, 134f
Davidson, Marama, 110
Dawn Raids
    1970s harassment and deportations, 13, 32–33, 91, 106, 180–81
    2021 apology for, 9–10, 85
    2023 reoccurrence of, 10, 85, 92
    disproportionate enforcement in, 85, 91, 180–81

Dawn Raids *(cont.)*
   inherited trauma of, 14, 184
   racial profiling, 13, 32–33, 59, 91–92, 180–81
Derrida, Jacques, 53–54
determinants of health, 126, 131–33, 134f, 143
discrimination, 1, 60, 108, 122, 124
   *see also* interpersonal racism; structural racism
discriminatory policies, 3, 5–6, 83, 103, 108, 124, 143, 180
'dog whistling', 2
Dole Pineapple Plantation, 28
Downs, Mathew, 187
du Plessis-Allan, Heather, 9
Durmont D'Urville, Jules, 22

education
   and the 'colonial gaze', 53
   as a luxury, 30
   marginalisation of minorities, 53–56, 154
   as training for manual labour, 23–24, 28–29, 42, 213n58
   as a vehicle for assimilation, 55, 60–61, 69
   as the way out of poverty, 29–30, 62, 83, 155, 157–58, 170
   *see also* compulsory education; tertiary education organisations; tertiary education students; universities
Education Act 1877, 61
Ellis, Albert, 40
Employment Contracts Act 1991, 46
ethnic identity, 62–64, 78
eugenics movement, 22
European explorers' characterisation of Pacific people, 21–23, 25, 31, 212n44

Fair Pay Agreements, 45–46
Fanon, Frantz, 53, 55, 56–57, 59
Fepulea'i, Damon, 60
*Fern and the Tiki, The* (Ausubel), 16, 211n33
Fiji, 15, 26, 28, 41, 85
Firth, Stewart, 18
'For Sia Fiegel' (Mila), 83
'Freedom Dreaming of Abolition in Aotearoa New Zealand' (Asafo), 197
*Freedom Dreams* (Kelley), 195
Fry, Ian, 113

Gonzalez, Carmen, 99, 113, 221n15, 221n16
Green List, 88–89, 93
Grey, George, 15
Gudgeon, Walter, 23

Hall, Stuart, 53–54, 56–57, 64
Harris, Ricci, 149
Hauʻofa, Epeli, 114–15, 195, 197
Hawaiʻi, 28
health
    child wellbeing and income inequality, 127f, 128
    determinants of health, 126, 131, 134f, 143
    inverse care law, 120, 121f
    Pacific health professionals, 141–42, 150, 169
    Pacific students' enrolment in health fields, 169t
health inequity
    access to determinants of health, 120, 131–33, 138, 143
    access to health services, 120, 121f, 129, 133, 135
    barriers causing, 129, 133, 135, 150
    changes needed, 140–41, 144–50
    costs of, 139, 151
    disparities, 117–19, 131
    health workforce and, 141–42, 150, 169
    internalised racism and, 122–23
    interpersonal racism and, 122, 124, 130
    opposition to equity policies, 141–42, 148
    Pacific communities' responses to, 122, 139–40, 144–45, 149–50
    quality of care and, 135, 149
    responsibility for rectifying, 139–40, 144
    structural racism and, 125, 128–31, 137–39, 149
Heron, Michael, 92
hierarchies based on race, 63, 78, 84, 88
higher education *see* tertiary education organisations; tertiary education students
Hipkins, Chris, 1
home ownership, 37, 143
Hugo, Graeme, 86–87
Human Rights Commission, 108

*Imagining Decolonisation* (Jackson in Elkington et al.), 197
Immigration Act 1968, 180
Immigration Act 2009, 108, 221n11
Immigration New Zealand, 10, 82, 85
immigration policies
    co-development/co-dependency, 82–83, 86–87
    Green List of preferred professions, 88–89
    and human rights, 108
    Pacific quota schemes, 89–90, 103, 106
    permanent resident (PR) status, 88–90, 98, 106
    privileging white migrants, 83, 88–89, 91–92, 100, 105
    as products of structural racism, 84, 86, 92, 108
    recommendations for change to, 93–94

immigration policies (*cont.*)
    review of dawn 'visits', 92
    and undesirable migrants, 86, 91, 100, 105, 107
    *see also* migration post-World War II; visas
imprisonment, 176, 184, 186, 188
incomes of Pacific people, 158, 158t
    *see also* Pacific pay gap
indentured labour, 26
Indigenous commonalities, 201–4
institutional racism, 67, 120, 124, 129, 130, 155–56
    *see also* structural racism; systemic racism
internalised racism, 35, 57, 60, 122–23, 191
interpersonal racism, 122, 124, 130, 137, 146
    *see also* discrimination; racial prejudice; racial slurs
inverse care law, 120, 121f
'island time', 25

Jackson, Moana, 108, 138, 197, 200
Johnson, Dwayne 'The Rock', 21
Jones, Camara Phyllis, 122–23, 130–31

Kalaniʻōpuʻu, 31
Kelley, Robin D. G., 195, 199
Kidman, Joanna, 67
Kiribati, 40–41, 85, 87, 102, 104
Krieger, Nancy, 139
Kukutai, Tahu, 111, 114

labour, exploitation of, 39, 42–44, 106, 180
labour mobility schemes *see* RSE (Recognised Seasonal Employer) scheme
land, exploitation of, 26, 40–41, 109
lay advocates, 190
Lealofi III, Tupua Tamasese, 179
'learned inferiority', 123
    *see also* internalised racism
'learned superiority', 123
Legal Services Amendment Bill, 191
Leong, Nancy, 99, 221n16
Letele, Dave, 132, 144
liberation for all marginalised peoples, 198–99, 201–4
Logan, Robert, 27, 179
Lolohea, Alice, 19
Lopesi, Lana, 106–7

'majoritarian stories', 177–78, 183, 191, 200
Mallon, Sean, 14, 63

manaakitanga, 111
Māori
    ancestral relationships with Pacific peoples, 93, 111–12, 197–98
    deprivation of, 100, 109, 125, 137, 186
    self-determination struggles, 58–59, 110, 128, 171, 198
Māori and Pacific Admission Scheme (MAPAS), 141–42
marking of difference, 19, 54–55, 56–60, 64
Marshall Islands, 40
Mau movement, 179
McAllister, Tara, 71, 156
Meihana, Peter, 17
meritocracy myth, 38
Middlemore Hospital, 129
migrant dream narrative
    education and employment opportunities, 4, 29–30, 62, 83
    land of milk and honey, 2, 4, 29, 196, 209n12
    questioning of, 49
    and upward economic mobility, 38, 44–45
migration post-World War II, 29, 106, 179–80
    *see also* immigration policies
Mila, Karlo, 83, 172–73
Mills, Charles, 5
Ministry for Pacific Peoples, 2, 18
model minorities, 3, 208n20

National Party, 2, 33
National/ACT/New Zealand First Government
    2024 budget cuts, 2–3, 191
    coalition agreement, 2
    dismantling equity measures, 2–3, 7, 46, 191, 196
    inciting prejudice and sowing division, 141–42
    'white grievance politics', 142, 148
    *see also* ACT party; National party
Nauru, 15, 40, 85
New Zealand economy
    1950s boom requiring cheap labour, 29, 106, 179–80
    1970s recession and deportations, 32–33, 91, 106, 180
    agriculture, 39–41, 94
    increasing inequality, 120, 124, 126, 140, 142
    and racial capitalism, 38, 44, 99–100, 105, 109
New Zealand First party, 2
New Zealand settler state
    climate justice and, 97–98, 112–13
    as a colonial power, 14–17, 21, 26, 179, 211n29
    definitions of, 206n2, 208n21, 233n3
    Eurocentric structures and institutions, 11–12, 125, 137

New Zealand settler state (*cont.*)
  government powers, 49, 108
  housing policies, 143
  human rights in, 108
  immigration policies, 5–6, 103, 105–8, 180
  and Māori whenua, 100, 109, 156, 221n17
  race relations, reputation of, 15–17, 108–9
  racial capitalism in, 38, 44, 99–100, 105, 109
  relationship with Pacific countries, 17, 82–83, 84, 87, 92, 180
  responsibility to Pacific peoples, 10, 18
  structural racism in, 2, 119, 124–25, 130–31, 136–37, 143–44
  *see also* Aotearoa New Zealand society; New Zealand economy
Ngata, Talavao, 143
'nice racism', 123, 144, 148–49
  *see also* unconscious bias
Niue, 15, 18, 31, 40
noble savage trope, 21, 212n44

'Ocean in Us, The' (Hauʻofa), 195
'Ofa Kolo, Finau, 59–60
Oranga Tamariki Act 1989, 190
Oranga Tamariki Act 2024, 196
othering, 53–55, 56–60, 64, 72, 109
  *see also* racial stereotyping

Pacific Access Category Resident Visa, 89–90, 103, 106
Pacific pay gap
  income inequity, 37, 39, 43–44, 49, 71–72, 156–57
  inquiry into, 43, 47–48
  possible solutions, 45–49, 157–58
  *see also* incomes of Pacific people; socioeconomic inequities
Pacific worldviews, 67, 69, 74–76, 145, 201
Pacific–Māori relationships, 93, 111–12, 197–98
Papa, Rahui, 198
Papua, 40
Papua New Guinea, 85
personal racism *see* interpersonal racism
Polynesian Panther Party, 13, 92
power
  defining legitimate knowledge and beliefs, 11, 58, 136
  defining what is normal, 26, 56–57, 68, 137
  defining what is racist, 124
  people with, 11, 99, 136, 143, 183–84
  perpetuation of, 68, 73
  *see also* structural racism
prejudice *see* racial prejudice

Quince, Khylee, 188–90

*R v Carr*, 187
Rabi island, 41
race, definition, 11
racial identities, 99–100, 105, 107, 109
racial prejudice, 9–12, 24, 122, 141–42
    *see also* interpersonal racism; racial stereotyping
racial slurs, 1, 12, 19–20
racial stereotyping
    historical foundations of, 4, 10–12, 18–19, 34–35, 56
    internalisation of, 24, 35, 57, 60
    inversion of, 12, 210n13
    marking as different, 54–55, 56–57
    racial identities, 99–100, 105–7, 109
    systemic racism and, 11–12, 34
    *see also* othering; stereotypes of Pacific people; structural racism
racialised bodies, 40, 42, 154, 214n7, 221n15
racism
    damaging consequences of, 78–79, 122, 123
    definitions, 1, 4–5
    denial of, 9, 124, 136
    experiences of minority groups, 9, 55–56, 122, 123, 135–36, 149, 157
    markers of, 56
    need for awareness of, 1, 123, 136–38, 144, 148–49
    public shift towards, 3
    *see also* institutional racism; interpersonal racism; structural racism; systemic racism
rainbow model of health determinants (Dahlgren and Whitehead), 133, 134f
Rata, Arama, 111, 114
Recognised Seasonal Employer scheme *see* RSE (Recognised Seasonal Employer) scheme
Refugee Convention, 113
Reid, Papaarangi, 138, 139, 147
Reti, Shane, 2
Ritskes, Eric, 199
Robson, Bridget, 139
Rousseau, Jean-Jacques, 212n44
RSE (Recognised Seasonal Employer) scheme
    as co-development, 82–83, 86–87
    as exploitation, 39, 42, 85–86, 106
    Human Rights Commission report on, 85
    and visa restrictions, 86, 104
    as a triple-win, 85
    wages, 93
*RSE Scheme in Aotearoa New Zealand: A Human Rights Review, The*, 85

Salesa, Damon, 15, 17, 30, 119
Sāmoa, 15, 26–27, 32, 85, 87, 178–79, 184
Samoan Quota Resident Visa, 89–90, 103, 106
Sankar, Anisha, 106–7
sentencing
    Criminal Justice Act 1985 s 16, 185, 188, 189
    family or community speakers, 188–90
    imprisonment, 176, 184, 186, 188
    'Pacific Peoples and the Criminal Justice System' report, 188–89
    section 27 reports, 185–89, 190–91
    Sentencing Act 2002, 185
    *see also* criminality
Seymour, David, 2, 10, 124
Shilliam, Robbie, 202
Sium, Aman, 199
Smith, Graham Hingangaroa, 72
Smith, Jo, 74
Smith, Linda Tuhiwai, 72
SmokeyGotBeatz, 14
socioeconomic inequities
    access to determinants of health, 120, 131–33, 138, 143
    correlation between income inequality and child wellbeing, 126, 127f, 176
    employment precarity, 30, 43, 46, 54, 72
    home ownership, 37, 143
    income inequity, 37, 39, 43–45, 49, 71–72, 156–57
    reasons for, 5, 14, 18, 29–30, 42, 142
    strategies for solving inequities, 45–49, 119, 157–58, 170
    unemployment and, 37, 43
    *see also* incomes of Pacific people
*Solicitor-General v Heta*, 186
Solomon Islands, 85
Special Issue of *Ethnographic Edge* journal, 75–77
SPYCC, 14, 34
Stanley, Elizabeth, 107
Stephens, Mamari, 189
stereotypes of Pacific people
    as childlike and lacking intelligence, 21–24, 32, 212n44
    as criminal and violent, 30–33, 60, 100, 107, 122
    by early Europeans, 18–19, 21–23, 25, 212n44
    as lacking self-control and responsibility, 22–23, 30
    as lazy, 24–27
    as opposite of Pālagi, 19
    as overstayers, 32, 59–60, 91, 107
    as poor, 27–30
    see also *Bunga* (short film); racial stereotyping
'straight-up racist', 123

structural racism
  definitions, 5, 124
  as foundational and embedded, 1–2, 119, 124–25, 136–37, 143–44
  how it works, 3, 4–6, 11, 44, 129–30, 143–44, 147
  opposition to structural change and, 125, 140–42, 148
  as the status quo, 128, 136–37, 138, 144
  *see also* discrimination; institutional racism; power; racial stereotyping; systemic racism
structural racism, dismantling strategies
  challenging by speaking out or writing, 45, 75–77
  decolonising, addressing inequities, 125, 138, 140
  focusing on structural change, 130, 137, 145–46
  Pacific solutions, 47, 120, 122, 144–45, 150
SWIDT, 12–14, 19–20
systemic racism
  and being tough on crime, 107
  consequences of, 2, 73, 117
  in education, 53, 73–74, 76–77
  and global responses to environmental crises, 98–99
  and racial stereotypes, 11–12, 34
  and racialised social systems, 5
  speaking out against, 45, 47
  *see also* structural racism

talatalanoa, 55, 64–66, 77
Tāmaki Makaurau *see* Auckland
Tasman, Abel, 31
tau talatalanoa, 65–66
'Te Kauae Paraoa', 141–42
Te Pūkenga, 164, 165t, 167t
Te Whare Tapa Whā, 58
Teaiwa, Teresia, 14, 63
Tecun, Arcia, 106–7
tertiary education organisations, 74–77
  business model of, 70
  disrupting institutional racism in, 171–72
  EFTs, 155
  equity and diversity strategies of, 54, 71, 78–79, 141–42
  equity funding, 172
  institutional and systemic racism in, 67–73, 75, 77–78, 155–57, 165, 170–71
  marginalisation of minorities, 53–56, 154
  Pacific staff in, 65, 67–68, 71–76, 78, 156–57
  Performance-Based Research Fund (PBRF), 70
  Te Pūkenga, 164, 165t, 167t
  types of, 155
  Western norms and systems in, 67–69, 73, 75

tertiary education organisations (*cont.*)
  *see also* universities
tertiary education students
  completion rates by ethnicity and qualification levels, 165, 166t
  completion rates of Pacific students, 154, 165, 167t, 169, 172
  dismantling structural racism in, 170–72
  enrolment of Pacific people by fields of study, 168, 168t
  enrolment of Pacific students by health fields of study, 169, 169t
  incomes from levels 1 to 3 qualifications, 163–64, 171–72
  incomes of Pacific people by qualifications, 158, 158t
  Pacific people by highest qualifications, 158–59, 159t
  Pacific people's participation by qualification levels, 159, 160t, 161
  Pacific students as percentage of total students by qualification levels, 162–63, 162t
  Pacific students' first-year retention rates, 164, 165t
  and the pipeline to success, 153–54, 157–58, 170
  student population by ethnicity and qualification level, 163t
  *see also* tertiary education organisations; universities
Thiong'o, Ngũgĩ wa, 77
tino rangatiratanga, 100, 108, 110, 112
Tiriti o Waitangi, 58, 100, 198
  *see also* constitutional transformation
Tokelau, 15, 18, 87
Tonga, 15, 28, 85, 87, 89–90
'Towards a New Oceania' (Wendt), 19
Trask, Haunani-Kay, 200
Tuiburelevu, Litia, 42, 106
Tukuitonga, Sir Collin, 3, 118–19
Tupua Tamasese Lealofi III *see* Lealofi III, Tupua Tamasese
Tuvalu, 85, 87, 97, 102, 104

unconscious bias, 129, 137
  *see also* 'nice racism'
universities
  Auckland University of Technology, 165t, 167t
  colonial foundations of, 156
  institutional habits, 155–56
  Lincoln University, 165t, 167t
  Massey University, 164, 165t, 166–67, 167t, 171
  Pacific staff, 156–57
  purpose of study, 155, 157
  University of Auckland, 156, 164, 165t, 167, 167t
  University of Canterbury, 164, 165t, 167t
  University of Otago, 156, 164, 165t, 166, 167, 167t
  University of Waikato, 156, 164, 165t, 167, 167t
  Victoria University of Wellington, 165t, 167, 167t
  *see also* tertiary education organisations; tertiary education students

vā fealoaloa'i (space of respect), 73, 76
Vanuatu, 85
Verner-Pula, Allyssa, 13
victim blaming, 26–27, 137–38
visas
    Accredited Employer Work Visas, 104, 106
    Immigration Act 2009, 221n11
    Pacific Access Category Resident Visas, 89–90, 103, 106
    Recognised Seasonal Employer (RSE) Limited Visas, 86–87, 104, 106
    Samoan Quota Resident Visas, 89–90, 103, 106
    Skilled Migrant Category Resident Visas, 88–89, 104, 105
    Straight to Residence Visas, 88
    temporary visas, 84–85, 92, 104
    Work to Residence Visas, 88
    *see also* immigration policies

Wagner-Hiliau, Hugo, 42, 106
Waititi, Taika, 9, 136
Wehipeihana, Emma, 141
Wendt, Albert, 19
Western norms
    about individuals, 67–68, 137
    about land, 26, 137
    about success, 57
    about time, 25
    about what is 'real', 58
    prioritising of, 56, 59–60, 136–37
Wetherell, Margaret, 56
Weymouth Boys' Home, 182
Whata, Christian, 186
'white gaze', 53
'white grievance politics', 125, 142, 148
White privilege
    and colonial systems, 11–12, 120
    denial of, 136, 209n8
    Western norms and, 56, 59–60, 136–37
    White fragility, 136
White supremacy, 5, 22, 136, 177–78, 196
Whitehead, Margaret, 133, 134f
Whiteness, 11, 39, 45, 57, 124, 136
Williams, Sir Joe, 183, 185, 187

Yao, Esther, 62, 78
Yates, Olivia, 98, 111

Zodgekar, Arvind, 63